Beyond Shariati

Ali Shariati (1933–1977) has been called by many the "ideologue of the Iranian Revolution." An inspiration to many of the revolutionary generation, Shariati's combination of Islamic political thought and Left-leaning ideology continues to influence both in Iran and across the wider Muslim world.

In this book, Siavash Saffari examines Shariati's long-standing legacy, and how new readings of his works by contemporary "neo-Shariatis" have contributed to a deconstruction of the false binaries of Islam/modernity, Islam/West, and East/West. Saffari argues that through their critique of Eurocentric metanarratives on the one hand, and the essentialist conceptions of Islam on the other, Shariati and neo-Shariatis have carved out a new space in Islamic thought beyond the traps of Orientalism and Occidentalism. This unique perspective will hold great appeal to researchers of the politics and intellectual thought of postrevolutionary Iran and the greater Middle East.

Siavash Saffari is an Assistant Professor of West Asian Studies, in the Department of Asian Languages and Civilizations, at Seoul National University. He received a PhD in Political Science from the University of Alberta, followed by a postdoctoral fellowship at Columbia University.

Beyond Shariati

Modernity, Cosmopolitanism, and Islam in Iranian Political Thought

SIAVASH SAFFARI
Seoul National University

CAMBRIDGE
UNIVERSITY PRESS

University Printing House, Cambridge CB2 8BS, United Kingdom
One Liberty Plaza, 20th Floor, New York, NY 10006, USA
477 Williamstown Road, Port Melbourne, VIC 3207, Australia
4843/24, 2nd Floor, Ansari Road, Daryaganj, Delhi – 110002, India
79 Anson Road, #06-04/06, Singapore 079906

Cambridge University Press is part of the University of Cambridge.

It furthers the University's mission by disseminating knowledge in the pursuit of
education, learning, and research at the highest international levels of excellence.

www.cambridge.org
Information on this title: www.cambridge.org/9781107164161
DOI: 10.1017/9781316686966

© Siavash Saffari 2017

This publication is in copyright. Subject to statutory exception
and to the provisions of relevant collective licensing agreements,
no reproduction of any part may take place without the written
permission of Cambridge University Press.

First published 2017

A catalog record for this publication is available from the British Library.

ISBN 978-1-107-16416-1 Hardback

Cambridge University Press has no responsibility for the persistence or accuracy of URLs
for external or third-party Internet Web sites referred to in this publication and does not
guarantee that any content on such Web sites is, or will remain, accurate or appropriate.

Contents

	Introduction: Between Cultural Essentialism and Hegemonic Universalism	*page* 1
	Unsettling a Hegemonic Paradigm	1
	The Life and Legacy of a Radical Islamic Thinker	5
	Islam and Modernity through the Lens of Dialogical Comparison	16
	Chapters' Summaries	18
1	Postrevolutionary Readings of a Revolutionary Islamic Discourse	21
	Revolution, Ideology, and the "Geography of Discourse"	21
	Shariati as the Ideologue of the 1979 Revolution	27
	An Unfinished Project of "Indigenous Modernity"	38
2	Islamic Thought in Encounter with Colonial Modernity	46
	What Is in a Term?	46
	Responses to an Encounter	52
	Contesting Genealogies of Emergent Islamic Modernities	65
3	A Postcolonial Discourse of Public Religion	74
	Reworking the Religious/Secular Binary	74
	"Islamic Protestantism" as a Methodology of Bottom-Up Change	81
	Progressive Public Religion under Islamist Ascendancy	86
	Neo-Shariatis and Islamic Liberalism	98
4	The Enlightenment Subject and a Religiously Mediated Subjectivity	102
	The Philosophical Foundations of an Islamic Discourse	102
	Modern Subjectivity and the Mediated Subject	107
	Secularization and the "Myth" of the Enlightenment	112

	The Descent: *A Theistic Narrative of Subjectivity*	120
	Religious Ontology and the Rights-Bearing Subject	126
5	Orientalism, Occidentalism, and the Civilizational Framework	134
	Civilization as a Critique of Westernization	134
	The Civilizational Framework Revisited	142
	Civilizational Analysis in Neo-Shariati Thought	156
	Reworking the Framework	160
	Conclusion: Toward a Postcolonial Cosmopolitanism	165
	A Postcolonial Reclaiming of Islam and Modernity	165
	Indigenous Modernity and the Post-Islamist Turn	169
	Indigenization and the Quest for Universalism from Below	177

Select Bibliography 181
   English Sources 181
   Persian Sources 193
Index 203

Introduction

Between Cultural Essentialism and Hegemonic Universalism

Unsettling a Hegemonic Paradigm

Since the late nineteenth century, discussions about a condition and project code-named *modernity* have occupied a critical space in many Middle Eastern and Islamicate societies at the theoretical as well as the practical level. Throughout this period, a perceived tension between modernity and the Islamic tradition has been one of the defining features of many social, political, philosophical, and cultural debates. The origins of this dichotomous discursive construct can be traced to the historical encounter of Muslim societies with modern Europe during the late phase of European colonialism. Since then, the binary view of Islam and modernity has been operative not only in Islamicate contexts but also in various sites within the West. Throughout the twentieth century, Western scholarship on Muslim politics and social life was largely shaped by two vaguely different articulations of this view. The first, represented by Orientalists such as Gustave E. von Grunebaum, held that Islam and Muslim societies were essentially incapable of reforming and adopting the achievements of the modern world. The second view, represented by modernization theorists such as Daniel Lerner, held that even though Islam lacked the necessary resources for initiating modernity, Muslim societies could still become modern by following the Western path of modernization. Although the second view may be said to have offered a somewhat more optimistic vision of the prospects for progressive change in Muslim societies, it is clear that in both accounts modernity was understood as a Western achievement and something alien and antithetical to Islam and Muslim cultures.

The occurrence of a number of events during the latter half of the previous century and the beginning of the present century reinforced the Western view about the irreconcilability of Islam and modernity. The first was the rise of Islamism during the 1970s and 1980s, which was interpreted by many Western observers as a turn against modernity. It was precisely through this lens that these commentators viewed the 1979 Iranian Revolution and the subsequent establishment of the Islamic Republic. Another event was the end of the Cold War. With the implosion of the Soviet Union and the collapse of the Eastern bloc Islam and Muslim societies came to be seen as the other of the West and the enemy of its modernity. As Mamdani notes, in the construction of the hegemonic post–Cold War narratives of the modern Western self, Muslim societies came to be seen not only as "incapable" of modernizing, but also as being inherently hostile and "resistant" to modernity.[1] In the post–Cold War context, the assumption of an imminent and inevitable clash between Western modernity and its Islamic nemesis found a clear manifestation in the civilizational clash discourse popularized by Bernard Lewis and Samuel Huntington.[2] Finally, there were the terrorist attacks of September 11, 2001 and the subsequent US-led invasions and occupations of Afghanistan and Iraq, in the aftermath of which the view of an insurmountable discord between Islam and modernity came to dominate both academic and mainstream debates.[3]

The Orientalist and modernist conceptions of Islam and Muslim cultures are often premised on a particular Eurocentric narrative of modernity developed by the leading figures of European Enlightenment and post-Enlightenment thought. Within this narrative, Europe was seen, in Walter Mignolo's apt description, as the singular "point of reference of global history" and the ultimate "point of arrival of human existence on the planet."[4] Negating the colonial and imperial constitution of

---

[1] Mahmood Mamdani, *Good Muslim, Bad Muslim: America, the Cold War, and the Roots of Terror* (New York: Three Leaves Press, 2005), 19.
[2] See: Bernard Lewis, "The Roots of Muslim Rage: Why So Many Muslims Deeply Resent the West, and Why Their Bitterness Will Not Be Easily Mollified," *The Atlantic Monthly* 26, no. 3 (September 1990): 47–58; Samuel P. Huntington, "The Clash of Civilizations?," *Foreign Affairs* 72, no. 3 (1993): 22–50; Samuel P. Huntington, *The Clash of Civilizations and the Remaking of World Order* (New York: Simon and Schuster, 1996).
[3] See: Bernard Lewis, *The Crisis of Islam: Holy War and Unholy Terror* (New York: Random House, 2004); Irshad Manji, *The Trouble with Islam* (Toronto: Random House, 2003); Salman Rushdie, "Yes, This Is about Islam," *New York Times*, November 02, 2001, A25.
[4] Walter Mignolo, *The Darker Side of Western Modernity: Global Futures, Decolonial Options* (Durham, NC and London: Duke University Press, 2011), xiv.

European modernity, and assuming an uninterrupted historical trajectory of Western civilizational development, this narrative privileged Europe's sociocultural and socioeconomic developments during the eighteenth and nineteenth centuries over other, non-Western modalities of social, cultural, political, and economic production and change. Among many other examples, the view of European modernity and its underlying Occidental rationalism as the universal expression of human progress manifested itself in Immanuel Kant's natural-historical account of racial differentiation, G. W. F. Hegel's juxtaposition of Occidental and Oriental reason, and Karl Marx's early views about the progressive impact of European colonialism in India and China.

At least since the mid-twentieth century, there has existed a sustained effort by a range of critical thinkers in the colonial periphery as well as in the metropolitan center to disrupt this hegemonic narrative and challenge its reproduction in contemporary debates. The thinkings of Mahatma Gandhi, Aimé Césaire, Frantz Fanon, and a subsequent generation of postcolonial theorists including Edward Said, Gayatri Spivak, Dipesh Chakrabarty, and Homi Bhabha have problematized the mono-civilizational and universalist disposition of Europe's Enlightenment modernity. Theories of multiple modernities, which emerged in the latter half of the twentieth century, have also critiqued Eurocentric and unilinear conceptions of human progress and development. Other theories, such as those describing modernity as a "global shift" and a universal condition, have sought to delink the category from its Eurocentric accounts and from the colonial trajectory of the modern West.[5] And yet others have rejected the possibility of delinking modernity from coloniality, identifying the latter as the darker side, the hidden agenda, and indeed constitutive of the former.[6]

The multifaceted and ongoing critique of the hegemonic historiography of modernity has further contributed to the unsettling of the Islam/modernity binary in the particular context of Muslim societies. A rich body of literature has emerged seeking to expose the multifarious and contested natures of both Islam and modernity by deconstructing discourses that reduce complex sociopolitical and socioeconomic challenges

---

[5] Sanjay Subrahmanyam, "Connected Histories: Notes towards a Reconfiguration of Early Modern Eurasia," *Modern Asian Studies* 31, no. 3 (1997): 737.
[6] See: Enrique Dussel, *The Underside of Modernity: Apel, Ricoeur, Rorty, Taylor, and the Philosophy of Liberation*, trans. Eduardo Mendieta (Atlantic Highland, NJ: Humanities Press, 1996); Mignolo, *Darker Side of Western Modernity*.

in Muslim societies to simplistic formulations such as the absence of modernity or its irreconcilability with Islam. A number of commentators have used the framework of multiple modernities to highlight the nuanced dynamics of lived Muslim experiences in diverse historical and contemporary contexts. Emphasizing at once cultural-historical difference and interconnectedness, these commentators advance a simultaneous critique of blind universalism and cultural relativism.[7] Others have used alternative categories such as post-Islamism to explain the discursive and political exhaustion of the dichotomous discourses of Islamism and modernism, especially in the context of the recent emergence of the Iranian Green Movement and the Arab Spring protests.[8] And yet others have focused on a sustained effort by a range of Muslim thinkers to dispel the view of an inherent clash between Islam and modernity. It is this latter effort that has given increased attention to the works of such contemporary Muslim reformers as Mohammed Arkoun, Nasr Hamid Abu Zayd, Fatima Mernissi, Leila Ahmed, Fethullah Gülen, Abdolkarim Soroush, Abdullahi Ahmed An-Na'im, and Tariq Ramadan.

The present book contributes to the emerging critical literature on the Islam/modernity binary by focusing on the ideas of Ali Shariati, one of the leading twentieth-century Muslim thinkers, and a group of his contemporary intellectual followers known collectively as neo-Shariatis. In its attempt to advance a contextually grounded discourse of progressive social and political change on the basis of a simultaneous critique of the Islamic tradition and Eurocentric modernization, Shariati's thought finds common ground with the projects of many of the aforementioned Muslim thinkers. However, what sets Shariati and neo-Shariatis apart from many of these Muslim thinkers is their concern and critical engagement with the concept of coloniality in relation to modern discursive and institutional formations in global and local contexts. Thus, even though Shariati and neo-Shariatis problematize the dichotomous construction of

---

[7] See: Nilüfer Göle, "Snapshots of Islamic Modernities," *Daedalus* 129, no. 1, *Multiple Modernities* (Winter, 2000): 91–117; Masoud Kamali, *Multiple Modernities, Civil Society and Islam: The Case of Iran and Turkey* (Liverpool: Liverpool University Press, 2006); Amyn B. Sajoo, ed., *Muslim Modernities: Expressions of the Civil Imagination* (London: I.B. Tauris, 2008); Modjtaba Sadria, ed., *Multiple Modernities in Muslim Societies: Tangible Elements and Abstract Perspectives* (London: I.B. Tauris, 2009).

[8] See: Joshua A. Stacher, "Post-Islamist Rumblings in Egypt: The Emergence of the Wasat Party," *Middle East Journal* 56, no. 3 (2002): 415–432; Mojtaba Mahdavi, "Post-Islamist Trends in Post-Revolutionary Iran," *Comparative Studies of South Asia, Africa, and the Middle East* 31, no. 1 (2011): 94–109; Asef Bayat, ed., *Post-Islamism: The Many Faces of Political Islam* (New York: Oxford University Press, 2013).

Islam and modernity and argue that the recognition of cultural plurality and difference makes possible the negotiation of diverse experiences of change in the modern world, they are also attentive to hegemony and global power asymmetries. In their radical critique of colonial and neo-colonial relations of domination, Shariati and neo-Shariatis challenge the hegemonic expansion of two particular socioeconomic and sociopolitical formations, namely, capitalism and liberal-democracy, in the course of the expansion of European modernity.

The central argument of this book is that in their simultaneous critique of the Eurocentric accounts of modernity, on the one hand, and the essentialist conceptions of Islam, on the other, Shariati and his followers advance a sociopolitically progressive discourse of indigenous modernity that engages freely and creatively with a wide range of emancipatory projects in the modern world. The book further argues that by stressing the need for the development of a critical consciousness about the operations and effects of Western colonialism and imperialism in the particular context of Muslim societies and by calling for a "return to the self" (*bazgasht beh khish*), Shariati and neo-Shariatis provide a contextually grounded view of cultural, social, and political change that gives attention both to global structures and local histories. A case is made that the search for a third way between hegemonic universalism and essentialist particularism by Shariati and neo-Shariatis opens up a new discursive space in Iranian and Islamic thought for engaging in cross-cultural encounters beyond Orientalism and Occidentalism. Finally, it is shown that for Shariati and neo-Shariatis, cultivating genuine cosmopolitanism requires recognizing diverse forms of locally mediated systems of knowledge production and political agency, and moving beyond the Eurocentric and monocivilizational paradigm that has shaped the interactions between the West and the non-West for roughly five centuries.

The Life and Legacy of a Radical Islamic Thinker

In his observations about the February 1979 Iranian Revolution, Michel Foucault made mention of Ali Shariati, whose invisible presence, he remarked, haunted "all political and religious life" in the country.[9] At the

---

[9] Michel Foucault, "What Are the Iranians Dreaming About?," *Le Nouvel Observateur*, October 16–22, 1978, quoted in Janet Afary and Kevin B. Anderson, *Foucault and the Iranian Revolution: Gender and the Seductions of Islamism* (Chicago: University of Chicago Press, 2005), 207.

time of the revolution, Shariati had already been dead for close to two years. There was (and is), however, little doubt about his significant influence in Iranian society during the 1960s and 1970s and in the formation and maturation of the popular uprising that led to the overthrow of the Pahlavi dynasty. It was this iconic and unrivaled status that gave Shariati, in Foucault's words, "the position, so privileged in Shi'ism, of the invisible Present, of the ever-present Absent."[10]

Shariati was born on November 23, 1933 in the desert village of Kahak in the northeastern province of Khorasan.[11] His father, Mohammad-Taghi, was a politically active and reform-minded Islamic preacher, whose religious and political ideas left a lasting influence on the young Shariati. In 1944, Mohammad-Taghi Shariati founded the Center for the Propagation of Islamic Truth (*kanun-e nashr-e haqayeq-e eslami*) in the provincial capital of Mashhad with the objective of disseminating a modernist interpretation of Islamic teachings. Soon after its founding, the center also became a hub for political activism in support of the nationalist leader Mohammad Mosaddegh and his National Front party. When Mosaddegh's tenure as prime minister came to an abrupt end in August 1953 through a British- and American-backed coup, the father and son were among the founding members of the Mashhad branch of the clandestine pro-Mosaddegh organization, the National Resistance Movement (*nehzat-e mogavemat-e melli*).[12]

In 1955, Shariati entered the newly inaugurated Faculty of Literature at the University of Mashhad. Upon completing his Bachelor of Arts degree, he received a government scholarship to continue his graduate studies abroad. In 1959, he arrived in Paris, where he enrolled at the Sorbonne, and four years later, in June 1963, he received a doctorate degree (*doctorat d'université*) from the Faculty of Arts and Social Sciences.[13] Despite majoring in History of Medieval Islam, during his doctoral studies Shariati reportedly created a program of study tailor-made to his own specific interests.[14] He spent much of his time at the Collège

---

[10] Ibid.

[11] Pouran Shariat-Razavi, *Tarhi az yek zendegi (Portrait of a Life)* (Tehran: Chapakhsh, 1376/1997), 3.

[12] Ibid., 41.

[13] Shariati's doctoral research, which was carried out under the supervision of French linguist and Iran scholar, Gilbert Lazard, included translating, correcting, and writing a commentary on *The Merits of Balkh (Fazayel-e Balkh)*, a thirteenth-century Persian work in Islamic hagiology by Safi al-Din Abu Bakr Balkhi.

[14] Ali Rahnema, *An Islamic Utopian: A Political Biography of Ali Shari'ati* (London and New York: I.B. Tauris, 2000), 117.

de France, auditing classes by French sociologist Georges Gurvitch and Islamic scholar Jacques Berque.[15] According to his political biographer, Ali Rahnema, aside from Gurvitch and Berque, three other figures left a deep and lasting impression on Shariati during his years in Paris. These included prominent French Orientalist Louis Massignon, Martinique-born revolutionary Frantz Fanon, and existentialist French philosopher Jean-Paul Sartre.[16]

In Paris, in addition to his involvement with the National Front and a number of other Iranian opposition groups, Shariati also immersed himself in various revolutionary debates and radical anticolonial and anti-imperialist activities taking place at the time. He was particularly influenced by the Algerian and Cuban revolutionaries, and even began translating, from French to Persian, Fanon's *A Dying Colonialism* (1959) and *The Wretched of the Earth* (1961), as well as Ernesto Che Guevara's *Guerrilla Warfare* (1961). He is also reported to have been arrested in February 1961 while participating in a rally in protest to the execution of Congolese independence leader Patrice Lumumba.[17] Despite his initial attraction to the Algerian and Cuban models of guerrilla warfare, Shariati gradually came to the belief that radical social and political transformation required not simply a change in power structures through a revolutionary takeover of the state, but rather a deep change in the consciousness of the masses. According to his wife, Pouran Shariat-Razavi, toward the end of his time in Paris, Shariati had arrived at the conclusion that the advocacy of armed struggle by the intellectual vanguard was a futile effort that only led to the further alienation of intellectuals from the mainstream of the society.[18] She believes that while Shariati was deeply sympathetic to a generation of young committed revolutionaries who had raised arms in their fight against injustice, he was nevertheless convinced of the primacy of raising the consciousness of the masses over waging armed struggle.[19] For Shariati, she argues, the task of revolutionary intellectuals was to develop a contextually grounded discourse of revolutionary awareness on the basis of the "extraction," "reformation," and "refinement" of local and popular cultural resources.[20]

---

[15] Shariat-Razavi, *Tarhi*, 69–70.
[16] Rahnema, *Islamic Utopian*, 120.
[17] Ibid.
[18] Shariat-Razavi, *Tarhi*, 83.
[19] Ibid., 166.
[20] Ibid., 83.

Returning to Iran in 1964, Shariati was arrested at the border and incarcerated briefly for his work with Iranian opposition groups in Europe. After his release, he returned to Mashhad where he began to work as a high school teacher. Two years later, he was hired as an Assistant Professor in History at the University of Mashhad, where he taught courses on Iranian history, history of Islamic civilization, and history of world civilizations. Shariati proved to be a popular teacher and a powerful orator, and very soon he was receiving invitations to deliver talks at university campuses across the country. In the late 1960s, he was invited to Tehran to speak at the Hosseinieh Ershad, a newly established modern religious institution aimed at engaging young educated urban classes in debates about Islamic thought, culture, and history. Between 1967 and 1972, Shariati was one of the main speakers at the Hosseinieh Ershad, and he was also heavily involved in organizing a wide range of activities at the center, from educational classes to theatrical plays and painting exhibitions.

At the Hosseinieh Ershad, Shariati found a site for sociopolitical engagement that was perhaps better suited for his revolutionary objectives than the academic setting of the University of Mashhad. Combining his subversive political message with a modern interpretation of traditional Islamic doctrines, he developed a revolutionary Islamic ideology that called for popular awareness, action, and movement in the face of oppression and injustice. His message was received enthusiastically by many young people, particularly the newly educated and socially and economically disenfranchised classes. His speeches attracted thousands of religious and nonreligious youth, and Hosseinieh Ershad became a major hub for oppositional activity against the Pahlavi regime.[21] Predictably, his political agitation angered both the Pahlavi regime and the traditionalist and conservative religious sectors. The regime's secret police and intelligence service (SAVAK) was alarmed by Shariati's increasing popularity and his revolutionary discourse. Many Shi'i clerics too were enraged by Shariati's radical criticism of traditional religious doctrines and the pro status-quo position of the clergy. By the early 1970s, a number of major Shi'i ulama including Abul Qasim Khoei, Sayyid Muhammad Hadi Milani, Sayyid Sadeq Rohani, and Muhammad Husayn Tabatabaei had

---

[21] Kamran Matin, "Decoding Political Islam: Uneven and Combined Development and Ai Shariati's Political Thought," in *International Relations and non-Western Thought: Imperialism, Colonialism, and Investigations of Global Modernity*, ed. Robbie Shilliam (London: Routledge, 2010), 115.

issued religious rulings (*fatwa*) against Shariati, accusing him of heresy and opposition to Islam. Soon after, the Pahlavi regime followed suit, and by the mid-1970s Shariati's books had been banned and possessing them could have been cause for arrest.[22]

In 1972, Hosseinieh Ershad was closed under pressure from SAVAK, and Shariati went into hiding. He was eventually arrested in 1973 and spent eighteen months in a prison in Tehran. Upon release, he returned to Mashhad, where he effectively lived under house arrest.[23] Unable to teach or to speak at any public forums, and growing increasingly impatient with his restricted condition, he decided to enter into a self-imposed exile. In May 1977, despite a government-imposed travel ban against him, Shariati managed to leave Iran, arriving first in Brussels and then in Southampton, England. Three weeks after his arrival there, on June 19, 1977, he died of a heart attack.[24] The news of his sudden death spread quickly and rumors implicating the SAVAK in a conspiracy to kill him soon elevated Shariati's position to that of a martyr. Fearing that the Pahlavi regime might use his popularity for its own propaganda purposes, a decision was made by Shariati's family and friends not to return his body to Iran. Instead, he was buried in the Sayyida Zeinab Mosque in Damascus, Syria, the site of the burial place of Zaynab bint Ali, the granddaughter of the prophet of Islam and the daughter of the first Shi'i imam.

According to a Shi'i tradition, the fortieth day of his death (*chehelom*) was marked by various ceremonies in Iran and abroad. Of these, the major event attended by Shariati's family and numerous prominent Iranian and non-Iranian intellectuals and activists took place in Beirut, Lebanon. The event, according to Rahnema, was "a mini-summit of liberation organizations." Some of the attendees included representatives from the Palestine Liberation Organization, the Lebanese Amal Movement, the People's Front for the Liberation of Eritrea, the National Liberation Movement of Zanzibar, the National Movement for the Freedom of Zimbabwe, the National Movement for the Freedom of Southern Philippines, the Militant Clergy of Iran, the Organization of Iranian Muslim Students in Europe, America, and Canada, and Iran Freedom Movement. Speaking at the ceremony on behalf of the PLO, Yasser Arafat praised Shariati as "an

---

[22] Ali Rahnema, "Ali Shariati: Teacher, Preacher, Rebel," in *Pioneers of Islamic Revival*, ed. Ali Rahnema (New York: Zed Books, 2005), 237–238.
[23] Shariat-Razavi, *Tarhi*, 195.
[24] Since no autopsy was conducted after Shariati's sudden death, the reasons for his heart attack remain unknown today.

international fighter,"[25] and Amal's leader, Musa al-Sadr, described him as a "transnational revolutionary" who sought to develop an indigenous discourse of emancipatory change in the context of Muslim societies.[26]

In the months after Shariati's death, his fiery speeches in support of revolutionary action were circulated widely in Iran, and in the mass protests of the late 1970s many protestors in Tehran and other cities carried banners displaying his pictures and quotes. Just weeks before the February 1979 revolution, one Iranian observer commented that despite the participation of a diverse range of political groups and social sectors, Shariati's portraits and words had become the symbols of the prevailing "ideological dimension" of the revolution.[27] Several other commentaries written throughout the 1980s described Shariati as the "teacher," "ideologue," and "architect" of the revolutionary movement.[28] Be that as it may, his family and friends have often maintained that had Shariati been alive in postrevolutionary Iran, he would have likely ended up in prison for his dissenting views. In fact, although in the immediate aftermath of the revolution the new ruling elites named streets and schools after Shariati and praised him as one of the teachers of the revolutionary movement, in the course of the last three and a half decades Shariati's Islamic discourse has fallen increasingly out of favor with the official guardians of the postrevolutionary regime. Throughout this period Shariati's intellectual followers have often faced censorship, imprisonment, and other restrictions, and various groups and political organizations associated with Shariati's thought have been declared unlawful and counterrevolutionary.[29]

---

[25] Rahnema, "Ali Shariati: Teacher, Preacher, Rebel," 243.

[26] Musa Sadr, "Sokhanrani emam Musa Sadr dar arbaeen-e Shariati" ("Lecture by Imam Musa Sadr at the Fortieth day of Shariati's Death"), http://drshariati.org/show/?id=182 (accessed on May 27, 2013).

[27] Mansour Farhang, "Resisting the Pharaohs: Ali Shariati on Oppression," *Race & Class* 21, no. 1 (July 1979): 31.

[28] See: Ervand Abrahamian, "Ali Shari'ati: Ideologue of the Iranian Revolution," *MERIP Reports*, no. 102, *Islam and Politics* (January 1982): 24–28; Abdulaziz Sachedina, "Ali Shariati: Ideologue of the Iranian Revolution," in *Voices of Resurgent Islam*, ed. John L. Esposito (New York: Oxford University Press, 1983), 191–214; Mehbi Abedi, "Ali Shariati: The Architect of the 1979 Islamic Revolution of Iran," *Iranian Studies* 19, no. 3–4 (1986): 229–234.

[29] Among the groups that claimed to follow Shariati's social and political path in postrevolutionary Iran, the largest was the Organization of the Vanguard Fighters of the Oppressed (*sazeman-e razmandegan-e pishgam-e mostazafin*), also known as Aspirations of the Oppressed (*arman-e mostazafin*). Some members of the group including the group's leader, Mohammad Bagher Borzoui, were jailed in the early 1980s. Another group with which some of Shariati's followers, including Reza Alijani and Taghi Rahmani, were involved during the late 1970s and early 1980s was the Organization of Revolutionary

While Shariati's radical Islamic discourse continues to irk the ruling class, his intellectual legacy remains a source of controversy and polarization in both academic and public discussions. The literature on Shariati seems to be permanently shaped by a series of unending debates. For some, he was a harbinger of the Islamist ascendancy during and after the 1979 revolution. They argue that in postrevolutionary Iran, Shariati's legacy has been kept alive in the major discourses and institutions of the Islamic Republic, including in the new regime's hostility toward the West and Western modernity as well as in the religiously mediated political construct of *velayat-e faqih* (the guardianship of the Islamic jurist).[30] Others suggest that Shariati's significance as an Islamic ideologue came to an end with the overthrow of the Pahlavi dynasty. According to the Iranian intellectual, Ehsan Naraghi, for example, Shariati's discourse was merely a reflection of the revolutionary, utopian, and ideological fervor that defined the 1960s and 1970s. In his view, "once [Iranian] society underwent a revolutionary phase, there was not much left in Shariati's thought that would be relevant for the postrevolutionary project."[31]

Despite Naraghi's pronouncement of his thought as an outdated and obsolete discourse, today Shariati's works continue to enjoy wide readership, including among the youth.[32] Each year, several books, conference proceedings, special journal and magazine issues, and newspaper articles are published examining Shariati's enduring relevance in ongoing social, political, cultural, and philosophical debates in Iranian society. Shariati's intellectual legacy has also been the subject of several

---

Monotheists (*sazman-e movahedin enghelabi*). Today, the most prominent group in Iran that is associated with Shariati's intellectual and political legacy is the Nationalist-Religious Coalition (*etelaaf-e mellimazhabi*), an opposition organization which pledges allegiance to the ideals of both Mosaddegh and Shariati and supports democratic social and political reforms.

[30] See: Abdolkarim Soroush, *Az Shariati (On Shariati)* (Tehran: Serat, 1384/2006), 8–9; Ali Mirsepassi, "Religious Intellectuals and Western Critiques of Secular Modernity," *Comparative Studies of South Asia, Africa and the Middle East* 26, no. 3 (2006): 416.

[31] Ehsan Naraghi, "Tafakor gheir-demokratik-e Shariati amel-e nakami eslahat" ("Shariati's anti-Democratic Thought Responsible for the Failure of Reformism"), *Etemad Melli* 29, Khordad 1385/19 June 2006, http://talar.shandel.info/showthread.php?tid=237#post_486 (accessed May 14, 2013).

[32] In 2012, the CD ROM of the complete collection of Shariati's works, released by Shariati's Cultural Foundation (*bonyad-e farhangi-e Shariati*), was in the best-selling book charts in Iran for several consecutive months. Also see: Shireen T. Hunter, "Islamic Reformist Discourses in Iran: Proponents and Prospects," in *Reformist Voices of Islam: Mediating Islam and Modernity*, ed. Shireen T. Hunter (Armonk, NY: M. E. Sharpe, 2008), 56.

graduate dissertations by a new generation of Iranian scholars.[33] These new readings reveal the multidimensionality of Shariati's body of work, drawing attention to some of the previously neglected aspects of his thought. Though attentive to his significance in the revolutionary movement, these contributions seek primarily to tease out the implications of Shariati's thought for addressing a range of topics in postrevolutionary Iran, including transition to democracy and secularism, demands for citizenship rights and gender equality, and the renegotiation of individual and collective identity in the face of the ongoing debasement of traditional sources of identity.

Outside of Iran too, in several other Middle Eastern countries, Shariati's thought continues to find new audiences and to influence social, political, and intellectual debates. As early as in the late 1970s, Shariati's works and their translations appeared in Afghanistan, Turkey, Algeria, Lebanon, Syria, and Egypt, and in more recent years the full collection of his writings has been released in both Arabic and Turkish. For many religious and Leftist intellectuals in these countries, Shariati's critical position toward Western hegemony and imperialist relations of domination, his critique of Westernization and Eurocentric modernization, his discourse of revolutionary consciousness and popular movement, his attention to local knowledge and his view about the limitations of Eurocentric analytical frameworks for understanding the particular condition of Muslim societies, his revolutionary and egalitarian interpretation of Islamic teachings, and his synthesis of Islam and socialism, offer a novel and contextually grounded discourse of social and political change. Another appealing aspect of Shariati's thought for his non-Iranian and non-Shi'i Muslim readers is the way in which his Islamic discourse transcends the sectarian divides between Shi'ism and Sunnism. As noted by a number of scholars, even though Shariati draws on concepts from the Shi'i tradition, by citing various Sunni scholars and by distinguishing between the oppressive and emancipatory aspects of Shi'ism, he effectively highlights the commonalities between progressive currents in the Shi'i and Sunni traditions.[34]

Beyond the immediate regional context of the Middle East, in recent years an increasing number of scholars have begun to see Shariati as one

---

[33] See: *Shariati dar daneshgah (Shariati in the Academy)*, ed. Bonyad Shariati (Tehran: Bonyad Farhangi-e Doctor Ali Shariati, 1390/2011).

[34] Syed Farid Alatas, "Goftegoo" ("Interview"), in *Shariati dar daneshgah (Shariati at the University)*, ed. Bonyad Shariati (Tehran: Bonyad Farhangi-e Doctor Ali Shariati, 1390/2011), 114; Hamid Algar, *The Roots of the Islamic Revolution* (Areekode, Kerala: Islamic Foundation Press, 1988), 49.

of the major voices of contemporary non-Western thought.[35] Many of these scholars have drawn attention to Shariati's contribution to unsettling the Islam/modernity binary and the hegemony of colonial modernity in the particular context of twentieth century Muslim societies. For Fred Dallmayr, Shariati's thought represents an effort to move beyond both Westerncentrism and culturalism and to invoke the liberating capacities of Islamic thought in conversation with other emancipatory theologies and philosophies.[36] Syed Farid Alatas describes Shariati as a pioneering critic of "the lingering psychological dimension of colonialism," who sought to replace the prevailing Eurocentric modes of analysis with a cosmopolitan frame of thought that gave recognition to social and cultural diversity and difference.[37] Walter Mignolo regards him as an early advocate of "de-coloniality" or an epistemic delinking from the colonial modes of knowledge and understanding.[38] And Raewyn Connell believes that Shariati was among the first anticolonial intellectuals in the global South who challenged the Eurocentric dynamics of knowledge production and advocated that freedom from imperial domination and Western hegemony required "the rediscovery of local identity or selfhood."[39]

To these contributions one must add a rich body of academic literature (in English) on Shariati's work by several scholars in the areas of Iranian and Islamic studies such as Mangol Bayat-Philipp, Ervand Abrahamian, Abdulaziz Sachedina, Hamid Algar, Shahrough Akhavi, Hamid Dabashi, Ali Rahnema, Ziba Mir-Hosseini, Yann Richard, Shireen Hunter, and Kingshuk Chatterjee, among others.[40] While the present book relies on

[35] See: Walter Mignolo, "Yes, We Can: Non-European Thinkers and Philosophers," Al-Jazeera, February 19, 2013, www.aljazeera.com/indepth/opinion/2013/02/20132672747320891.html (accessed March 13, 2013).
[36] Fred Dallmayr, *Alternative Visions: Paths in the Global Village* (Lanham, MD: Rowman & Littlefield Publishers, 1998), 92–94.
[37] Syed Farid Alatas, *Alternative Discourses in Asian Social Science: Responses to Eurocentrism* (London and California: Sage Publications, 2006), 52.
[38] Walter Mignolo, "Delinking: The Rhetoric of Modernity, the Logic of Coloniality and the Grammar of De-Coloniality," *Cultural Studies* 21, no. 2 (2007): 449–514; Mignolo, *Darker Side of Western Modernity*, xxx.
[39] Raewyn Connell, *Southern Theory: The Global Dynamics of Knowledge in Social Science* (Cambridge: Polity Press, 2007), 134.
[40] See: Mangol Bayat-Philipp, "Shi'ism in Contemporary Iranian Politics: The Case of Ali Shari'ati," in *Towards a Modern Iran: Studies in Thought, Politics and Society*, ed. E. Kedourie, and S. G. Haim (London: Frank Cass Co. Ltd., 1980), 155–168; Ervand Abrahamian, "Ali Shari'ati: Ideologue of the Iranian Revolution," *MERIP Reports*, no. 102, *Islam and Politics* (January 1982): 24–28; Abdulaziz Sachedina, "Ali Shariati: Ideologue of the Iranian Revolution," in *Voices of Resurgent Islam*, ed. John L. Esposito (New York: Oxford University Press, 1983), 191–214; Algar, *Roots of the Islamic*

this vast body of research and discusses at length the analyses of some of these scholars, it also presents a unique approach for examining Shariati's intellectual legacy in Iran and beyond. The attention to and close reading of the works by Shariati's intellectual followers in postrevolutionary Iran is one feature that sets this work apart from the numerous other titles that have been published on Shariati since the early 1980s. Though important in shedding light on various aspects of Shariati's life and thinking, the aforementioned contributions have been largely inattentive to the ways in which Shariati's thought and legacy are understood by his present-day followers. The postrevolutionary rise of the neo-Shariati current, however, deserves close attention for at least two separate sets of reasons. First, the neo-Shariati reclaiming and rereading of Shariati as one of the major advocates of a revolutionary Islamic discourse in Iran during the 1960s and 1970s is not only an intellectual but also an inherently political exercise. To reread Shariati is, in effect, to reread the intellectual foundations of the 1979 revolution. Second, during the last two decades, neo-Shariatis have been an important force in Iran's democratic reform movement and opposition to Islamism. Some of the leading figures of this current, including Reza Alijani, Taghi Rahmani, and Hassan Yousefi Eshkevari have faced imprisonment and exile, while others such as Ehsan Shariati and Hashem Aghajari have been banned from teaching in universities. Examining the rise of neo-Shariatis, therefore, helps to understand not only the intellectual and sociopolitical dynamics of an indigenous and grassroots democratic movement in Iran, but also the gradual exhaustion of Islamist politics and the Islam/modernity binary that has helped to sustain and legitimize it.

Another novel feature of this book is its dialogical reading of Shariati's thought, a methodological feature, which will be discussed in more detail in the following section. Though the arguments that I present are

---

Revolution; Shahrough Akhavi, "Islam, Politics and Society in the Thought of Ayatullah Khomeini, Ayatullah Taliqani and Ali Shariati," *Middle Eastern Studies* 24, no. 4 (October 1988): 404–431; Hamid Dabashi, *Theology of Discontent: The Ideological Foundation of the Islamic Revolution in Iran* (New York and London: New York University Press, 1993); Rahnema, *Islamic Utopian*; Ziba Mir-Hosseini, "Religious Modernists and the 'Woman Question': Challenges and Complicities," in *Twenty Years of Islamic Revolution: Political and Social Transition in Iran since 1979*, ed. Eric Hooglund (Syracuse University Press, 2002), 74–95; Yann Richard, "Contemporary Shi'i Thought," in *Modern Iran: Roots and Results of Revolution*, ed. Nikki R. Keddie (New Haven, CT: Yale University Press, 2003), 202–229; Hunter, "Islamic Reformist Discourses," 33–95; Kingshuk Chatterjee, *'Ali Shari'ati and the Shaping of Political Islam in Iran* (New York: Palgrave Macmillan, 2011).

sustained primarily through a textual analysis of works by Shariati and neo-Shariatis, I take caution not to treat these texts as if they exist, or are produced and read, in a social or historical vacuum. As such, in the first two chapters I make the case that Shariati's thought must be properly understood as part of a broader attempt within modern Islamic thought to reconcile the Islamic tradition with contemporary challenges and realities. Locating Shariati's discourse of indigenous modernity in the wider context of debates on modernization, secularization, and Westernization in contemporary Islamic thought, Chapter 2 in particular draws several parallels between Shariati's thought (and its new readings) and the discourses of a range of Muslim modernists and reformists, while at the same time making a clear demarcation between Shariati's brand of Islamic thought and Islamism. In this regard, particular attention is paid to Shariati's and neo-Shariatis' rejection of the notion of the Islamic state which, as I argue, is the very heart of Islamist thinking. In introducing this demarcation, I am careful not to reduce to Islamism all modes of critical engagement with Western modernity that appeal to Islam either for its mobilizational capacity or its ontological insight. I am also cautious to avoid reducing Islamism to the singular antagonist of Western modernity and in doing so to perpetuate the myth of Islamic exceptionalism.

Proceeding with this comparative approach, in the subsequent three chapters I take a number of analytical steps to reveal the ways in which Shariati's thought finds common ground with a range of global discourses that treat Europe's Enlightenment modernity, its metanarratives of modernization and secularization, and its associated sociopolitical and socioeconomic formations (i.e., the nation-state structure and capitalist economics) as objects of reform and critique. In Chapter 3, this is accomplished by probing similarities between Shariati's vision of a religiously mediated indigenous modernity and the analytical frameworks of public religion, as articulated by José Casanova, and multiple modernities, as defined by Shmuel N. Eisenstadt. Chapter 4 focuses on Shariati's philosophical engagement with Enlightenment modernity and his attempt to identify Islam's *tawhidi* worldview as an alternative ontological ground for the negotiation of human subjectivity. Here, Shariati's Islamic thought is placed in dialogue with Charles Taylor's communitarian thought, Cornel West's liberation theology, and Fred Dallmayr's Gadamerian phenomenology. Chapter 5 continues to investigate Shariati's critical engagement with Western modernity, this time by focusing on his views regarding the colonial construction of the civilizational binary of East/West. Though the chapter notes that, perhaps under the influence of

European orientalist discourses, Shariati's thought reproduces certain articulations of this civilizational binary, it nevertheless draws parallels between Shariati's critique and the contributions of postcolonial theorists such as Edward Said, Prasenjit Duara, and Hamid Dabashi.

Islam and Modernity through the Lens of Dialogical Comparison

In examining Shariati's thought and its new readings in relation to the ongoing debates on Islam and modernity, the primary method used in this book is dialogical comparison. The method is often associated with the work of comparative political theorist Fred Dallmayr. It encourages "mutual interpretation" through attentiveness not only to difference, but also to border-crossings, cross-cultural encounters, and cross-linguistic equivalences.[41] Unlike conventional comparative analysis, dialogical comparison seeks to arrive not at a universal standard for measurement and understanding, but rather at "shared meanings and practices" through close attention to "lateral interaction, negotiation, and contestation among different, historically grown cultural frameworks."[42] Applied to the analysis of texts, the method is essentially a "hermeneutical" approach intended "to gain understanding through an intensive dialogue ... between reader and text, between self and other, between indigenous traditions and alien life-forms."[43] Drawing on the contributions of German philosopher Hans-Georg Gadamer, and building on the work of a number of comparative political theorists including Anthony Parel, Hwa Yol Jung, and Bhikhu Parekh, Dallmayr's work throughout the past four decades has underscored dialogical possibilities in European, East Asian, Indian, and Muslim intellectual traditions.

Dialogical comparison, as defined by Dallmayr and others, entails not only a methodological commitment to the hermeneutical understanding of cross-cultural encounters, but also a political commitment to challenging and critiquing power relations that undermine cosmopolitan visions of the world. It may thus be argued that developing and implementing this method is part of an effort to negotiate a third way between the normative poles of universalism and parochialism.[44] As noted by Roxanne

---

[41] Fred Dallmayr, "Beyond Monologue: For a Comparative Political Theory," *Perspectives on Politics* 2, no. 2 (June 2004): 249.
[42] Ibid.
[43] Ibid., 250.
[44] Ibid., 254.

Euben, comparative political theory's logic of dialogical comparison works on the assumption that "disparate cultures are not worlds apart, morally and cognitively incommensurable, but exist in conversation with one another, even if they have serious moral and political disagreements."[45] This assumption, according to Euben, does not automatically suggest that political questions and debates are essentially universal dilemmas that surface in all human societies uniformly, irrespective of really existing material and cultural differences. Instead, the assumption is reflective of a certain feature of the modern world, namely the globalization of Western colonial modernity and many of its socioeconomic, sociopolitical, and sociocultural constellations. Euben argues that the exercise of dialogical comparison begins with the acknowledgment that colonialism and globalization have brought diverse cultures and peoples into unprecedented proximity, while also producing highly asymmetrical global power relations. In this context, dialogical comparison challenges the condition of hegemony and Westerncentrism and seeks to give recognition to the "possibility that there is humanly significant knowledge outside the confines of the Western canon." It does so, however, not by appealing to universal truth claims, but rather by "emphasizing shared dilemmas and questions."[46]

In developing the theoretical framework of this book, I have drawn on both normative and methodological insights of comparative political theory. Essential to this framework is the assumption that the globalization of Europe's colonial modernity since the fifteenth century has brought dispersed human societies into close proximity and made possible the opening up of new dialogical sites for rethinking not only coloniality and modernity, but also cosmopolitanism and active global solidarity. Moreover, in employing the method of dialogical comparison, I have made a conscious effort in this book to avoid the problematic exercise of assessing the content and the normative claims of Shariati and neo-Shariatis against an established Western canonical yardstick. Instead, the Islamic discourse of Shariati and neo-Shariatis is put in conversation with some of the other responses to European Enlightenment and colonial modernity in Islamic thought, postcolonial thought, and contemporary

---

[45] Roxanne L. Euben, *Enemy in the Mirror: Islamic Fundamentalism and the Limits of Modern Rationalism: A Work of Comparative Political Theory* (Princeton, NJ: Princeton University Press, 1999), 10. Also see: Roxanne L. Euben, "Contingent Borders, Syncretic Perspectives: Globalization, Political Theory, and Islamizing Knowledge," *International Studies Review* 4, no. 1 (2002): 26.

[46] Ibid., 10.

Western normative thought along the axis of four major themes: the genealogy of modernity, the Islam/modernity binary, colonial legacy and Eurocentrism, and identity and identitarianism.

What is revealed in these dialogical readings is not only the deficiency of the Eurocentric metanarratives of modernization and secularization for analyzing the complex and multifaceted processes of sociocultural, sociopolitical, and socioeconomic change in both Western and non-Western contexts, but also the existence of many similarities and equivalences between Shariati's thought and other regional and global responses to modernity. In Chapter 2 for example, I reject the juxtaposition of Shariati's thought with the discourse of Islamic reformism and highlight the overlaps between his intellectual project and those of contemporary Muslim reformers including Mohammed Arkoun, Nasr Hamid Abu Zayd, Fethullah Gülen, and Abdolkarim Soroush. Similarly, in comparing and contrasting Shariati's critique of the philosophical foundations of Enlightenment modernity with some of the Western critiques of Enlightenment thought, Chapter 4 draws attention to some of the ways in which Shariati's views about the capacities of emancipatory Islamic thought for negotiating an alternative ontology to that of Enlightenment rationalism find common ground with the views of Cornel West about the antidomination ontology of prophetic Christianity and those of Max Horkheimer and Theodor Adorno about the progressive inspirational capacities of the Jewish tradition. In these and other discussions, the book seeks to identify the particularities of Shariati's discourse without assuming the irreconcilability of difference and the impossibility of "mutual" understanding and "shared meaning," and to find its common ground with other local and global emancipatory discourses without taking the stance of a "universal spectator" possessing a "global yardstick."[47]

Chapters' Summaries

Chapter 1 examines the various readings of Ali Shariati's work and intellectual legacy by his critics and sympathizers in the post-1979 revolution context. This is done, first, by making a distinction between the contesting readings of Shariati's thought as a finished and as an unfinished project, and second, by comparing and contrasting these readings in relation to ongoing debates on the Islam/modernity binary. The chapter argues that in

---

[47] Dallmayr, "Introduction," 421–422.

its neo-Shariati reading, Shariati's thought presents itself as an unfinished project of indigenous modernity aimed at advancing a bottom-up cultural, intellectual, and sociopolitical transformation of Iranian society and presenting a third way between the dichotomous discourses of modernism and Islamism.

To locate Shariati's particular vision of indigenous modernity within the broader setting of contemporary Islamic thought, Chapter 2 provides an overview of some of the major debates among leading Muslim thinkers about the condition, content, and consequences of the late-nineteenth-century encounter with European colonial modernity in Islamicate contexts. Distinguishing between the currents of traditionalism, modernism, Islamism, and reformism, the chapter argues that the discourses of Shariati and neo-Shariatis find common ground with those of a range of contemporary Muslim modernists and reformists who have contributed to the negotiation of contextually grounded visions of sociopolitical change in Muslim societies. To further explore the content of his particular vision of indigenous modernity, Chapter 3 focuses on the articulation by Shariati of a postcolonial discourse of public religion that utilizes Islam's ontological-inspirational as well as social-mobilizational capacities for a bottom-up advancement of sociocultural and sociopolitical development in Iran and other Muslim societies. The chapter also examines the effort by neo-Shariatis to move forward Shariati's unfinished project by way of highlighting his spiritual, humanist, and egalitarian interpretation of Islamic thought and emphasizing the role of intellectuals as agents of cultural-intellectual change within civil society.

Chapter 4 probes the philosophical foundations of Shariati's religiously mediated theory of indigenous modernity. It begins with a critical assessment of some of the ways in which his philosophical premises have been the subject of critique by a number of contemporary scholars. Notably, the chapter focuses on the views of two prominent Iranian-American social theorists, Ali Mirsepassi and Farzin Vahdat, who in a number of works over the last decade have described Shariati's religious ontology as antithetical to the modern notion of individual subjectivity. After a critical assessment of these accounts and their normative underpinnings, the chapter turns to the new philosophical readings of Shariati's thought by his contemporary intellectual followers. A case is made that contrary to the views of Mirsepassi and Vahdat, in both pre- and postrevolutionary Iran, Shariati's thought and its new readings have contributed to the negotiation of a contextually grounded account of an autonomous human subject and the rights-bearing individual. I argue that the critical engagement of Shariati and neo-Shariatis with the philosophical foundations of Enlightenment modernity is informed to a large extent by their view of the crisis of the modern subject in Western modernity and their attempt to redefine the relationship between the modern self and its others through a religiously mediated account of subjectivity.

Chapter 5 asks if Shariati's critique of Enlightenment modernity and Westernization amounts to an anti-Western stance or to Orientalism in reverse. The chapter begins with a discussion about the civilizational framework of Shariati's thought. It is shown that Shariati saw the discourse of civilization (*tamadon*) as a counter-hegemonic alternative to the prevailing and state-sponsored discourse of modernization (*tajadod*). I argue that for Shariati, the negotiation of indigenous modernities in Iran and other non-Western contexts is necessary not only for facilitating progressive and bottom-up change, but also for moving toward a postcolonial condition of localized cosmopolitanism and civilizational diversity. After identifying some of the conceptual limitations and political pitfalls of the civilizational frame of analysis, the final section discusses some of the ways in which neo-Shariatis have sought to critically reexamine and to go beyond Shariati's civilizational framework. The chapter's conclusion suggests that in a critical and constructive conversation with other contemporary advocates of post-Orientalism and post-Occidentalism, neo-Shariatis can further advance Shariati's simultaneous and radical deconstruction of hegemonic universalism and essentialist particularism in contemporary Iranian society, and expand on his cosmopolitan solidarities with global emancipatory discourses and struggles.

Finally, the Conclusion identifies some of the potential sites of dialogue and creative engagement between Shariati and a number of contemporary critics of colonial modernity such as Enrique Dussel, Walter Mignolo, Sanjay Subrahmanyam, and Hamid Dabashi. After presenting some brief observations about the potential bearings of Shariati's thought and its new readings in the context of the present sociopolitical developments in the Middle East and North Africa, the Conclusion asks how the neo-Shariati variant of Islamic thought may contribute to debates about the decolonization and indigenization of knowledge that have gained ground in recent decades in a number of Muslim societies.

I

Postrevolutionary Readings of a Revolutionary Islamic Discourse

Revolution, Ideology, and the "Geography of Discourse"

Returning to Iran from Paris in 1964, and convinced that a progressive transformation in Iranian society would be impossible without a radical change in the consciousness of the masses, Shariati focused his efforts on articulating a contextually grounded revolutionary ideology by appealing to what he saw as the emancipatory potential of the local cultural and religious traditions. For him, one of the major hindrances to genuine development in Iran, as in many other non-Western societies, was the inability of intellectuals to communicate effectively with the masses. Critiquing the Eurocentricity of educated elites, Shariati wrote about a class of intellectuals in early-twentieth-century Iran, "whose most recognizable characteristic was that the further they pursued their intellectualism the further away they removed themselves from their own people; they felt estranged from their own society while feeling ever closer to Europeans."[1] These intellectuals, many of them graduates of European universities, resented what they saw as the backwardness of their own societies vis-à-vis Europe, rejected all indigenous sources of knowledge, and "judged their history, culture, religion, and themselves, against the only frame of reference that they knew," namely European modernity.[2]

---

[1] Ali Shariati, *Ma va Iqbal: majmooeh asar 5 (Iqbal and Us: Collected Works 5)*, (Aachen, Germany: Hosseinieh Ershad, 1978), 230.
[2] Ibid., 231.

Shariati's views about the estrangement of modern Iranian intellectuals from their indigenous sources of identity and their assessment of their society and culture from a Eurocentric perspective echoes Frantz Fanon's analysis about the self-alienating effects of colonialism on the colonized. In *Black Skin, White Masks* (1952), Fanon defined "alienation" as a "psychic" form of violence and a colonial byproduct, as a result of which the colonized come to see themselves from the perspective of, and thus inferior to, their colonizers.[3] Similarly, Shariati saw Eurocentrism or "Westoxication" (*gharbzadegi*) as a cultural consequence of colonialism with varied intellectual and social manifestations in the colonial periphery.[4] In his view, though the phenomenon also took the form of adopting Western "consumption patterns and lifestyles," its most devastating and paralyzing effect was the "Westoxication of the intellect."[5] Thus, in *Iqbal and Us* (*Ma va Iqbal*) Shariati wrote, "there is nothing more tragic than when our intellectuals see themselves through the eyes of the other and use foreign points of reference and analytical tools to gain knowledge of their own thoughts, culture, history, and religion."[6]

Like Fanon, Shariati believed that self-alienation was most pronouncedly evident among the educated elites who were deeply integrated into the colonial and imperial structures of power and their associated modes of economic and knowledge production. He argued that the encounter with and the hegemony of European modernity created a chasm between the masses of the people and the intellectual class. The majority of the population at the time was under the influence of traditional sources of authority, namely the clerical institution, monarchy, and local landowning elites. Faced with and attempting to fundamentally challenge these traditional power structures, the new educated class sought to realize its modernist vision primarily by renouncing local cultural traditions and popular religious beliefs.[7] "As a result," Shariati wrote, "this intellectual minority alienated itself from the masses of the people, and rather

---

[3] Frantz Fanon, *Black Skin, White Masks* (Originally published 1952), trans. Charles Lam Markmann (London: Pluto Press, 1986), 34.

[4] Ali Shariati, "Bazgasht beh kodam khish?" ("Return to Which Self?") 1350/1971, C.W. 4, *Ali Shariati: The Complete Collection of Works* [CD ROM], Tehran: Shariati Cultural Foundation, 2010. The term *gharbzadegi* was coined originally by prominent Iranian writer Jalal Ale Ahmad in a book with the same title published in 1962.

[5] Ibid.

[6] Shariati, *Ma va Iqbal*, 152.

[7] Ali Shariati, "Nameh beh Ehsan" ("Letter to Ehsan") Farvardin-Ordibehesht 1356/April–May 1977, C.W. 1, *Ali Shariati: The Complete Collection of Works* [CD ROM], Tehran: Shariati Cultural Foundation, 2010.

than contributing to the organic evolution of our society it became an inorganic entity dependent on alien histories, cultures, and political agendas."[8] Though he credited the secular Left with developing a clear analysis about the economic aspects of colonialism, he nevertheless charged them with failing to see the cultural consequences of the colonial condition and even acting as the agents of the project of Westernization.[9]

In contradistinction to Westoxicated, Eurocentric, and self-alienated intellectuals, Shariati introduced another category of intellectuals to whom he referred as "authentic." Whereas the former group often spoke "Anglicized or Frenchified versions of their mother tongue," the latter group spoke the language of the masses.[10] Unlike Eurocentric intellectuals who depended entirely on Western frames of analysis and lacked a thorough knowledge of their local cultures and histories, authentic intellectuals were able to formulate contextually relevant analyses that addressed the particular challenges of their society and epoch.[11] These intellectuals, Shariati argued, were keenly mindful of the cultural embeddedness and the indigenous sources of the self, which included "historical and civilizational elements demarcating one's identity from other categories of identification such as Westerner or Easterner, American or African."[12] In his view, Sayyid Jamal al-Din Afghani, Muhammad Abduh, and Muhammad Iqbal were some of the archetypal figures of authentic intellectualism in Islamicate contexts who combined their anticolonial analysis with a deep knowledge of local traditions and a firm commitment to improve the objective conditions of the Muslim masses.[13] On the other hand, Mirza Malkom Khan and Seyed Hassan Taghizadeh, who were among the leading intellectual figures of the Constitutional Movement, were regarded by Shariati as stereotypical examples of self-alienated intellectuals. The latter had reportedly called for the "total Westernization of Iranian society, from head to toe."[14]

Shariati's critical position toward Eurocentric metanarratives of modernity and his emphasis on the contextual determinants of knowledge

---

[8] Ibid.
[9] Shariati, "Bazgasht beh khodam khish?"
[10] Shariati, *Ma va Iqbal*, 157.
[11] Ali Rahnema, *An Islamic Utopian: A Political Biography of Ali Shari'ati* (London and New York: I.B. Tauris, 2000), 196, 250.
[12] Ali Shariati, *Bazgasht: majmooeh asar 4 (Return: Collected Works 4)* (Tehran: Entesharat-e Elham, 1373/1994), 18.
[13] Shariati, *Ma va Iqbal*, 73–105.
[14] Shariati, *Bazgasht*, 243.

production particularly in the area of social sciences also echoed calls for the decolonization of knowledge in the latter half of the twentieth century by such non-European social scientists as Orlando Fals Borda, Lloyd Best, and Syed Hussein Alatas. Highlighting the link between the global expansion of Europe's colonial modernity and the hegemony of Eurocentric discourses of sociocultural development in the non-Western world, Shariati called on Iranian intellectuals to be mindful of what he termed the "geography of discourse" (*joghrafia-ye harf*).[15] According to him, in social and political matters it was not possible to simply import a theory or ideology from one context and apply it to another. A critical task for authentic intellectuals then was to gain knowledge of their local context and of a range of contextual determinants of change including the prevailing social and cultural attitudes, predominant power relations, and the consequences of colonial and imperial relations of domination.[16] In *Return* (*Bazgasht*), Shariati posited that theories and methodologies of social and political change were always relative and context-dependent. Whereas in natural sciences ideas or concepts could be examined on their own merits and vis-à-vis a set of known, rational, and scientific variables, "in the production of social and political knowledge, geography must be taken into account as a major component of analysis."[17] Each society, he claimed, was "a living and dynamic" organism with a collective consciousness which had to be studied and analyzed with respect to its particularities.[18]

Shariati further believed that by developing a deep understanding of indigenous cultures, local traditions, and popular beliefs, authentic intellectuals could contribute to the articulation of a revolutionary ideology that resonated with the masses of the people. Witnessing the fervent ideological battles of the mid-twentieth century in Europe and around the world, he was convinced that ideological conviction was a vital component of any revolutionary movement. In his view, ideology served the purpose of raising self-consciousness among and empowering the masses, who had been traditionally excluded from the political process. He defined ideology as a coherent awareness of the existing contradictions within a society with the power of mobilizing the masses and giving direction to their popular movements.[19] Identifying "ideological

---

[15] Ibid., 276.
[16] Shariati, *Ma va Iqbal*, 92.
[17] Shariati, *Bazgasht*, 276.
[18] Ibid., 279.
[19] Ibid., 144.

awareness" as a major component of all anticolonial struggles throughout the Third World, Shariati wrote:

> We can see in our present time ... that many colonized nations have, through a nationalist or class-based ideology, achieved national rebirths, and within a relatively short period have accomplished a significant level of progress, empowerment, and civilization. Ideological awareness, working as a powerful spirit, gives life to the dead body of a race, nation, and society that has been captive to the forces of stagnation. And through this ideological awareness the dead rise from their graves and embark on a revolution of life, vitality, evolution, creativity, ingenuity, culture, science, philosophy, and art.[20]

In the context of twentieth-century Iran, Shariati regarded Islam and Shi'ism as the two vital components of Iranian collective identity and called for the development of an Islamic or Shi'i ideology as a contextually grounded discourse of progressive change. Such an ideology, he held, had the capacity to bridge the chasm between the educated elites and the religious masses, and to enable anti-status quo intellectuals to introduce new ideas into society using a language and idioms that were familiar to the Muslim masses. At the same time, by releasing the emancipatory capacities of the local cultural and religious traditions this ideological project could facilitate the emergence of a self-conscious and empowered citizenry.[21] For Shariati, ideologization of religion was an attempt "to transform Islam from an assortment of unconscious, habitual, and useless rituals, prayers, mottos, and practices, into a self-conscious, dynamic, and emancipatory faith that creates agency and gives birth to a new set of values, and harbingers social rebirth and movement."[22]

Shariati's revolutionary Islamic ideology was constructed in opposition to and as a call for mass mobilization against an authoritarian and dependent Pahlavi regime and its forceful imposition of a capitalist modernization and Westernization program on various aspects of social, cultural, and economic life in Iran. It was also presented as an alternative to socialist and Marxist, and to a lesser extent secular liberal nationalist, discourses that opposed the Pahlavi regime and its dependency on imperial powers but were unable to effectively mobilize Iranian masses. Therefore, Shariati often referred to Western imperialism and domestic tyranny as the

---

[20] Ibid., 150.
[21] Ali Shariati, "Nameh beh Ehsan."
[22] Ali Shariati, "Nameh beh aghayan Homayoun va Minachi," ("Letter to Mr. Homayoun and Mr. Minachi") 1351/1972, C.W. 1, *Ali Shariati: The Complete Collection of Works* [CD ROM], Tehran: Shariati Cultural Foundation, 2010.

"enemy" (*doshman*) and to socialist and Marxist revolutionary discourses as the "competition" (*raghib*).[23] Despite maintaining a sympathetic position toward and freely borrowing from socialist and Marxist revolutionary thought, Shariati's critique of the representatives of these traditions in Iran was not simply their failure to communicate effectively with the religious masses. As I will argue in the following chapters, in calling for a return to the indigenous Iranian self, Shariati sought not only to draw on the social-mobilizational capacities of the local sources of identity, but also to articulate an alternative vision of progress to that of Enlightenment modernity on the basis of the ontological-inspirational capacities of the local cultural and religious traditions. In his view, socialist and Marxist thought represented extensions, albeit progressive, of the Enlightenment tradition and their introduction into Iranian society, as in other non-Western societies, was a function of the globalization of Europe's colonial modernity.

There are, to be sure, undeniable overlaps between Shariati's Islamic ideology and Marxism. For one thing, Shariati's ideological reading of Islam and Shi'ism contains within it a modified version of the Hegelian-Marxian view of a dialectical movement in history. Thus, in retelling the story of the revolt of the third Shi'i Imam, Hussain ibn Ali, against the Umayyad Caliphate, Shariati explains that the ideological core of Shi'ism is a conviction that the progression of history is the result of a clash, in various spheres and periods, between justice and injustice. History, in this ideology, begins with the conflict between Cain and Abel and ends with the revolt of Imam Mahdi (the last Shi'i imam and a messianic figure who is believed to have been in occultation since the late ninth century and expected to return in an undetermined future). The ultimate result of this dialectic will be the victory of "the wretched of the earth" and the triumph of "equality, fraternity, peace, and light." The sociopolitical implication of such an ideology, Shariati held, was that "in each context and epoch" individuals must attempt to correctly identify the main contradictions and to fulfill the historical obligation of fighting on behalf of justice and the transcendental values of freedom and equality.[24] Despite sharing with Marxism a dialectical view of history and an egalitarian orientation, Shariati maintained that his Islamic ideology was more than simply

[23] Ali Shariati, "Chegooneh mandan" ("How to Stay"), 1355/1976, C.W. 2, *Ali Shariati: The Complete Collection of Works* [CD ROM], Tehran: Shariati Cultural Foundation, 2010; Ali Shariati, "Nameh beh yek baradar," ("Letter to a Brother"), 1355/1976, C.W. 1, *Ali Shariati: The Complete Collection of Works* [CD ROM], Tehran: Shariati Cultural Foundation, 2010.

[24] Ali Shariati, "Horr," 1355/1976, C.W. 2, *Ali Shariati: The Complete Collection of Works* [CD ROM], Tehran: Shariati Cultural Foundation, 2010.

an indigenous or Islamized version of the former ideology. An Islamic or *tawhidi* (monotheistic) ideology, he argued, provided an alternative "to a vision of egalitarianism based on a materialistic worldview."[25]

Though his Islamic ideology gained enormous popularity among many of those who joined the revolutionary uprising of the late 1970s, Shariati himself did not live to see the revolution and its aftermath. Nevertheless, in the nearly four decades since his death, debates have continued about the substance of his intellectual project, and a wide range of commentators have sought to determine the relationship between Shariati's religious discourse, the 1979 revolution, and the ascendency of Islamism in postrevolutionary Iran. In a very broad sense, it may be possible to distinguish between two readings of Shariati's thought: one that regards it as an Islamist revolutionary discourse that reached its zenith with the 1979 revolution, and another that sees it as a vision of bottom-up and progressive sociocultural and sociopolitical change that remains relevant in postrevolutionary Iran. Even though some variations of the first reading suggest that Shariati's ideas are embodied in the discourses and institutions of the Islamic Republic, they nevertheless hold that his revolutionary discourse no longer corresponds to the contemporary realities of Iranian society. For many of those who adhere to this reading, Shariati's emphasis on intellectual responsibility and the revolutionary role of authentic intellectuals represents a statist and vanguardist view of social and political change. Furthermore, in this reading Shariati's critical position toward the European Enlightenment and his emphasis on indigenous religious, cultural, and civilizational sources of identity are seen as a rejection of modernity and a range of modern values. While the second reading acknowledges the revolutionary character of Shariati's thought, it nevertheless differentiates Shariati's Islamic discourse from the Islamist discourses that rose to ascendancy in the course of the revolution and after the establishment of the Islamic state. Shariati's work, in this reading, constitutes an unfinished project of indigenous modernity, advanced primarily through a radical restructuring of local religious and cultural traditions.

Shariati as the Ideologue of the 1979 Revolution

Ervand Abrahamian's "Ali Shari'ati: Ideologue of the Iranian Revolution" (1982) is one of the earliest works examining the relationship between

---

[25] Shariati, "Chegooneh."

Shariati's radical Islamic discourse and the 1979 revolution. Identifying him as the main ideological icon of the revolutionary movement, Abrahamian argues that Shariati's Islamic ideology successfully blended "traditional Shi'ism" with "modern socialism" and Fanonian Third Worldism.[26] In this essay, as well as in his seminal book, *Iran between Two Revolutions* (1982), Abrahamian asserts that in developing a radical Islamic discourse, Shariati set out to show that Islam is neither a "conservative and fatalistic creed" nor an "apolitical personal faith," but instead an emancipatory revolutionary ideology "that permeates all spheres of life, especially politics, and inspires true believers to fight against all forms of oppression, exploitation, and social injustice." For Shariati, he argues, Islam's anti-oppression and anti-exploitation orientation is inherent in its *tawhidi* worldview which requires believers to constantly strive "toward justice, equity, human brotherhood, public ownership of wealth, and, most important of all, a classless society."[27]

Returning to the ontological foundations of Shariati's revolutionary ideology in a subsequent work, titled *Radical Islam: The Iranian Mojahedin* (1989), Abrahamian argues that Shariati saw history as an evolutionary and dialectical process of human development. The driving force behind this dialectical movement was a combination of "God's will," an innate human desire "to reach a higher stage of consciousness," and "class struggle" between the oppressors and the oppressed. Abrahamian notes that in a number of his works including *Religion versus Religion*, Shariati made the case that out of the historical conflict between the two classes, two clashing religions had emerged: "that of the rulers sanctifying oppression, illegitimate power, and the status quo; and that of the ruled articulating a true sense of right and wrong, of good and evil, and of justice and injustice." In this view, all of human history could be seen as the battle between the religion of oppression and the religion of liberation. Shariati, it is further argued, believed that while the initial and true message of Islam was one of "permanent revolution" toward the realization of "social justice, human brotherhood, and eventually a classless society," the post-Muhammad caliphate "created a new imperial ruling class and ... transformed the religion of liberation into one of oppression." Thus

---

[26] Ervand Abrahamian, "Ali Shari'ati: Ideologue of the Iranian Revolution," *MERIP Reports*, no. 102, *Islam and Politics* (January 1982): 24.

[27] Ervand Abrahamian, *Iran between Two Revolutions* (Princeton, NJ: Princeton University Press, 1982), 466.

Shi'ism, as the path of the prophet's rightful heirs, rose the "banner of revolt and [showed] the world that the caliphs had betrayed the revolutionary message of Islam."[28] Yet, Shi'ism too had been "expropriated" and "institutionalized" by the official clerical class. It was now up to the authentic Muslim intellectuals to uphold the banner of revolt by "raising 'public consciousness', injecting dynamic thinking into people's awareness, and hastening the 'dialectical process': in short, leading the way towards the revolution."[29]

Throughout the 1980s and 1990s, Shariati's Islamic ideology and its relation to the 1979 revolution was the subject of analyses by a number of other commentators. Among these, Hamid Algar, in *The Roots of the Islamic Revolution* (1988), argues that while the revolutionary movement was led primarily by the Shi'i ulama, Shariati played a key role in preparing a large segment of Iran's younger educated class "to accept and follow with devotion and courage the leadership given by Ayatollah Khomeini."[30] Another commentator, Abdulaziz Sachedina, who studied under Shariati at the University of Mashhad during the late 1960s, posits that in a social context shaped on the one hand by the Pahlavi state's forceful "Westernization" program, and on the other by the inability of traditional religious and secular elites to present an alternative social and political agenda, Shariati's construction of Islam into a modern ideology led to an "Islamic revival among Iranian youth" and a regeneration of "the revolutionary and reformative aspects of early Islam."[31]

Also describing Shariati as a leading ideologue of the 1979 revolution is Hamid Dabashi's 1992 book, titled *Theology of Discontent: The Ideological Foundations of the Islamic Revolution in Iran*. Shariati's Islamic radicalism, Dabashi argues, "energized the Iranian political culture ... beyond anything known in its modern history."[32] According to him, Shariati's ultimate aim was to construct a revolutionary ideology capable of initiating a "massive ideological reconstitution of the status

---

[28] Ervand Abrahamian, *Radical Islam: The Iranian Mojahedin* (New Haven, CT: Yale University Press, 1989), 111–112.
[29] Ibid., 113.
[30] Hamid Algar, *The Roots of the Islamic Revolution* (Areekode, Kerala: Islamic Foundation Press, 1988), 49.
[31] Abdulaziz Sachedina, "Ali Shariati: Ideologue of the Iranian Revolution," in *Voices of Resurgent Islam*, ed. John L. Esposito (New York: Oxford University Press, 1983), 212.
[32] Hamid Dabashi, *Theology of Discontent: The Ideological Foundation of the Islamic Revolution in Iran* (New York and London: New York University Press, 1993), 103.

quo," and transforming "private pieties into public virtues."³³ In his reading of the Islamic language and content of Shariati's revolutionary thought, Dabashi identifies a dilemma that Shariati, as a Muslim revolutionary who believed in "the necessity of ideological convictions to augment, or advance, the 'material conditions' of any revolution," had to overcome. On the one hand, Shariati "witnessed the failure of radical 'Western' ideologies, transplanted from their native soil, attempting to take root in the political consciousness of the masses." On the other hand, however, he aimed "to mobilize the masses for political ends" articulated by those very same secular ideologies. Faced with this dilemma, Dabashi argues, "Shariati sought to achieve his revolutionary ends through the same ancient traditions that other secular ideologies considered as the opium of the masses."³⁴ Shariati, he further posits, aimed to rewrite "the entire Islamic history in a utopian language that would convince his young constituency of the political viability of his version of Shi'ite Islam," a project that included reinterpreting "Marxist utopian motifs based on specifically Shi'ite terms."³⁵

A more detailed analysis of Shariati's Islamic ideology is developed by Ali Rahnema in *An Islamic Utopian: A Political Biography of Ali Shariati* (2000), as well as in an essay, titled "Ali Shariati: Teacher, Preacher, Rebel" (2005). According to Rahnema, though a synthesis of many contradictory currents, Shariati's revolutionary thought is ultimately an egalitarian ideology based on a spiritual ontology. Shariati's ideal society, he argues "is founded on a socialist economic system governed by ethical and spiritual values firmly based on the Islamic belief in God."³⁶ Rahnema further identifies five distinct phases in the development of Shariati's political thought and his Islamic ideology. The first phase begins with Shariati's early enchantment with the character of Abu Zar (Abu Dharr al-Ghifari) (d. 652), an early convert to Islam known for his strict piety and opposition to corruption in the post-Muhammad institution of the caliphate during the rule of Caliph Uthman ibn Affan (577–656). Shariati considered Abu Zar to be the first Islamic socialist, and even referred to him as "the forefather of all post French Revolution egalitarian schools." Shariati's Abu Zar, Rahnema argues, is a "symbolic

---

³³ Ibid., 106.
³⁴ Ibid., 110.
³⁵ Ibid., 114.
³⁶ Ali Rahnema, "Ali Shariati: Teacher, Preacher, Rebel," in *Pioneers of Islamic Revival*, ed. Ali Rahnema (New York: Zed Books, 2005), 242.

creation" representing "the signal, code or allegory for the committed, defiant, revolutionary Muslim who preaches equality, fraternity, justice and liberation."[37] This early phase, we are told, is also marked in the early 1950s by Shariati's involvement with the Movement of God-Worshipping Socialists, an organization that "blended Islam with socialism and maintained that Islam's socio-economic system was that of scientific socialism based on monotheism."[38]

The second phase begins in the early 1960s during Shariati's time in Paris when in the course of his activism in support of the Algerian independence movement he became familiar with and came to be inspired by the strategy of armed struggle employed by the National Liberation Front. The success of this strategy convinced Shariati "of the necessity of military action by a small group of highly dedicated, well-trained, professional, organizationally independent and clandestine revolutionaries."[39] This was a shortlived phase in Shariati's revolutionary thought. The third phase begins in the mid-1960s, when Shariati came to see ideological awareness as the main prerequisite for launching a genuine revolutionary movement.[40] It was in this period that he began "a life of total dedication to the cause of articulating, formulating and propagating a radical Islamic ideology which he hoped would lead to a radical Islamic political movement among the Iranian youth."[41] Emphasizing the necessity of bridging the gap between intellectuals and the predominantly religious masses, Shariati "set out to show that irrespective of their faith in religion, militant intellectuals who sought social and political change in Iran were obliged to learn their religious heritage and speak its language."[42]

The fourth phase in the evolution of Shariati's revolutionary thought begins in October 1971, when he became a regular lecturer at the Hosseinieh Ershad in Tehran.[43] Mere months before this, in February 1971, the Siahkal uprising had occurred. This was an unsuccessful

[37] Ibid., 213.
[38] Ibid., 214–215.
[39] Ibid., 223.
[40] Rahnema, *Islamic Utopian*, 194.
[41] Rahnema, "Ali Shariati: Teacher, Preacher, Rebel," 225.
[42] Ibid., 228.
[43] Hosseinieh Ershad was founded in Tehran in the mid-1960s as a religious institute dedicated to the propagation of Islamic thought. The facility, which includes a large lecture hall and a public library, quickly became a popular hub for many young Muslims who attended public lectures and courses taught by Shariati and a number of other prominent anti-Shah religious figures. It was shut down by the government in the early 1970s and reopened again after the revolution.

guerrilla operation carried out in northern Iran by the Leftist group, the Iranian People's Fadaee Guerrillas (*cherik-hayeh fadaeyeh khalgheh Iran*). Seeing the increasing influence of Marxist ideas on young Iranians, Shariati sought "to formulate a coherent radical and revolutionary Islamic doctrine," to compete with other well-established ideologies, particularly revolutionary Marxism.⁴⁴ By the summer of 1971, the Organization of the People's Mojahedin of Iran (*sazman-e mojahedin khalgh-e Iran*), an Islamic-Marxist opposition group, was also engaged in armed struggle. Hosseinieh Ershad and Shariati's lectures became a recruiting ground for these new guerrilla groups, particularly the Mojahedin. Pointing to the dynamism between Shariati's teachings and the highly volatile political environment in Iran, Rahnema writes: "While [Shariati's] fiery speeches aroused the high school and university students and mentally prepared them for engaging in armed struggle, the daring and selfless revolutionary acts of this same youth moved and impressed him, further radicalizing his message."⁴⁵ This phase ends with the closure of Hosseinieh Ershad in November 1972 and Shariati's eventual imprisonment.

The final phase in the development of Shariati's Islamic discourse begins after his release from prison in March 1975. According to Rahnema, this phase "is characterized by a return to revolutionary intellectual rhetoric, recommending theoretical and ideological engagement rather than armed revolutionary struggle."⁴⁶ During this phase, Rahnema further argues, Shariati placed greater emphasis on spirituality and came to believe that "revolutionary Puritanism [*khodsazi-ye enqelabi*], essentially based on gnosticism [*sic*] was a prerequisite to social transformation."⁴⁷ In his final analysis, Rahnema assesses Shariati's revolutionary Islamic discourse as a utopian vision of a revolution without a clear strategy and objectives. In the Conclusion of *An Islamic Utopian*, Rahnema writes: "Shariati was a romantic and not a practitioner of revolutions. A firm believer in platonic relations, he did not, perhaps, want to lose the immaculate vision that he held of the revolution. The utopian idea was too good to be put to test."⁴⁸

Among the more recent contributions, Shireen Hunter's *Reformist Voices of Islam: Mediating Islam and Modernity* (2008) dedicates a

---

⁴⁴ Rahnema, *Islamic Utopian*, 287.
⁴⁵ Ibid., 280.
⁴⁶ Ibid., 356.
⁴⁷ Ibid., 361.
⁴⁸ Ibid., 370.

section to examining Shariati's revolutionary Islamic ideology. For Hunter, Shariati was first and foremost "a Leftist intellectual who believed in revolutionary action and assigned an important role for a revolutionary vanguard in creating the new society after having dismissed the old system." Nevertheless, she asserts that Islam constituted "the cornerstone of [Shariati's] ideology and worldview." According to her, the Islamic character of Shariati's revolutionary ideology was, in part, informed by his religious beliefs and family background, and, in part, by his "authenticist tendencies, which had been sharpened by his becoming acquainted with similar ideas developed by Third World intellectuals, most notably Franz Fanon."[49] In evaluating Shariati's influence on the revolutionary uprising of the late 1970s, she concludes that Shariati's Islamic ideology "won large numbers of Iranian youth to the idea of Islamic Revolution," and quotes Iranian intellectual, Ehsan Naraghi, that "[Shariati] made people fall in love with revolution."[50]

In addition to the assessments of Shariati's revolutionary ideology by academic commentators, many of which are in English, a different and more critical account of his radical Islamic discourse has been advanced in postrevolutionary Iran by a number of prominent intellectuals who critique Shariati for what they see as the direct consequences of his project of ideologizing religion. Defining ideology as a closed and dogmatic system of action-oriented thought that cultivates blind imitation, these critics argue that as the leading ideologue of the Iranian revolution Shariati paved the way for the postrevolutionary revival and reappropriation of the Islamic tradition, thus delaying the negotiation of modernity in Iranian society.[51] This charge is leveled not only by secular intellectuals such as Dariush Shayegan and Javad Tabatabaei, but also by an intellectual current which has come to be known in recent decades as religious intellectualism (*roshanfekri-ye dini*). Some of the leading figures of this current, including Abdolkarim Soroush, were themselves among the

---

[49] Shireen T. Hunter, "Islamic Reformist Discourses in Iran: Proponents and Prospects," in *Reformist Voices of Islam: Mediating Islam and Modernity*, ed. Shireen T. Hunter (Armonk, NY: M. E. Sharpe, 2008), 55.
[50] Ibid., 56.
[51] See: Seyyed Javad Tabatabaei, *Ibn-e Khaldun va oloom ejtemaei (Ibn Khaldun and Social Sciences)*, (Tehran: Tarh-e No, 1374/1994); Dariush Shayegan, "Ayin hendoo va erfan eslami" ("Hindu Tradition and Islamic Mysticism"), interview with Aliasghar Seyed Abadi, *Baztab-e Andisheh*, no. 77 (Shahrivar 1385/September 2006); Ramin Jahanbegloo, *Zir asmanhay-e jahan: goftegooye Dariush Shayegan ba Ramin Jahanbegloo (Under the World's Skies: Dariush Shayegan in Conversation with Ramin Jahanbegloo)* (Tehran: Farzan Rooz, 1387/2008).

young students who attended Shariati's lectures at the Hosseinieh Ershad and were influenced by his teachings and ideas.

Distinguishing between Shariati's religious discourse and the discourses of postrevolutionary religious intellectuals, Soroush argues that while the former sought to advance a synthesis of "Islam and revolution," the latter's aim has been to reconcile "Islam and democracy."[52] According to Soroush, Shariati lived in the age of ideologies and was thus convinced that to revolt against the ruling regime his predominantly religious society needed to have a unifying and action-oriented ideology. Shariati's most important achievement, in his view, was to turn Islam and its traditional doctrines into a modern ideology at the service of mobilizing the masses against the status quo.[53] Soroush further believes that in the aftermath of the revolution, Shariati's ideological project proved to be an effective weapon in the hands of the Islamic Republic. According to him, "the terminology and concepts that Shariati extracted from ancient religious texts and teachings are today among the key concepts and terms in the language with which the Islamic Republic speaks."[54] He sees the rise of an official (clerical) class of the interpreters of revolutionary ideology and the augmentation of a sense of national unity on the basis of a common hatred for a perceived enemy (i.e., the West) as some of the negative consequences of Shariati's ideologization of religion. Soroush, nevertheless, maintains that these negative consequences were the unintended effects of Shariati's project. "Ideas," he writes, "always find a life of their own, independently of the intentions of their authors." The negative consequences of ideologization of religion, then, are "unfortunate fruits" that have grown on the tree of Shariati's ideas, even though they may be unrecognizable to the author himself.[55]

The charge of antimodernism, leveled against Shariati by Shayegan, Tabatabaei, and Soroush, is echoed by another group of commentators who regard Shariati as the proponent of a discourse of Islamic nativism that called for a turn away from modernity and the Western other, and toward an authentic Islamic or Shi'i self. Among these commentators, Mehrzad Boroujerdi, in *Iranian Intellectuals and the West: The Tormented Triumph of Nativism* (1996), argues that the ultimate objective of Shariati's ideological discourse was to reconstruct the authentic

---

[52] Abdolkarim Soroush, *Az Shariati (On Shariati)* (Tehran: Serat, 1384/2006), 1.
[53] Ibid., 8.
[54] Ibid., 8–9.
[55] Ibid., 11.

existence of his Islamic and Oriental society by juxtaposing the latter against a monolithic entity called the West or the Occident. According to Boroujerdi, in Shariati's thought the Islamic Orient and the Christian Occident are deceptively presented as archetypically different entities with distinct ontologies and epistemologies. Shariati, he claims, described Christianity as a passive and apolitical religion and Islam as a revolutionary and emancipatory faith, while being fully aware of the fraudulency of such a dichotomy. He posits that Shariati had been exposed to the ideas of Christian liberation theology during his time in Paris, and "knew all too well that his dichotomy between Christian passivity and Islamic militancy was fraudulent."[56] Boroujerdi further asserts that despite his nativist position toward modernity and the West, Shariati's Islamic discourse drew heavily on modern Western thought.[57] Describing Shariati's thesis of "return to the self" as "a replica of Fanon's discourse of 'return of the oppressed' but with a peculiarly Iranian twist," he argues that whereas Fanon stressed "the racial, historical, and linguistic features of Third World struggles," Shariati put emphasis on "Islamic roots."[58]

Ali Mirsepassi too, in a number of his works, has described Shariati's revolutionary Islamic ideology as a discourse of authenticity.[59] According to him, Shariati's critique and reconfiguration of Western modernity was ultimately aimed at reconciling "the experience of modernization with Iranian traditional life."[60] He, nevertheless, remains skeptical about the nature of this reconciliatory project. According to him, while Enlightenment modernity and its philosophical foundations present a set of "universal and normative standards of human behavior and ethics based on a rational, democratic, and humanist model of society,"[61] Shariati's "alternative modernity" departed from modernity's "cosmopolitan humanist position."[62] Pointing to a tension between Enlightenment and counter-Enlightenment currents in the context of Western modernity, Mirsepassi argues that Shariati's thought challenged a conception of

---

[56] Mehrzad Boroujerdi, *Iranian Intellectuals and the West: The Tormented Triumph of Nativism* (New York: Syracuse University Press, 1996), 109.
[57] Ibid., 110–113.
[58] Ibid., 112.
[59] Ali Mirsepassi, "Religious Intellectuals and Western Critiques of Secular Modernity," *Comparative Studies of South Asia, Africa and the Middle East* 26, no. 3 (2006): 417.
[60] Ali Mirsepassi, *Intellectual Discourse and the Politics of Modernization: Negotiating Modernity in Iran* (Cambridge: Cambridge University Press, 2000), 116.
[61] Ibid., 19.
[62] Ali Mirsepassi, "Intellectual Life after the 1979 Revolution: Radical Hope and Nihilistic Dreams," *Radical History Review* 2009, no. 105 (October 2009): 172.

universalism advanced by Enlightenment modernity. In Shariati's authenticist discourse, he asserts, "In place of a universal and secular truth is an equally modern championing and politicization of the truth in cultural tradition, or a defense of a single overarching sociocultural meaning as both an ontology and a mode of political organization." Mirsepassi believes that in the context of twentieth century Iran where democratic institutions were not consolidated, Shariati's appeal to authenticity had particularly "disastrous" political consequences as it put forth a narrative that was "inherently hostile to even the very concept of formal democracy and *pluralism*."[63] According to him, much like Heidegger's counter-Enlightenment discourse, Shariati's vision of authenticity and his call for a return to the self were "fraught with the dangers of authoritarianism and cultural particularism."[64]

Like Boroujerdi and Mirsepassi, Farzin Vahdat believes that although Shariati's Islamic discourse did not reject modernity in its entirety it was nevertheless constructed as an authentic response to "the cultural aspects of the modern world."[65] In examining the negotiation between modern and non-modern elements in Shariati's thought, Vahdat is particularly interested in Shariati's engagement with the autonomous subject of the European Enlightenment. Shariati, in Vahdat's view, was highly suspicious of and ultimately renounced the notion of an autonomous, self-conscious, and willful individual subject, theorized by such European thinkers as Descartes, Kant, and Hegel. In his reading, "horrified by the solitude of subjectivity," Shariati found serenity in a religious belief in an ontological bond between the individual and the metaphysics, and in "submission to the Being, in annihilation of the self in God, and in finding a 'new' self, who, in cooperation with God and Love, would create the universe anew."[66] Vahdat further argues that by conceptualizing human agency as an attribute of divine sovereignty, Shariati's thought constantly vacillated between confirming and denying modern subjectivity.[67] He is, nevertheless, less skeptical than Mirsepassi about Shariati's particular articulation of an Islamic modernity, and considers this religiously

---

[63] Mirsepassi, "Religious Intellectuals," 416.

[64] Ali Mirsepassi, *Political Islam, Iran, and the Enlightenment: Philosophies of Hope and Despair* (New York: Cambridge University Press, 2011), 128.

[65] Farzin Vahdat, "Religious Modernity in Iran: Dilemmas of Islamic Democracy in the Discourse of Mohammad Khatami," *Comparative Studies of South Asia, Africa and the Middle East* 25, no. 3 (2005): 650.

[66] Farzin Vahdat, *God and Juggernaut: Iran's Intellectual Encounter with Modernity* (Syracuse: Syracuse University Press, 2002), 145.

[67] Vahdat, "Religious Modernity in Iran," 652.

mediated account of subjectivity as a "transitory discourse with a possibility of translating itself and society."[68] The full transition, according to him, would depend on the emergence and gradual consolidation of a secular discourse in the public sphere and the recognition of absolute and unmediated subjectivity.

Taking a different position than those of Boroujerdi, Mirsepassi, and Vahdat, and echoing the views of Abrahamian and Dabashi, Kamran Matin describes Shariati's radical Islamic authenticity as a contextually grounded theory of modern sociopolitical transformation along the lines of the Iranian Leftist tradition.[69] Examining a national context conditioned by the rise of the urban middle and working classes and their unmet expectations, and an international context shaped by the Cold War and a host of anticolonial and independence movements, Matin makes a case that Shariati's radical Islamic discourse was more effective than its secular-Leftist rivals in communicating with and mobilizing the emerging social classes in Iranian society and placing its "ideological stamp on the revolutionary movement that was already in active gesture."[70] According to him, based on the analysis that modern classes did not exist in Iran "as they had historically developed in the West," Shariati posited that in order to bring about transformative consciousness a political ideology had to be "capable of engaging and positively provoking the cultural-emotional sensibilities of the principal agency of the revolution, 'the people' and *not* the proletariat or 'national bourgeoisie'."[71] In Matin's reading, by identifying and mobilizing the contextually appropriate agency of the Iranian masses Shariati's discourse of radical Islamic authenticity succeeded in reconstructing "the dominant, but largely conservative and passive, discourses of Shi'ism into a modern popular ideological force marked by an innovative combination of modern revolutionary zeal and a radically reformed sense of Muslimhood."[72]

---

[68] Farzin Vahdat, "Metaphysical Foundations of Islamic Revolutionary Discourse in Iran: Vacillations on Human Subjectivity," *Critique: Critical Middle Eastern Studies* 8, no. 14 (1999): 72.
[69] Kamran Matin, "Decoding Political Islam: Uneven and Combined Development and Ai Shariati's Political Thought," in *International Relations and non-Western Thought: Imperialism, Colonialism, and Investigations of Global Modernity*, ed. Robbie Shilliam (London: Routledge, 2010), 108.
[70] Ibid., 114.
[71] Ibid., 116.
[72] Ibid., 121.

An Unfinished Project of "Indigenous Modernity"

While for his religious and secular critics Shariati is the chief exponent of an ideological Islamic discourse aimed at reviving a lost traditional authenticity, a number of other commentators have offered an account of his work as an attempt to negotiate a third way between authoritarian modernism and conservative traditionalism. For the former group, Shariati's radical religious discourse represents a misguided response to the modernization policies of the Pahlavi state, and one that no longer corresponds to the objective realities of Iranian society under the reign of the Islamic state. The latter group, however, finds Shariati's attention to the contextual determinants of change and his simultaneous critique of modernity and tradition to be a relevant approach for advancing a progressive vision of sociocultural and sociopolitical development in postrevolutionary Iran. One such commentator, Maghsoud Farasatkhah, believes that Shariati's critical position toward Western hegemony and his modern interpretation of Islamic thought continue to have social and political appeal in contemporary Iranian society.[73] For Mohammad Amin Ghaneirad too, Shariati's simultaneous critique of traditionalism and modernism remains a major intellectual challenge to both "Westernism" and "nativism." Shariati's lasting legacy, he contends, is his call for a "third way" between the blind imitation of the West and the uncritical embrace of tradition.[74] Ghaneirad further credits Shariati with pioneering an "indigenous social theory" that continues to offer a unique perspective for understanding the nuances of social and political change in contemporary Iran.[75]

Echoing the views of Farasatkhah and Ghaneirad, Bijan Abdolkarimi describes Shariati's critical engagement with modernity and tradition as

---

[73] Maghsoud Farasatkhah, "Shesh tip roshanfekri dini" ("Six Types of Religious Intellectualism"), Islah Web, November 15, 2009, www.islahweb.org/node/2879 (accessed November 17, 2012).

[74] Mohammad Amin Ghaneirad, "A Critical Review of the Iranian Attempts at the Development of Alternative Sociologies," in *Facing Unequal World: Challenges For a Global Sociology*, Volume Two: Asia, ed. Michael Burawoy, Mau-kuei Chang, and Michelle Fei-yu Hsieh (Taiwan: Institute of Sociology at Academia Sinica, Council of National Association of the International Sociological Association, and Academia Sinica, 2010), 39.

[75] Mohammad Amin Ghaneirad, *Tabarshenasi-e aghlaniat-e modern: ghera'ati postmodern az andisheh doctor Ali Shariati (The Genealogy of Modern Rationality: A Postmodern Reading of Dr. Ali Shariati's Thought)*, (Tehran: Naghd-e farhang, 1381/2002), 275.

an unfinished project, the revival of which can serve a progressive role in dealing with a range of sociocultural and sociopolitical challenges in Iran today.⁷⁶ In Abdolkarimi's reading, Shariati accepts neither a total embrace of modernity nor an uncritical return to tradition, and instead proposes a dialectical approach for understanding both categories. According to him, in its concurrent acknowledgment of the emancipatory potential and the dark side of Western modernity, Shariati's thought finds common ground with European critical theory and the Frankfurt School. He, nevertheless, posits that by appealing to the epistemological and ontological resources of local religious and cultural traditions Shariati emerges as a distinctly Iranian and Muslim thinker. Abdolkarimi further believes that by adopting a phenomenological vantage point and giving recognition to an ongoing dialectic between "modern rationality" and "local traditions," Shariati's thought deconstructs the dichotomous constructs of East/West and Islam/modernity.⁷⁷

Also regarding Shariati's work as an unfinished project, Mojtaba Mahdavi argues that Shariati sought to identify a theoretical and practical potential "for combining traditional and modern models [of development]."⁷⁸ In two essays, one "Radicalism from Two Perspectives: The Classical Discourse and Shariati's Neo-Radicalism" (2002), and the other "One Bed and Two Dreams? Contentious Public Religion in the Discourses of Ayatollah Khomeini and Ali Shariati" (2014), he draws attention to two major themes in Shariati's analysis about the conditions for bottom-up and sustainable change. First, the need for a critical engagement with the past (i.e., religion, traditional culture, etc.) in light of present needs and future objectives. And second, the responsibility of intellectuals to become agents of change. For Shariati, he argues, "the future is but a synthesis of the present and the past" and no sustainable project of change can be advanced by

---

⁷⁶ Bijan Abdolkarimi, "Davate bozorg-e Shariati, tajdid-e ahd ba sonat-e tarikhi-e mast," ("Shariati's Major Invitation Was to Renew Our Historical Traditions)," January 17, 2012, Academy of Iranian Studies in London, http://iranianstudies.org/fa/ (accessed August 23, 2012).
⁷⁷ Bijan Abdolkarimi, "Ma va moderniteh beh revaiat-e Shariati" (Modernity and Us as Narrated by Shariati), June 22, 2013, Bijan Abdolkarimi Information Center, http://abdolkarimi.blogfa.com/post/83 (accessed November 29, 2014).
⁷⁸ Mojtaba Mahdavi, "Radikalism az do didgah: gofteman-e kelasik va noradikalism-e Shariati" ("Radicalism from Two Perspectives: The Classical Discourse and Shariati's Neo-Radicalism"), in *Ghoghnoos-e ssian: revaiati digar az andisheh doktor Shariati (The Rebellious Phoenix: Another Account of the Thought of Dr. Shariati)*, ed. Amir Rezaei (Tehran: Ghasidehsara, 2002), 248.

negating historical trajectories and prevailing traditions.[79] It is for this reason, Mahdavi believes, that Shariati calls upon intellectuals to initiate "a deep transformation in the prevailing religious thought and a revolution in traditions in order to change their content and preserve their revised forms."[80] In Mahdavi's reading, Shariati's thought essentially "rejects the unilinear trajectories of modernism, the monolithic conceptualization of modernization, and the mechanical dichotomization of tradition and modernity." Shariati, it is argued, regards such modern concepts as human freedom, equality, and democracy to be universal values "reflecting the shared experiences of humanity" and having emerged out of a historical process of "restructuring traditional institutions and norms." Thus, for Mahdavi, Shariati's thought advances a vision of human societies and civilizations "as products of intermixing rather than authenticity."[81]

In another essay, titled "Post-Islamist Trends in Post-Revolutionary Iran" (2011), Mahdavi discusses new readings of Shariati's thought by neo-Shariatis and their significance for challenging the dominant Islamist discourse. Leading neo-Shariati figures, he argues, have contributed to the advancement of the religious reform movement and contextually grounded discourses of democratization in postrevolutionary Iran.[82] According to him, while neo-Shariatis problematize and ultimately reject the notion of a religious state they nevertheless hold that "modern spirituality, not organized religion, can play a constructive role in the public sphere."[83] Citing a number of prominent neo-Shariati figures, Mahdavi makes the case that in its neo-Shariati reading Shariati's thought is "a humanistic Islamic discourse in [which] people are the only true representatives of God on Earth." He also draws attention to neo-Shariatis' support for a democratic secular governance model that separates the "religious and political institutions," but gives recognition to religion as a source of inspiration for normative values "in the individual, social, and political sphere."[84]

---

[79] Mojtaba Mahdavi, "One Bed and Two Dreams? Contentious Public Religion in the Discourses of Ayatollah Khomeini and Ali Shariati," *Studies in Religion / Sciences Religieuses* 43, no. 1 (2014): 45.
[80] Ibid., 44.
[81] Mahdavi, "Radikalism az do didgah," 248.
[82] Mojtaba Mahdavi, "Post-Islamist Trends in Post-Revolutionary Iran," *Comparative Studies of South Asia, Africa, and the Middle East* 31, no. 1 (2011): 95.
[83] Ibid., 104.
[84] Ibid., 105–106.

Other commentators too have drawn attention to neo-Shariatis' democratic readings of Shariati's religious and political thought in post-revolutionary Iran. Mohammad Ghouchani, for example, believes that Shariati's contemporary intellectual followers seek to balance his critique of modernity with an espousal of secularism, democracy, and some form of republicanism.[85] Similarly, Farasatkhah maintains that in their engagement with Shariati's intellectual project neo-Shariatis distinguish the utopia of his Islamic ideology from Islamist discourses and their associated visions. According to him, neo-Shariatis continue Shariati's unfinished project through a twofold effort of critiquing traditionalism and Islamism, and identifying the progressive capacities of the Islamic faith for advancing a bottom-up transformation in Iranian society.[86] He further argues that by reviving the radical and egalitarian orientation of Shariati's thought neo-Shariatis present a "social democratic" alternative to the emerging "bourgeois" and "liberal" currents in contemporary religious reform thought in Iran.[87] Likewise, Hunter describes neo-Shariatis as a Leftist group of dissident Iranian intellectuals and activists who continue to favor a reformist Islamic discourse on the basis of a new interpretation of Shariati's ideas. According to Hunter, in the postrevolutionary context neo-Shariatis "portray [Shariati] as a democrat, believing first and foremost in the cultural transformation of society."[88]

Though neo-Shariatis regard Shariati as a "teacher of revolution," they nevertheless challenge the conventional understanding of the substance of his radical Islamic discourse.[89] According to Susan Shariati, Shariati's approach was based neither on "revolutionary idealism" and the pursuit of change by any means and at any price, nor simply on "reformism." Instead, she argues, Shariati was a theorist and practitioner of

[85] Mohammad Ghouchani, "Shesh nasl farzandan-e Shariati" ("Six Generations of Shariati's Children"), *Khordad*, 28, Khordad 1383/ June 17, 2004. Also see: Mohammad Ghouchani, *Seh eslam: maktab-e Najaf, maktab-e Ghom, maktab-e Tehran (Three Islams: Najaf School, Qom School, Tehran School)* (Tehran: Saraee, 1385/2006).
[86] Maghsoud Farasatkhah, "Roshanfekri dini: istadeh bar sar" ("Religious Intellectuals: Standing on Its Head,") (paper presented at Religion and Modernity seminar, Tehran, September 2007) http://e-b-a.blogfa.com/post-11.aspx (accessed February 20, 2012).
[87] Farasatkhah, "Shesh tip."
[88] Hunter, "Islamic Reformist Discourses," 55.
[89] Susan Shariati, "Shariati, moalem kodam enghelab?" ("Shariati, the Teacher of Which Revolution?"), *Shahrvand Emrooz*, Bahman 1386/February 2008, www.slideshare.net/sco1385/ss-1762422 (accessed July 11, 2011). Also see: Susan Shariati, "Shaieh-ei beh nam-e Shariati" ("A Rumor Called Shariati"), *Etemad*, 2 Esfand 1386/February 21, 2008, www.slideshare.net/sco1385/ss-1762423 (accessed July 11, 2011).

"revolutionary reform." Shariati, she contends, was acutely aware of the dangers of a revolutionary change at the political level without a deep prior transformation at the sociocultural level and, hence, believed that "revolution before awareness is nothing short of disaster."[90] Similarly, Ehsan Shariati notes that in the mid-1970s, and as the revolutionary movement was on the rise, Shariati insisted on introducing an alternative paradigm to the prevailing paradigm of armed resistance. According to him, while the defining characteristic of Iranian society at the time was an overriding revolutionary spirit, Shariati tried to persuade "a radicalized generation ready for battle to turn its attention to sustainable change." He further problematizes Soroush's assertion that while Shariati reconciled Islam and revolution, postrevolutionary religious intellectuals must reconcile Islam and democracy. Pointing to the historical links between popular revolutionary movements and the expansion of political and economic democracy in Europe and elsewhere, he argues that far from being opposing objectives revolution and democracy can be seen as one and the same.[91]

Moreover, while many neo-Shariatis acknowledge the "ideological" character of Shariati's discourse, they reject the logic of Shayegan, Tabatabaei, and Soroush in equating ideology with dogma. Hossein Mesbahian, for instance, points to a European "ideological tradition" (represented by figures such as Destutt de Tracy and György Lukács) of critiquing the status quo and the prevailing sociocultural norms that legitimize and sustain dominant power relations.[92] According to him, Shariati was the first Iranian intellectual to attempt to revive the "neglected foundations" of this progressive tradition.[93] True to the original meaning of ideology, he posits, Shariati sought to identify an alternative and

---

[90] Ibid. Also see: Susan Shariati, "Simay-e yek zendani: negahi beh ketab-e Shariati beh revaiat-e asnad-e savak," ("The Portrait of a Prisoner: A Look at a Book Titled Shariati as Narrated by SAVAK Documents"), in *Ghoghnoos-e osian: revaiati digar az andisheh doktor Shariati (The Rebellious Phoenix: Another Account of the Thought of Dr. Shariati)*, ed. Amir Rezaei (Tehran: Ghasidehsara, 2002), 133–178.

[91] Ehsan Shariati, "*Hamchenan armangara, enghelabi, va ideolojik hastam*," ("I Remain Utopian, Revolutionary, and Ideological"), interview with Susan Shariati, *Shahrvand-e Emrooz*, 10 Tir 1387/ June 30, 2008, http://shahrvandemroz.blogfa.com/post-557.aspx (accessed November 3, 2011).

[92] Hossein (Mesbahian) Rahyab, "Defa-e johari az mantegh darooni-e ideolojy: rooya-rooyee ba bardasht-haye nadorost," ("A Foundational Defense of the Internal Logic of Ideology: Challenging Misconceptions"), in *Dar hashiyeh matn* (On the Margins of the Text), ed. Bonyad Shariati (Tehran: Shahr-e Aftab, 1379/2000), 40.

[93] Ibid., 99.

contextually grounded worldview from the vantage point of which to critique hegemonic norms and to identify counter-hegemonic modes of action.[94] Citing passages from Shariati's text about the definition and function of ideology, he notes that Shariati distinguished between three distinct but interconnected components of ideological thinking: "First, a worldview informing one's general assumptions about being, life, and the role of the individual; second, a critical analysis of the really existing conditions and the various factors that inform collective understandings of these conditions; and third, realistic alternatives and practical solutions."[95]

It is in light of this alternative definition of ideology that Shariati's contemporary followers defend his notion of ideological religion.[96] According to Ehsan Shariati, for instance, far from constituting a project against critical rationality, Shariati's attempt at ideologization of religion involved a critical engagement with Islam's history aimed at "identifying the religion's internal dynamism, critiquing the class function of its jurisprudential tradition, and preserving its spiritual and transcendental core."[97] Noting the rationalizing effect of the project of ideologization of faith, he argues that by distinguishing between the different historical manifestations, social functions, and political orientations of religion Shariati's notion of Islam as ideology contributed to the secularization of Islamic religious thought in contemporary Iranian society. He nevertheless believes that in rereading Shariati's thought in postrevolutionary Iran it is vital to emphasize the separation between the realms of ideology and governance. According to him, though ideology may determine one's general orientation in social and political realms, its institutionalization and formalization at the state level is undesirable and potentially disastrous. He suggests that the separation of ideology (including religious ideology) from the state is assumed in Shariati's thought and must be effectively protected under any democratic political order.[98]

Finally, while neo-Shariatis acknowledge that Shariati's Islamic discourse was articulated in response to the dominant modernization discourse of the Pahlavi state and the Eurocentric discourses of Iranian elites, they reject the reading of Shariati's thought as an authenticist turn

---

[94] Ibid., 117.
[95] Ali Shariati, C.W. 23, 70–71, quoted in (Mesbahian) Rahyab, "Defa-e Johari," 116.
[96] See: Reza Alijani, ed., *Ideolojy: zaroorat ya parhiz va goriz (Ideology: Necessity or Avoidance)* (Tehran: Chapakhsh, 1380/2001).
[97] Ehsan Shariati, "Hamchenan armangara."
[98] Ibid.

against modernity, rationality, progress, and development. According to Sara Shariati, Shariati's "selective approach" toward tradition and modernity defied the logic of the metanarratives of modernism and traditionalism, and drew attention instead to contextual particularities and contingencies. Shariati, she argues, favored adopting "the universal fruits of modernity (i.e., science, technology, and democracy as a means of controlling and distributing power)," while also taking into account "the plural conceptions, historical trajectories, and cultural experiences of modernity."[99] Noting Shariati's rejection of the dichotomous construction of tradition/modernity and his view of the historical role of the Protestant Reformation in the emergence of the European Enlightenment, she argues that for Shariati each society arrives at its own indigenous modernity through a radical restructuring of its prevailing traditions.[100] Shariati, she further contends, believed that by undertaking a project of religious and cultural reform, authentic intellectuals who speak the language of the masses and are thoroughly familiar with local traditions can "manipulate the force of historical determinism" and expedite the negotiation of modernity in their societies.[101]

For neo-Shariatis, the occurrence of the revolution and the coming to power of an Islamic state at a time when Shariati's revolutionary ideology was still incomplete and fragile left unfinished the work that he had initiated. They argue that in a postrevolutionary context where the amalgamation of religious and political power has reinforced the tradition/modernity dichotomy, the revival and continuation of the project of indigenous modernity has become a more urgent task than before.[102] At the same time, by drawing attention to the major changes that have taken place in Iran over the last four decades, neo-Shariatis also stress the "unthoughts" of Shariati's thought as well as the need to adopt new strategies for advancing his unfinished project in the new context. In "The Philosophical Unthoughts of Shariati's Thought," for example, Ehsan

---

[99] Sara Shariati, "Dar bareh sharaiet-e emkan-e moderniteh dini," ("On the Conditions for the Possibility of Religious Modernity"), in *Dar hashiyeh matn (On the Margins of the Text)*, ed. Bonyad Shariati (Tehran: Shahr-e Aftab, 1379/2000), 159.
[100] Ibid., 160.
[101] Ibid., 159.
[102] Ehsan Shariati, "Nayandishideh mandeh haye falsafi andisheh ye mo'alem Shariati" ("The Philosophical Unthoughts of Shariati's Thought,"), in *Dar hashiyeh matn (On the Margins of the Text)*, ed. Bonyad Shariati (Tehran: Shahr-e Aftab, 1379/2000), 9; Sara Shariati, "Dar bareh sharaiet-e emkan-e moderniteh dini," 162–163; Hassan Yousefi Eshkevari, "Edameh projeh na-tamam" ("Continuing an Unfinished Project"), interview with Reza Khojasteh Rahimi, *Toos* no. 764, Khordad 1377/June 1998, 30.

Shariati makes a case that while Shariati's thesis of "return to the self" was proposed as a counter-discourse to the prevailing Western cultural imperialism and the Pahlavi regime's imported modernization agenda, in the postrevolutionary context the "return" thesis ought to be replaced with the thesis of "revisiting and restructuring of the self."[103]

As demonstrated in the following chapters, in postrevolutionary Iran neo-Shariatis have sought to resuscitate and move forward Shariati's "unfinished project" in three major ways. First, they have advanced a concurrent deconstruction of modernity and tradition, arguing that neither category is totalizing, constant, and unique to one civilization or another. Like Shariati, they reject a view of modernity as essentially European and reducible to the experiences and consequences of the European Enlightenment, and instead emphasize the universal nature and the cross-cultural development of concepts such as human reason and individual autonomy, popular sovereignty, and equal citizenship rights. Second, by advocating a non-state-centric approach to sociopolitical transformation and emphasizing the dialectic between normative and structural change, neo-Shariatis have sought to raise a change-oriented consciousness not only through religious reformation, but also through grassroots activism and sustained civil society engagement. Third, in their engagement with Islamic history and intellectual traditions, neo-Shariatis have sought to identify some of the ways in which Islam's ontological and epistemological resources can contribute to the negotiation of an alternative vision of human subjectivity and progress to that of Enlightenment modernity. I shall return to this last point later in the book. But in the chapter that follows, and in order to locate Shariati's thought and its new readings in the broader context of contemporary Islamic thought, I will examine some of the major responses by Muslim thinkers to the late nineteenth-century encounter with colonial modernity in Islamicate contexts.

---

[103] Ehsan Shariati, "Nayandishideh mandeh haye falsafi," 10.

2

Islamic Thought in Encounter with Colonial Modernity

What Is in a Term?

In "Modernity: An Unfinished Project" (1997), Jürgen Habermas argues that at different historical turns the idea of "modernity" has come to articulate "the consciousness of an era that refers back to the past of classical antiquity precisely in order to comprehend itself as the result of a transition from the old to new."[1] According to him, while the term "modern" was first used in the late fifth century to distinguish the Christian era from the pagan past, what is known as the "project of modernity" essentially began with the European Enlightenment. Modernity, in this sense, meant "the relentless development of the objectivating sciences, of the universalistic foundations of morality and law, and of autonomous art," as well as the idea of "the rational organization of social relations." This is what Habermas regards as the "unfinished" project, which needs to be revisited and revived in the face of a growing skepticism about modernity and its claims.[2]

Habermas's critics often highlight the lopsidedness and the Eurocentric bias of his account of modernity. Commenting on Habermas's *The Philosophical Discourse of Modernity* (1985), Fred Dallmayr, for instance, argues that while in its idealistic claims it sets out to emancipate humans from the chains of political and ecclesiastical tutelage and "to inaugurate a new age of ... self-determination," in its historical

---

[1] Jürgen Habermas, "Modernity: An Unfinished Project," in *Habermas and the Unfinished Project of Modernity*, ed. Maurizio Passerin d'Entreves and Seyla Benhabib (Cambridge, MA: The MIT Press, 1997), 39.
[2] Ibid., 45.

experiences, modernity has been a project of imposing the mastery of the modern European subject over nature and the non-modern other.³ Drawing on the work of Enrique Dussel, Dallmayr contends that in the context of the prevailing global power asymmetries, "the totalizing ambitions of Western modernity" have created sharply different experiences in the hegemonic global North and the dominated global South.⁴

For another group of commentators, Eurocentric narratives of modernity such as Habermas's are constructed and sustained through the omission of a range of precolonial and non-European experiences of social, political, and economic change. Among them, Sanjay Subrahmanyam regards modernity to be a global phenomenon with distinct and multilingual histories. In "Connected Histories: Notes towards a Reconfiguration of Early Modern Eurasia" (1997), he proposes a conception of modernity delinked "from a particular European trajectory" and one which represents "a more-or-less global shift, with many different sources and roots, and – inevitably – many different forms and meanings depending on which society we look at it from."⁵ Similarly, in examining the historical context of what he calls a "Persianate modernity," Mohamad Tavakoli-Targhi rejects the "conventional" story of modernity as a product of "Occidental rationalism," defining it instead as a historical-global process that began to unfold around the sixteenth century with divergent manifestations in different cultural and geographical zones.⁶

Notwithstanding their distinct perspectives, most critics of the Eurocentric discourses of modernity agree that European colonialism and the globalization of the Western order altered the precolonial non-European trajectories of change and shaped, directly or indirectly, subsequent developments throughout the non-West.⁷ As José Casanova points out, it is an undeniable reality of our world that capitalism and

---

³ Fred Dallmayr, "The Underside of Modernity: Adorno, Heidegger, and Dussel," *Constellations* 11, no 1 (2004): 102.
⁴ Ibid., 101.
⁵ Sanjay Subrahmanyam, "Connected Histories: Notes towards a Reconfiguration of Early Modern Eurasia," *Modern Asian Studies* 31, no. 3 (July 1997): 737.
⁶ Mohamad Tavakoli-Targhi, "The Homeless Texts of Persianate Modernity," *Cultural Dynamics* 13, no. 3 (November 2001): 263–291, 265. Also see: Abbas Milani, *Lost Wisdom: Rethinking Modernity in Iran* (Washington: Mage, 2004), 10–11.
⁷ See: Hamid Dabashi, *Islamic Liberation Theology: Resisting the Empire* (New York: Routledge, 2008), 62; Bassam Tibi, *The Crisis of Modern Islam: A Preindustrial Culture in the Scientific-Technological Age*, trans., Judith von Sivers (Salt Lake City: University of Utah Press, 1988), 2; Enrique Dussel, "World-System and 'Trans'-Modernity," *Nepantla: Views from South* 3, no. 2 (2002): 222.

the nation-state structure have been on a "self-propelled march toward a world system," challenging and wrecking all other socioeconomic and sociopolitical formations that stand in their way.[8] The condition to which Casanova points has given modernity different meanings and contents throughout the non-Western world. On the one hand, the global expansion of Europe's colonial modernity has created, among certain sectors, a pull toward modernity and a desire to adapt to a condition that claims universality. On the other hand, however, it has also created a push against modernity among other sectors that regard its claim of universality as a threat against particularity and difference. As Dallmayr and Devy (1998) note, this condition has further given modernity a dual function in many non-Western societies as a "vehicle of colonialism" as well as "the harbinger of social transformation and emancipation."[9]

The experiences of Muslim societies with colonial modernity were not radically different from those of most other non-Western societies. While Europe's colonial conquests in the Middle East can be traced back to the sixteenth century, the real encounter with European modernity followed a series of nineteenth-century Russian military advances against Iran and British-French expansions into other parts of the Middle East and North Africa. The post-World War I partitioning of the Ottoman Empire further facilitated the acceleration of "Western cultural penetration and military domination" over Muslim territories.[10] Ever since this initial encounter, the question of modernity has been front and center in Islamic political thought. In contemporary Muslim societies, debates on a wide range of topics, from democratization, socioeconomic development, and globalization, to cultural identity, the status of women, and the trajectories of change in social values continue to be examined with reference to the analytical framework of Islam and modernity.

Similarly, in the Western academy the question of compatibility or incompatibility of Islam and modernity has long preoccupied Orientalists and many other historians, anthropologists, sociologists, and political

---

[8] José Casanova, *Public Religions in the Modern World* (Chicago and London: University of Chicago Press, 1994), 234.

[9] Fred Dallmayr, G. N. Devy, "Introduction," in *Between Tradition and Modernity: India's Search for Identity: A Twentieth Century Anthology*, ed. Fred Dallmayr, G. N. Devy (Walnut Creek, CA: Altamira Press, 1998), 16.

[10] Yvonne Yazbeck Haddad, "The Revivalist Literature and the Literature on Revival: An Introduction," in Yvonne Yazbeck et al., *The Contemporary Islamic Revival: A Critical Survey and Bibliography* (Westport, CT: Greenwood Press, 1991), 3. Also see: John Esposito, *Islam and Politics* (Syracuse, NY: Syracuse University Press, 1984), 43.

scientists. One of the leading figures of nineteenth century Orientalism, Ernest Renan, held that Islam and Muslim societies were particularly hostile to modernity. Renan famously argued that as the antithesis of Europe, "Islam is the disdain of science, the suppression of civil society; it is the appalling simplicity of the Semitic spirit, restricting the human mind, closing it to all delicate ideas, to all refined sentiment, to all rational research, in order to keep it facing an eternal tautology: God is God."[11] Analogous views to those of Renan were articulated throughout the twentieth century. With the fall of the Communist Soviet Union near the end of the century, Islam became the new perceived enemy of the West and its liberal democracy. A decade later, the terrorist attacks of September 11, 2001, and the subsequent launch of the United States-led War on Terrorism in Afghanistan and Iraq (as well as in Pakistan, Yemen, Somalia, Mali, and elsewhere) brought new attention to sociocultural and sociopolitical discourses about the inherent inability or unwillingness of Muslims to embrace modern notions of secularism, democracy, and pluralism.[12]

Increasingly, however, Muslim and non-Muslim commentators are challenging the dichotomous construct of the modern West versus the non-modern rest. Among the better-known contemporary formulations of the West/rest binary, Samuel Huntington's clash of civilizations and Francis Fukuyama's end of history theses have been the subject of numerous critiques.[13] Emphasizing cultural hybridity and historical interactions between diverse cultural traditions, some critics have highlighted the universality of many modern norms and practices, arguing that as a category of representation "the West" is in fact "an amalgamation of multiple traditions, including the Greek, Roman, Judaic, Christian, and Islamic."[14] Moreover, a range of theories of multiple modernities have

---

[11] Ernest Renan, *Oeuvres complètes (Complete Works)* (Paris: Calmann-Livy, 1947), volume 2, 333, quoted in Charles Kurzman, ed., *Liberal Islam: A Sourcebook* (New York: Oxford University Press, 1998), 3.

[12] Talal Asad, *Formations of the Secular: Christianity, Islam, Modernity* (Stanford University Press, 2003), 9–10.

[13] For some examples see: Edward Said, "The Clash of Ignorance," *The Nation* 273, no. 12 (October 22, 2001): 11–14; Tariq Ali, *The Clash of Fundamentalisms: Crusades, Jihads and Modernity* (New York: Verso, 2003); Mojtaba Mahdavi and Andy Knight, "On the 'Dignity of Difference': Neither the 'End of History' nor the 'Clash of Civilizations,' " *Journal for the Study of Peace and Conflict* (Winter 2008): 27–41; Hamid Dabashi, "For the Last Time: Civilizations," *International Sociology* 16, no. 3 (September 2001): 361–368.

[14] Roxanne L. Euben and Muhammad Qasim Zaman, "Introduction," in *Princeton Readings in Islamist Thought: Texts and Contexts from al-Banna to Bin Laden*, ed.

questioned the dominant Eurocentric and monocivilizational view of modernity, drawing attention to the unique modern experiences of social, cultural, political, and economic formation and change in Western and non-Western contexts.[15]

These critical discourses have also contributed to the radical deconstruction of the dichotomous and coconstitutive paradigms of hegemonic universalism and essentialist particularism. In its various manifestations, the former paradigm advances a narrative of the West as the universal trajectory of modernity and progress, thus dismissing the histories and experiences of the non-West. The paradigm has informed a great deal of academic debates as well as various, and largely failed, top-down modernization and secularization programs seeking to transform Muslim societies in the image of European modernity. Viewing Western and Islamic traditions as culturally homogenous and mutually exclusive units, the latter paradigm presents a picture of constant collision and clash between nations, civilizations, and cultural traditions. In the aftermath of the events of September 2001 this dichotomous depiction of Islam and modernity came to inform a great deal of the political rhetoric and modes of political mobilization in both Western and Muslim societies.[16]

The critique of hegemonic universalism and essentialist particularism in recent years has also had the effect of shedding light on a sustained effort within contemporary Islamic thought to negotiate a third way between the total acceptance and the total rejection of modernity. Since the late nineteenth century, the former position has often been championed by a group of Western-oriented (and often Western-educated) elites who call for the modernization of their societies through Westernization and top-down secularization.[17] In Iran for instance, prominent intellectuals

Roxanne L. Euben and Muhammad Qasim Zaman (Princeton, NJ: Princeton University Press, 2009), 32.

[15] See: Charles Taylor, *Modern Social Imaginaries* (Durham and London: Duke University Press, 2004); Masoud Kamali, *Multiple Modernities, Civil Society and Islam: The Case of Iran and Turkey* (Liverpool: Liverpool University Press, 2005); S. N. Eisenstadt, ed., *Multiple Modernities* (New Brunswick, NJ: Transaction, 2002); Modjtaba Sadria, ed., *Multiple Modernities in Muslim Societies* (London: I.B. Tauris, 2009); Amyn B. Sajoo, ed., *Muslim Modernities: Expressions of the Civil Imagination* (London: I.B. Tauris, 2008).

[16] See: Edward Said, "The Clash of Definitions," in *The New Crusades: Constructing the Muslim Enemy*, ed. Emran Qureshi and Michael A. Sells (New York: Columbia University Press, 2003): 68–88.

[17] Shireen T. Hunter, "Introduction," in *Reformist Voices of Islam: Mediating Islam and Modernity*, ed. Shireen T. Hunter (Armonk, NY: M. E. Sharpe, 2008), 14.

such as Mirza Fatali Akhundzadeh (1812–1878) and Hassan Taghizadeh (1878–1970) called for the unequivocal embrace of Western civilization and culture.[18] The latter position, or that of the total rejection of modernity, is advocated primarily by some of the Islamic ulama as well as by contemporary Muslim traditionalists who call for bypassing modernity and returning to Islamic traditions in the face of modern challenges. Leading contemporary traditionalists such as Seyed Hossein Nasr reject not only what they see as the "Western" notions of "democracy," "popular sovereignty," and "republicanism," but also any attempt to deviate from traditional Islamic teachings through the introduction of such categories as "Islamic ideology," "political Islam," and "Islamic democracy."[19] Against the dichotomous forces of modernism and traditionalism, a host of contemporary Muslim thinkers have sought to advance a simultaneous critique of Western modernity and local traditions and to identify, in the words of one scholar, "strategies for successfully being-in-the-(modern)-world and not exiting from it."[20] Thus, even when Islamist thinkers such as Qutb, Maududi, and Khomeini position themselves against modernity and call for alternatives to modern norms and structures, they nevertheless advance a nontraditionalist reading of Islam by advocating a revision in conventional religious understandings, the adoption of modern science and technology, and the utilization of the capacities of the modern nation-state to implement their particular interpretations of Islam.

While the following discussion is attentive to continuities and overlaps in modern Islamic thought, it also highlights the diversity and differences that characterize the discourses of a wide range of post-nineteenth century Muslim thinkers. Far from having fixed meanings and sociopolitical connotations, in modern Islamic thought modernity and Islam serve as floating signifiers reflecting contesting normative assumptions and distinct contextual determinants. As a floating signifier, modernity represents a plurality of concepts, values, and institutions, from industrialization and socioeconomic development (both capitalist and socialist)

---

[18] Mashallah Ajoudani, *Mashrooteh Irani (Iranian Constitutionalism)* (Tehran: Akhtaran, 1387/2008), 220–222, 282–289.
[19] Seyyed Hossein Nasr, "Goftam ba taraghi mokhalefam, cheh resad beh kanoon taraghi" ("Firmly Opposed to Taraghi Center") interview with Hamed Zare, *Mehrnameh* 23, 30 Tir 1391/20 July 2012: 115.
[20] Kamran Matin, "Decoding Political Islam: Uneven and Combined Development and Ai Shariati's Political Thought," in *International Relations and non-Western Thought: Imperialism, Colonialism, and Investigations of Global Modernity*, ed. Robbie Shilliam (London: Routledge, 2010), 111.

to secularism, individual rights and freedoms, pluralism, and democracy. Similarly, Islam is at once a source of methodological and/or ontological-inspirational, a discourse of mass mobilization, a call for the recognition of cultural difference, and a shield against modern relativism and the crisis of identity.

Responses to an Encounter

Commentators often distinguish between three major currents within modern Islamic thought.[21] In much of the academic literature the genesis of this broad and diverse body of thinking begins in the late nineteenth century with the rise of Islamic modernism, and continues throughout the twentieth century and presently with Islamism and Islamic reformism. Far from representing monolithic, neatly packaged, and clearly divisible categories, these currents represent diverse, and at times contesting, philosophical, religious, social, political, and economic orientations. The categorization is nevertheless useful for comparing and contrasting some of the ways in which contemporary Muslim thinkers have addressed the question of modernity, and for highlighting their points of convergence and divergence. Though marked by major differences, these currents represent a continuous effort by Muslim thinkers to respond to the challenges of colonial modernity on the basis of their nontraditionalist interpretations of Islamic thought.

Islamic Modernism

The late nineteenth century encounter with colonial modernity led, in the words of one commentator, to a "deep soul-searching" in Muslim societies and an effort to identify and overcome the causes of decline.[22] It was following this encounter that many prominent Muslim thinkers began to call for the modernization of Islamic thought and the adoption

---

[21] See: Roxanne L. Euben, "Mapping Modernities, 'Islamic' and 'Western'," in *Border Crossings: Toward a Comparative Political Theory*, ed. Fred Dallmayr (New York: Lexington Books, 1999), 11–37; Hamid Enayat, *Modern Islamic Political Thought: The Response of the Shi'I and Sunni Muslims to the Twentieth Century* New Edition (New York: I.B. Tauris, 2005); Ibrahim M. Abu-Rabi, "Editor's Introduction: Contemporary Islamic Thought: One or Many?," in *The Blackwell Companion to Contemporary Islamic Thought*, ed. Ibrahim M. Abu-Rabi (Malden, MA: Blackwell Publishing, 2006), 1–20; Euben and Zaman, "Introduction", 1–48; Mehran Kamrava, ed. *The New Voices of Islam: Reforming Politics and Modernity: A Reader* (London: I.B. Tauris, 2006).

[22] Hunter, "Introduction," 13.

in their societies of scientific, industrial, military, and other features of Western modernity.²³ Indian Islamic scholar Syed Ahmad Khan (1817–1898), Iranian-born pan-Islamic ideologue Sayyid Jamal al Din Afghani (1838–1897), Egyptian religious reformer Muhammad Abduh (1845–1905), Syrian theologian Muhammad Rashid Rida (1865–1935), and Indian-born poet and philosopher Muhammad Iqbal (1877–1938) are regarded as some of the most influential figures of Islamic modernism. Despite a shared commitment to reviving and modernizing Islamic thought these modernists advanced radically different social and intellectual projects. Afghani, for instance, was a passionate advocate of Muslim unity in resistance to British colonialism, whereas Ahmad Khan opposed the call for *jihad* against foreign occupiers and advocated political quietism.²⁴

The enterprise of reconciling Islam with a range of modern values and institutions effectively distinguished Islamic modernism from both traditionalism and secular modernism. Unlike the latter two, Islamic modernism maintained that far from being incompatible with modernity and scientific rationality, Islam was an inherently rational religion.²⁵ Some Muslim modernists even believed that Islam's scientific spirit, once manifested in a vast and thriving Islamic civilization, had in the course of historical interactions been passed on to Europe and embodied in different aspects of European modernity.²⁶ Yet faced with the reality of Europe's scientific, technological, and military superiority and the state of stagnation and decline in their own societies, they called for modernization without Westernization and sought to theorize "options for renaissance" and change from within.²⁷ This approach, based on selectivity and synthesis, was most pronounced in the modernist discourses of Afghani, Abduh, and Iqbal.

For Afghani, European colonial expansion in Muslim societies was a consequence of Europe's scientific and material advancement on the one

---

²³ Ibrahim M. Abu-Rabi, *Intellectual Origins of Islamic Resurgence in the Modern Arab World* (Albany: State University of New York Press, 1996), 6. Also see: Mahmoud M. Ayoub, "Forward," in Ibrahim M. Abu-Rabi, *Intellectual Origins of Islamic Resurgence in the Modern Arab World* (Albany: State University of New York Press, 1996), x.
²⁴ Ali Rahnema, "Introduction to 2nd Edition: Contextualizing the Pioneers of Islamic Revival," in *Pioneers of Islamic Revival* – Second Edition, ed. Ali Rahnema (New York: Zed Books, 2005), xxxii.
²⁵ Abu-Rabi, *Intellectual Origins*, 9. Also see: Ayoub, "Forward," x.
²⁶ Hunter, "Introduction," 15.
²⁷ Abu-Rabi, *Intellectual Origins*, 8.

hand, and centuries of intellectual stagnation in Muslim societies on the other.[28] In his view, by adopting the technological and industrial achievements of the West, Muslim societies could overcome the onslaught of colonialism and imperialism. Islam, according to him, had the capacity not only to be reconciled with modernity, but also to serve as a strong force for mobilizing the masses against the imperialists.[29] He argued that reversing the state of halt in "philosophical or intellectual movement" in the Muslim world required fighting against traditional religious "dogma" and interpreting Islamic doctrines in accordance with the needs and challenges of the modern era.[30] Responding to Renan and rejecting his assertion that "Islam" and "the Semitic spirit" were responsible for the state of backwardness and decline in Muslim societies, Afghani asserted that during the height of the Islamic civilization "the sciences made astonishing progress among the Arabs and in all the countries under their domination."[31]

Afghani's modernist efforts were continued after his death by his students and followers in various Muslim societies. Among them was Muhammad Abduh, widely regarded as the founder of Islamic modernism in the Arab world.[32] Like Afghani, Abduh was critical of the traditionalist ulama and called for a reformative project to "extract from the foundations all those ... superstitions attributed to religion that really have nothing to do with it."[33] Such a project, he argued, would be "an important social revolution" as it would alleviate many "social illnesses in the Orient" including a prevailing sense of "inferiority" vis-à-vis "Western nations."[34] According to Euben, by emphasizing Islam's rationalist core, Abduh's discourse of Islamic modernism rejected the binary construction

---

[28] Bassam Tibi, *The Crisis of Modern Islam: A Preindustrial Culture in the Scientific-Technological Age*, trans. Judith von Sivers (Salt Lake City: University of Utah Press, 1988), 92.

[29] Ervand Abrahamian, *Iran between Two Revolutions* (Princeton, NJ: Princeton University Press, 1982), 63.

[30] Jamal al-Din al-Afghani, "Answer of Jamal al-Din to Renan," *Journal des Débats*, May 18, 1883, in Nikki Keddie, *An Islamic Response to Imperialism: Political and Religious Writings of Sayyid Jamāl Ad-Dīn "al-Afghānī,"* (Berkeley and Los Angeles: University of California Press, 1983), 183.

[31] Ibid., 184.

[32] Hunter, "Introduction," 5.

[33] Muhammad Abduh, "The True Reform and its Necessity for Al-Azhar," *al-Manar* 10: 28, February 1906, trans. Kamran Talattof, in Mansoor Moaddel, and Kamran Talattof, *Contemporary Debates in Islam: An Anthology of Modernist and Fundamentalist Thought* (New York: St. Martin's Press, 2000), 47.

[34] Ibid., 48.

of Islam and modernity and instead proposed "that modern reason and its fruits [were] universal inheritance consistent with, and supportive of, Islamic truths rightly interpreted."³⁵

In the Indian subcontinent, it was Muhammad Iqbal who sought to advance Afghani's intellectual legacy and his modernist approach to Islam. Iqbal regarded Afghani as the first Muslim thinker to fully realize "the importance and immensity" of the project of modernizing Islamic thought. Nevertheless, in Iqbal's view, Afghani's "indefatigable energy" had been too divided for him to develop a coherent outline of the project that he had himself initiated.³⁶ Thus, in his own attempt to systematize the modernization of Islamic thought, Iqbal made a case for reviving the religious practice of *ijtihad* (independent reasoning), which refers to the application of individual reason to Islamic law independently of the views of traditional schools of *fiqh* (jurisprudence).³⁷ Iqbal's appeal to the historically neglected principle of *ijtihad* was informed by his belief that Islam was at its core a rational religion. He described the prophet of Islam as someone who stood "between the ancient and the modern world," and asserted that the Quran's designation of Muhammad as the Seal of the Prophets (*khatam an-nabiyyin*) was an indication that "in order to achieve full self-consciousness man [sic] must finally be thrown back on his own resources."³⁸

In his major work in Islamic philosophy, *The Reconstruction of Religious Thought in Islam* (1930), Iqbal made the case that the critical task before "the modern Muslim" was "to rethink the whole system of Islam without completely breaking with the past."³⁹ For him, the project of rethinking Islamic religious thought was a prerequisite for sustained social and cultural change in Muslim societies. He argued that modern developments around the world had created "new cultural necessities, and, thus, Islamic jurisprudential reason, which the masses of people regard as the rule of Sharia, is now in need of revision."⁴⁰ Challenging

---

35 Euben, "Mapping Modernities," 16.
36 Muhammad Iqbal, *The Reconstruction of Religious Thought in Islam* (Lahore: Ashraf, 1962), 97.
37 Riffat Hassan, "Islamic Modernist and Reformist Discourse in South Asia," in *Reformist Voices of Islam: Mediating Islam and Modernity*, ed. Shireen T. Hunter (Armonk, NY: M. E. Sharpe, 2008), 168.
38 Iqbal, *The Reconstruction of Religious Thought*, 126
39 Ibid., 97.
40 Muhammad Iqbal, quoted in Jawid Iqbal, "Moghaddameh" ("Introduction"), in *Kolliat-e Iqbal Lahori (The Poetry Collection of Iqbal Lahori)* (Tehran: Elham, 1384/2005), 24–25.

the claims of the traditional Islamic ulama about the finality of the historical schools of jurisprudence,[41] he maintained that the historical contributions of earlier Muslim thinkers were only to be seen in light of the prevailing contextual particularities.[42] Appealing to the Quranic teaching that "life is a process of progressive creation," Iqbal reasoned that each generation "should be permitted to solve its own problems."[43] For him, the task of rethinking and reconstructing Islamic thought meant developing a set of moral, social, and political ideals that corresponded to contemporary conditions and that were based on the "original simplicity and universality" of the monotheistic notions of "freedom, equality, and solidarity."[44]

The Islamic modernism of Afghani, Abduh, Iqbal, and others is often seen as having left a mixed legacy. According to Abu-Rabi, Islamic modernism sought to develop a new terminology to replace "the preindustrial and precapitalist notions and concepts of Muslim thought."[45] Islamic modernism is also credited with having initiated debates on a wide range of issues including cultural identity, the relationship between Muslim societies and the West, the status of women, and political rights and freedoms. Furthermore, the intellectual legacy of Islamic modernism is said to have paved the way for the subsequent rise of secular nationalist movements, as well as early women's emancipation movements.[46] On the other hand, however, commentators have also pointed to the shortcomings and failures of the modernist project during the early half of the twentieth century.[47] By the beginning of the century it was clear that Islamic modernism was not becoming a popular discourse of social change. While the masses of people remained loyal to the traditional religious establishment and its predominantly theological interpretation of religious doctrines, the educated elites insisted on pursuing a project of Westernization of their societies through top-down modernization measures. In this context, throughout the twentieth century the legacy of Islamic modernism was claimed and advanced by two distinct and contesting currents, namely Islamism and reformism.

---

[41] Iqbal, *The Reconstruction of Religious Thought*, 168.
[42] Ibid., 3.
[43] Ibid., 168.
[44] Ibid., 156.
[45] Abu-Rabi, *Intellectual Origins*, 9.
[46] John Esposito, *Islam and Politics* (Syracuse, NY: Syracuse University Press, 1984), 60.
[47] Enayat, *Modern Islamic Political Thought*, 53.

Islamism

One important consequence of the expansion of European colonialism in Islamicate context and the decline of major Muslim empires in South Asia, the Middle East, and North Africa, was the emergence throughout these lands of modern nation-states and the subsequent rise of nationalist movements. Seeking to reverse the weakness of their respective societies vis-à-vis the West, modern Muslim states and secular nationalist elites began to advance a series of modernization programs on the basis of Westerncentric models of development. Though limited modernization measures had already begun in the nineteenth century, during the period between 1920s and 1970s, a number of countries including Afghanistan, Turkey, Egypt, and Iran aggressively pursued a range of policies to adopt Western military, legal, educational, and economic institutions.

The advent of Islamist currents in the twentieth century has been attributed by several commentators to the failure of secular nationalism and the crisis of the modern nation-state. Abu-Rabi, for instance, argues that the Islamist turn was as much a product of the inability of Islamic modernism to achieve its initial vision of renaissance, as it was a consequence of the failure of secular nationalist states to adequately address the challenges of the postcolonial era.[48] Similarly, Sayyid links the popular attractiveness of Islamist discourses to "the inability of the secular elites, which succeeded the European colonial regimes, to meet the hopes and aspirations of their people."[49] According to him, the inadequate integration of the new petty bourgeoisie in political and economic structures of the newly independent states, the unevenness of economic development, and the effects of cultural erosion of "Muslim identities" were major factors that contributed to the inception and augmentation of Islamist currents.[50]

Challenging what they regarded as the disruptive effects of Westernization in their societies, Islamist discourses first emerged near the middle of the twentieth century calling for Islamic alternatives to modern ideas, values, and institutions.[51] Iranian religious and political

---

[48] Ibrahim M. Abu-Rabi, "Editor's Introduction: Islamism from the Standpoint of Critical Theory," in *Contemporary Arab Reader on Political Islam*, ed. Ibrahim M. Abu-Rabi (London and Edmonton: Pluto Press and University of Alberta Press, 2010), ix.

[49] S. Sayyid, *A Fundamental Fear: Eurocentrism and the Emergence of Islamism* (London and New York: Zed Books, 1997), 19.

[50] Ibid., 18–22. Also see: Michael Fischer, "Islam and the Revolt of Petit Bourgeoisie," *Daedalus* 3, no. 1 (1982): 101–122.

[51] Rahnema, "Introduction," 2.

leader Ruhollah Khomeini (1902–1989), Pakistani theologian Abul Ala Maududi (1903–1979), Egyptian preacher and the founder of the Muslim Brotherhood Hassan al-Banna (1906–1949), Egyptian author and Muslim Brotherhood member Sayyid Qutb (1906–1966), and Indian Islamic scholar Abul Hassan Ali Nadwi (1913–1999) are some of the major figures of mid-twentieth century Islamism. Among the prominent contemporary Islamist figures are Egyptian theologian Yusuf al-Qaradawi (b. 1926), Sudanese religious leader and founder of Sudan's Muslim Brotherhood Hassan al-Turabi (b. 1932), and Iran's current Supreme Leader Ali Khamenei (b. 1939). Like Islamic modernism, Islamism is also characterized as much by continuities and overlaps as it is by diversity and difference. As a result, some commentators distinguish between various forms of Islamism: nonviolent and violent, democratic and nondemocratic, moderate and extreme.[52]

Seeking to identify a total alternative to Western modernity, Islamist thinkers turned Islam into the "master signifier" and the "unifying point" of their discursive productions.[53] As such, within Islamist thinking Islam came to represent "the authentic characteristic of the collective 'self' in opposition to the European 'other'."[54] In practice, however, the claim to authenticity and the project of articulating a total Islamic alternative to modernity meant first and foremost advocating the establishment of an Islamic state and the implementation of sharia law. While such leading modernists as Ali Abdel Raziq (1888–1966) had argued that the Quran and the Islamic tradition did not endorse any particular form of government,[55] Islamists like Nadwi, al-Banna, and Maududi saw the reign of the prophet of Islam and the first four caliphs as a governance model to be restored in the modern age. Nadwi traced the beginning of the Islamic stagnation to what he saw as the "de facto separation between religion and state" after the establishment of the Umayyad Caliphate in 661 AD.[56] For Al-Banna, the founding of an Islamic state was the only way to revive Muslim societies and to resist Western domination.[57] Maududi,

---

[52] See: Abu-Rabi, "Editor's Introduction: Islamism from the Standpoint of Critical Theory," xiii–xiv.
[53] Sayyid, *A Fundamental Fear*, 158.
[54] Nasr Hamid Abu Zayd, "The Modernization of Islam or the Islamization of Modernity," in *Cosmopolitanism, Identity and Authenticity in the Middle East*, ed. Roel Meijer (London: Routledge Curzon Press, 1999), 79–80.
[55] Tibi, *The Crisis of Modern Islam*, 45.
[56] Abu-Rabi, *Intellectual Origins*, 18.
[57] Rahnema, "Introduction to 2nd Edition," 4.

too, believed that it was imperative for Muslims to strive to establish a state committed to the implementation of sharia.⁵⁸ Still, the most detailed and forceful theories of the Islamic state were developed by Qutb in his account of the absolute sovereignty of God, and by Khomeini in his doctrine of the guardianship of the jurist (*velayat-e faqih*).

Qutb's Islamist views were expressed in his later works, particularly in *Milestones (ma'alim fi al-tariq)*, written while he was in prison under the rule of Gamal Abdel Nasser, and published in 1964.⁵⁹ There, he used the Quranic term *jahiliyya* (barbarism or ignorance) to describe the modern condition in Egypt and around the world. While in the Quran the term generally refers to the condition of pre-Islamic Arabia, in Qutb's political thought *jahiliyya* came to represent the sovereignty of the individual and the rejection of divine authority.⁶⁰ Describing the postcolonial Egyptian state as an instrument for preserving the sovereignty of Nasser's totalitarian rule, Qutb called for the establishment of a new political order based on the absolute sovereignty of God and the rule of sharia.⁶¹ In his view, the restoration of divine sovereignty required a committed Muslim vanguard whose tasks included developing social programs on the basis of the Islamic law. Thus, in *Milestones* he called upon the Muslim vanguard to eliminate the reign of man and to establish the kingdom of God on earth.⁶²

Whereas Qutb's vision of the kingdom of God on earth came to an end with his execution in 1966, his Iranian contemporary, Khomeini, was the first Islamist to both articulate and implement his idea of the Islamic state.⁶³ For centuries, the Shi'i ulama had deferred the founding of an Islamic state to the return of the Shi'i messianic figure, Imam Mahdi. It was believed that until the return of the hidden Imam, the role of the Shi'i jurists was to provide believers with religious guidance, oversee religious practices, and collect and distribute religious taxes (*khums*) from and among the believers on behalf of the Imam. In a radical reformulation

---

[58] Euben and Zaman, "Introduction," 12.
[59] Gilles Kepel, *Muslim Extremism in Egypt*, trans., Jon Rothschild (Berkeley: University of California Press, 1986), 13.
[60] Ibid., 53–55.
[61] Euben, "Mapping Modernities," 20. Also see: Charles Tripp, "Sayyid Qutb: The Political Vision," in *Pioneers of Islamic Revival*, ed. Ali Rahnema (New York: Zed Books, 2005), 154–183.
[62] Sayed Khatab, *The Political Thought of Sayyid Qutb: The Theory of Jahiliyyah* (London & New York: Routledge, 2006), 169.
[63] Baqer Moin, "Khomeini's Search for Perfection: Theory and Reality," in *Pioneers of Islamic Revival* Second Edition, ed. Ali Rahnema (New York: Zed Books, 2005), 64.

of this traditional Shi'i clerical doctrine, Khomeini argued that in the absence of the hidden Imam the deputyship of the ulama extended to all facets of social and political life.[64]

From his first book, *Secrets Unveiled (kashf al-asrar)*, published in 1944, to his 1970 book, *Guardianship of the Jurist (velayat-e faqih)*, Khomeini introduced and expanded on the notion of a theocratic state. His views in *Secrets Unveiled* resembled Qutb's arguments in *Milestones*. There, Khomeini argued that sovereignty only belonged to God and in the absence of prophetic authority the most important qualification for political leadership was knowledge of the Islamic law. Like Qutb, Khomeini also rejected the idea of human legislation.[65] According to him, under the leadership of the guardian-jurist, the state is only subject to "conditions that are set forth in the Noble Quran and the *Sunna* of the Most Nobel Messenger."[66] As noted by some commentators, however, Khomeini took an entirely different position after the establishment of the Islamic Republic, arguing that the authority of the state transcended the provisions of Islamic law and that the state was the final arbiter of the interest of Islam.[67]

Highlighting its antidemocratic and antirationalist features, some critics see Islamism as a rejection of "the dominant features of modernity."[68] Critics also describe the Islamists' claims of authenticity as a position against the universality of modern norms and structures.[69] However, as Abu-Rabi correctly points out, while Islamism strives "to replace modernity [...] with an Islamic *Weltanschauung*," it would be a mistake to "juxtapose Islamism and modernity or [to] argue in binary terms" because the former's emergence in the Muslim world was itself facilitated by modernity.[70] Similarly, Tibi argues that the formulation of the concept of an

---

[64] Roxanne L. Euben and Muhammad Qasim Zaman, "Ayatollah Ruhollah Khomeini," in *Princeton Readings in Islamist Thought: Texts and Contexts from al-Banna to Bin Laden*, ed. Roxanne L. Euben and Muhammad Qasim Zaman (Princeton, NJ: Princeton University Press, 2009), 158.

[65] Farzin Vahdat, *God and Juggernaut: Iran's Intellectual Encounter with Modernity* (Syracuse, NY: Syracuse University Press, 2002), 163.

[66] Ruhollah Khomeini (1981), 55, quoted in Mojtaba Mahdavi, "Islam/Muslims and Political Leadership," in *The Ashgate Research Companion to Political Leadership*, ed. Joseph Masciulli, Mikhail A. Molchanov, and W. Andy Knight (Burlington, VT: Ashgate, 2009), 296.

[67] Euben and Zaman, "Ayatollah Ruhollah Khomeini," 160.

[68] Nilüfer Göle, "Snapshots of Islamic Modernities," *Daedalus* 129, no. 1, *Multiple Modernities* (Winter, 2000): 92–93.

[69] Aziz Al-Azmeh, *Islam and Modernities* (London and New York: Verso, 1993), 92.

[70] Abu-Rabi, "Editor's Introduction: Islamism from the Standpoint of Critical Theory," xi.

"Islamic Republic" in the aftermath of the 1979 revolution in Iran points to the negotiation between modern and traditional concepts in Islamist thought. According to him, while Islamist discourses that claim "authenticity" can generally be termed "defensive-cultural mechanisms," they are nevertheless modern discourses, which display varying degrees of hybridity and engagement with modern Western thought.[71]

Like their modernist predecessors, leading twentieth-century Islamists called on Muslims to pursue scientific and technological advancement.[72] Also like modernists, they criticized the traditional ulama for fixating on religious rituals, failing to adjust themselves to the realities of the modern world, and advocating political quietism. Maududi, among others, was highly critical of the ulama's preoccupation with "ritual practices [...] at the expense of 'the real spirit of the religion'."[73] Qutb, too, saw the traditional ulama as "'opportunists' who transformed religion into a profession, manipulated religious texts to serve their own material interests, and, in so doing, paralyzed and deceived Muslims 'in the name of religion'."[74] Likewise, Khomeini condemned the political quietism of "pseudo-saints" who aided imperialist domination, and called on the youth to "strip them of their turbans."[75]

The rise of Islamism is also said to have facilitated the social and political participation of many Muslims in the modern world. Even its critics acknowledge that by challenging the "traditional subjugation of Muslim identity" and the "monocivilizational impositions of Western modernity," Islamism has served as "a critical introduction of Muslim agency into the modern arenas of social life."[76] According to Göle, as a contemporary phenomenon that simultaneously seeks continuity with and breaks from the past, Islamism provides Muslims with a sense of collective agency, a modern political vocabulary, and the means for participation and communication in "urban and public spaces of modernity."[77] Moreover,

[71] Tibi, *The Crisis of Modern Islam*, 6.
[72] Euben, "Mapping Modernities," 21; Abu-Rabi, *Intellectual Origins*, 20.
[73] Roxanne L. Euben and Muhammad Qasim Zaman, "Sayyid Abu'l-A'la Mawdudi" in *Princeton Readings in Islamist Thought: Texts and Contexts from al-Banna to Bin Laden*, ed. Roxanne L. Euben and Muhammad Qasim Zaman (Princeton, NJ: Princeton University Press, 2009), 81.
[74] Roxanne L. Euben and Muhammad Qasim Zaman, "Sayyid Qutb," in *Princeton Readings in Islamist Thought: Texts and Contexts from al-Banna to Bin Laden*, ed. Roxanne L. Euben and Muhammad Qasim Zaman (Princeton, NJ: Princeton University Press, 2009), 133.
[75] Euben and Zaman, "Ayatollah Ruhollah Khomeini," 160–161.
[76] Göle, "Snapshots of Islamic Modernities," 93.
[77] Ibid., 114.

Abu-Rabi describes Islamism as "a powerful source of critical debate in the struggle against the undemocratic imposition of a new world order by the United States, and against the economic and ecological violence of neoliberalism."[78]

Reformism
While Islamism's advocacy of the Islamic state and the rule of sharia as an alternative to Western modernity constituted a conservative turn in the evolution of modern Islamic thought, the mid- and late-twentieth century also witnessed the emergence of a number of reformist discourses aimed at continuing the progressive legacies of Afghani, Abduh, and Iqbal. In addition to Ali Shariati, whom will be discussed separately in the next section, some of the most prominent twentieth-century Muslim reformers included Iranian religious and political activist Mehdi Bazargan (1907–1995), Sudanese Muslim thinker Mahmoud Mohammad Taha (1909–1985), Iranian theologian Mahmoud Taliqani (1911–1979), Algerian-French scholar of Islamic studies Mohammed Arkoun (1928–2010), Egyptian Quranic scholar Nasr Hamid Abu Zayd (1943–2010), and Moroccan feminist and sociologist Fatima Mernissi (1940–2015). Among the leading contemporary Muslim reformists are Egyptian-American Muslim feminist Leila Ahmed (b. 1940), Turkish author and educator Fethullah Gülen (b. 1941), Iranian dissident intellectual Abdolkarim Soroush (b. 1945), Sudanese-American Islamic and legal scholar Abdullahi Ahmed An-Na'im (b. 1950), and Swiss academic Tariq Ramadan (b. 1962). Like Islamism, Islamic reformism encompasses a wide range of religious, philosophical, sociopolitical, and socioeconomic views and projects. Nevertheless, the common denominator between the distinct variations of reformism (and one which connects reformism to the late nineteenth- and early twentieth-century modernism) is the rejection of the mutually exclusive binary of Islam and modernity, and the attempt to advance a religiously mediated discourse of indigenous modernity.

The emergence of Islamic reformism was a challenge not only to Eurocentric modernism and Islamic traditionalism, but also to Islamism. While such leading Islamists as Maududi, Qutb, and Khomeini called for the establishment of an Islamic state based on the absolute sovereignty of God and the rule of sharia, their reformist counterparts – including

---

[78] Abu-Rabi, "Editor's Introduction: Islamism from the Standpoint of Critical Theory," vii.

Bazargan, Taliqani, and Taha – advocated various accounts of Islamic humanism and rejected authoritarian and statist readings of Islam's religious doctrines. Bazargan, who served as Iran's first postrevolution Prime Minister from February 1979 to November 1979, was a critic of Khomeini's Islamist vision and argued that the absolute guardianship of the jurist was tantamount to religious despotism.[79] Taliqani, a highly regarded senior Shi'i cleric who died shortly after the revolution, supported democratic governance and was critical of the turn toward authoritarian Islamism under the Islamic Republic. Taha too rejected the implementation of sharia law in Sudan and challenged traditionalist interpretations of religious doctrines. His position was harshly criticized by the advocates of traditionalism and Islamism and he was eventually charged with heresy and executed in 1985 during the presidency of Gaafar Nimeiry.

Since its advent in the mid-twentieth century and continuing today, the question of the relationship between Islam and modernity has been one of the central preoccupations of Islamic reformism. As two leading figures of this intellectual current in the late twentieth century, Abu Zayd and Arkoun rejected Orientalist and Islamist claims about the irreconcilability of Islam and modernity and the inherently European nature of the latter. Their views on the compatibility of Islam and modernity were advanced through two distinct but interrelated lines of argumentation. On the one hand, citing the intellectual legacies of the Mutazila movement (a rationalist school of theology which came to prominence between the eighth and eleventh centuries) and of Muslim rationalists such as Al-Jahiz, Al-Kindi, Al-Razi, Al-Farabi, Al-Tawhidi, Ibn Miskawayh, Ibn Sina (Avicenna), and Ibn Rushd (Averroes), these reformists highlighted a tradition of Islamic rationalism and its contributions to the European Enlightenment thought. On the other hand, however, in their critique of scientific positivism and the binary construction of reason and revelation, they distinguished Islam's rationalist tradition from that of Enlightenment rationality. Arkoun, for instance, believed that unlike the "neutral," "cold," and "calculating" rationality of the Aristotelian reason, Islamic reason was a creative force oriented toward fundamental human needs and everyday challenges.[80] Arkoun also argued for the necessity of

---

[79] Mehdi Moslemi, *Factional Politics in Post-Khomeini Iran* (Syracuse, NY: Syracuse University Press, 2002), 14.

[80] Mohammed Arkoun, "Naghd-e aghl-e eslami va mafhoom-e khoda" ("The Critique of Islamic Reason and the Concept of God"), interview with Hashim Salih, trans. Mehdi Khalaji, *Kian* 27, Khordad-Tir 1378/June-July 1999: 22.

finding a third way between the "abstract rationalism" of Enlightenment's scientific positivism and the dogmatism and conservatism of traditional Islamic jurisprudence.[81] Abu Zayd made a similar point by arguing that contrary to Greek philosophy, which only recognized reason and logos, the history of Islamic philosophy was characterized by an effort to bring together reason and revelation and to "upgrade the meaning of revelation to meet the findings of reason."[82]

Among the leading contemporary advocates of the compatibility of Islam and modernity, Gülen argues that the traditional Islamic principle of the absolute sovereignty of God does not contradict the modern principle of popular sovereignty. According to Gülen, since sovereignty has been entrusted to humans by God, people are "free to make choices with regard to their social and political actions."[83] While rejecting the notion of the Islamic state and endorsing a secular model of governance, Gülen nevertheless calls for an active role for religion in social, ethical, educational, and intellectual realms.[84] He also favors the reinterpretation of sharia in accordance with the modern principles of human rights and freedom. In his view, a revisited and reinterpreted sharia could present "higher principles" to guide the community in addition to "laws made by humans."[85]

Another prominent voice of contemporary Islamic reformism, Soroush also argues for the compatibility of "reason and faith," and "spiritual authority and political liberty."[86] In Soroush's view, modernity marks a set of changes as a result of which human beings turn from "passive objects" in a fixed and predetermined world into "active subjects" who

[81] Mohammed Arkoun, "Positivism and Tradition in an Islamic Perspective: Kemalism," *Diogenes* 32, no. 127 (1984): 82–100.

[82] Nasr Hamid Abu Zayd, "The Other as Mirror of Selfunderstanding. Comparing Two Traditions," Reset-DOC: Dialogues on Civilizations, July 18, 2011, www.resetdoc.org/story/00000021674 (accessed August 4, 2012).

[83] Fethullah Gülen, "An Interview with Fethullah Gülen," interview and translation by Zeki Saritoprak and Ali Unal, *The Muslim World* 95, no. 3: 453, quoted in John Esposito and Ihsan Yilmaz, *Islam and Peacebuilding: Gulen Movement Initiatives* (New York: Blue Dome, 2010), 31.

[84] Abu-Rabi, "Editor's Introduction," in Nevval Sevindi, *Contemporary Islamic Conversations: M. Fethullah Gulen on Turkey, Islam, and the West*, ed. Ibrahim M. Abu-Rabi, trans. Abdulah T. Antepli (New York: State University of New York, 2008), xi-xii. Also see: John Esposito and Ihsan Yilmaz, *Islam and Peacebuilding: Gulen Movement Initiatives* (New York: Blue Dome, 2010), 33–36.

[85] Gülen, "An Interview," 450.

[86] Mahmoud Sadri and Ahmad Sadri, "Introduction," in *Reason, Freedom, and Democracy in Islam: Essential Writings of Abdolkarim Soroush*, ed. Mahmoud Sadri and Ahmad Sadri (New York: Oxford University Press, 2000), xi.

can transform the world.[87] For him, the premodern age is defined by "the hegemony of metaphysical thought in political, economic, and social realms." Modernity, he thus contends, secularized politics by subjecting the state to "criticism, checks, and balances."[88] For Soroush, the modern secular state, then, is "a regime in whose polity no values and rules are beyond human appraisal and verification and in which no protocol, status, position, or ordinance is above public scrutiny." Soroush nevertheless critiques the exclusion of God in Western liberal thought and argues that the main challenge for contemporary Muslim societies is to make politics "desacralized," "rational," and "scientific" without antagonizing religion.[89] Thus, while rejecting the theory of *velayat-e faqih*,[90] he remains hopeful about the possibility of a "democratic religious government."[91]

Contesting Genealogies of Emergent Islamic Modernities

Increasingly in recent years, commentators are pointing to the emergence of religiously grounded discourses of sociocultural and sociopolitical development in the Muslim world exemplified by the works of such leading Muslim reformists as Arkoun, Abu Zayd, Gülen, and Soroush. These commentators contend that in the twenty-first century Islamic reformism has emerged as a force that can align itself with the more progressive sectors of Muslim societies in the ongoing quest for democracy, secularism, and human rights. Hunter, for example, argues that by advancing a synthesis of modernity and Islam, contemporary Muslim reformists are introducing "an indigenous concept of modernity."[92] Similarly, Mirsepassi notes a growing tendency among Islamic reformists toward offering "a

---

[87] Abdolkarim Soroush, "The Sense and Essence of Secularism," in *Reason, Freedom, and Democracy in Islam: Essential Writings of Abdolkarim Soroush*, ed. Mahmoud Sadri and Ahmad Sadri (New York: Oxford University Press, 2000), 54.
[88] Ibid., 59–60.
[89] Ibid., 60.
[90] Ibid., 63.
[91] Abdolkarim Soroush, "The Idea of Democratic Religious Government," in *Reason, Freedom, and Democracy in Islam: Essential Writings of Abdolkarim Soroush*, ed. Mahmoud Sadri and Ahmad Sadri (New York: Oxford University Press, 2000), 122. Soroush writes: "The problem of religious democratic governments is threefold: to reconcile people's satisfaction with God's approval; to strike a balance between the religious and the nonreligious; and to do right by both the people and by God, acknowledging at once the integrity of human beings and of religion."
[92] Shireen T. Hunter, "Preface," in *Reformist Voices of Islam: Mediating Islam and Modernity*, ed. Shireen T. Hunter (Armonk, NY: M. E. Sharpe, 2008), xx.

more enlightened understanding of historical and contemporary relations between Islam and the West, as well as venturing profound criticism and interpretation of historical and contemporary Islamic thought and culture with a view to developing more democratic forms in existing Islamic societies." Referring to Arkoun's notion of the "unthoughts" of Islamic thought, he argues that in their modern "reconstruction" and "reconsiderations" of Islamic thought and history, Muslim reformists are engaged in advancing "alternative democratic possibilities while also showing an often-overlooked dimension of contemporary Islamic culture and religious discourse."[93]

Taking into account, as the previous section did, the historical trajectory of modern Islamic thought since the late-nineteenth-century encounter of Muslim societies with colonial modernity, and attending not only to breaks but also to continuities in this intellectual tradition, particularly the connections between Islamic modernism and reformism, it is possible to arrive at a different genealogy of what may be referred to as discourses of indigenous modernity in Islamicate contexts. In this alternative genealogy, Shariati occupies a salient position as a link between Muslim modernists and reformists. Reading his work in light of this historical trajectory also reveals important common grounds between Shariati's thought and the works of notable reformists such as Arkoun, Abu Zayd, Gülen, and Soroush. These common grounds are often overlooked as several academic commentaries have erroneously placed Shariati in the same category with Islamists such as Maududi, Qutb, and Khomeini. Hunter, for instance, sees Shariati as having shared Qutb's apprehensions "regarding the despiritualizing and alienating aspects of modern socioeconomic systems."[94] Mirsepassi, too, views Shariati as a leading "Islamist" whose Heideggerian rejection of Enlightenment modernity and whose articulation of an Islamic ideology "paved the way" for the ascendency of Islamism in Iran during and in the aftermath of the 1979 revolution.[95]

In his own writings and lectures, Shariati often describes his work as a continuation of the modernist works of Afghani and Iqbal. These figures are, for Shariati, the pioneers of a contextually grounded project of radical transformation and progressive change in Muslim societies. In *Iqbal*

---

[93] Ali Mirsepassi, *Political Islam, Iran, and the Enlightenment: Philosophies of Hope and Despair* (New York: Cambridge University Press, 2011), 11.
[94] Hunter, "Introduction," 7, 18–19.
[95] Mirsepassi, *Political Islam*, 1–5.

and Us (*Ma va Iqbal*), he distinguishes the politically charged discourses of Afghani and Iqbal from the quietist and apolitical discourses of Indian modernist Syed Ahmad Khan and his followers, arguing that the latter group mistakenly believed that "Islamic revival would be possible simply through philosophical reasoning and a modern, scientific, rational, twentieth-century interpretation of Islamic beliefs and Quranic teachings, irrespective of the prevailing social conditions, which included continued British imperialism."[96] The radical and anticolonial discourses of Afghani and Iqbal, on the other hand, are seen by Shariati as efforts to transcend the confines of theological, philosophical, and metaphysical debates and to address the prevailing social and political challenges of their societies.[97] Shariati also contrasts the reform-minded visions of Afghani and Iqbal with the statist and authoritarian projects of social and political change seeking to "radically alter norms and beliefs and reorganize social relations and ways of human upbringing through the force of compulsion and violence."[98]

In his reading of Afghani and Iqbal, Shariati underscores what he regards as the open and synthetic nature of their intellectual projects. It is precisely this quality that, in his view, sets the discourses of these pioneering modernists apart from culturalist discourses that advocated a "dogmatic, backwards, and racist turn to the past." According to him, without denying the achievements of Europe, Afghani and Iqbal drew attention to the diversity of civilizational traditions. Defying the monocivilizational narrative of European modernity, they conceived of Islamic and European traditions as two interconnected entities that influenced one another in the course of ongoing historical interactions. He thus contends that although Afghani and Iqbal were attentive to the sociopolitical and sociocultural consequences of European colonialism, they nonetheless acknowledged the transformative potential of modern normative and intellectual transformations in Europe, exemplified by the Renaissance, the Reformation, and the Enlightenment.[99]

While accentuating their selective approach to tradition and modernity, Shariati also praises Afghani and Iqbal for confronting the myth of Europe as "the universal trajectory of progress and the most complete

---

[96] Ali Shariati, *Ma va Iqbal: majmooeh asar 5 (Iqbal and Us: Collected Works)*, (Aachen, Germany: Hosseinieh Ershad, 1978), 34.
[97] Ibid., 53.
[98] Ibid., 34.
[99] Ibid., 74.

vision of human ideals and values."[100] Afghani, in his view, pioneered a movement that aimed not only to liberate Muslim nations from the political and economic force of European colonialism, but also to challenge a savage colonial modernity that denied and obliterated all other cultures and civilizations. Afghani's call for turning away from the West, he posits, came approximately a century before the provincialization of Europe by such well-known twentieth century anticolonial figures as Sarvepalli Radhakrishnan, Jomo Kenyatta, Léopold Sédar Senghor, Kwame Nkrumah, Ahmed Sékou Touré, Julius Nyerere, Aimé Césaire, Frantz Fanon, Kateb Yacine, and Albert Memmi.[101]

If Afghani is credited with initiating the postcolonial turn away from Europe, Iqbal is recognized for giving "ideological substance" to Afghani's vision.[102] According to Shariati, in his reconstruction of Islamic thought Iqbal sought to reexamine local cultural and intellectual resources in the Islamic tradition, identify their capacities, and utilize those capacities in a project of renewal. Iqbal's work, he maintains, provided a blueprint for transforming Islam from a "static and stagnant" culture of hopelessness, determinism, and fixation with the afterlife, into a change-oriented, future-oriented, and this-worldly vision of existence.[103] In his view, unlike Westerncentric and secular ideologies that had little influence on the religious masses, Iqbal's indigenous ideology sought to "awaken Muslims" precisely by drawing on the familiar and local cultural and civilizational resources.[104] He argues that by developing a modern and contextually negotiated ideology of social and political development on the basis of the restructuring of Islamic thought, Iqbal also showed the continued relevance of religious thought in the intellectual and philosophical debates of the modern age.[105]

Building on the modernist discourses of Afghani and Iqbal, Shariati makes a case for the compatibility of religious revelation with human reason and will. According to him, instead of emphasizing the notion of "divine destiny" in which human will is entirely inconsequential, the Quran emphasizes "human destiny" in which the individual is regarded as an agent of change.[106] In defense of such a view, he cites the Quranic

---

[100] Ibid., 79–80.
[101] Ibid., 79–85.
[102] Ibid., 28, 142, 180.
[103] Ibid., 32–33.
[104] Ibid., 12.
[105] Ibid., 11.
[106] Ibid., 36–37.

teaching that "Allah will not change the condition of a people until they change what is in themselves" (13:11).[107] He argues that by stressing "human autonomy and responsibility" Iqbal's thought reaches similar conclusions as those of modern humanism and existentialism. However, while the latter two traditions make a case for individual autonomy by negating religion, Iqbal arrives at this conclusion "in the course of his spiritual journey."[108]

Shariati's own view on human will recognizes individual autonomy and agency while simultaneously acknowledging its limitations. According to him, since the nineteenth century Western "individualists" and "radical humanists" have promoted the idea that "the individual is the prime mover in all social and historical processes of change." "Socialists, naturalists, and social Darwinists," on the other hand, have highlighted contextual "determinants" that limit human agency. Seeking to reconcile these contesting views, he favors a dialectical approach, which he attributes to Russian-French sociologist and his Sorbonne professor Georges Gurvitch (1894–1969). Within this approach, he asserts, "the individual and society are seen as being in a constant process of constructing and influencing one another."[109] Thus, while social and environmental factors may impose particular limitations on one's agency, the individual can also influence and alter the prevailing "social, historical, cultural, economic, and natural" determinants.[110]

Modernity, for Shariati, is a condition that enhances human agency, thus altering the dialectic between autonomous will and contextual determinants in favor of the former.[111] Noting the influence of the Christian Reformation in giving recognition to autonomous human will in the course of the European modernity, he applauds Afghani and Iqbal for initiating a similar project in Muslim societies and calls on other Muslim intellectuals to follow this progressive reformist path.[112] Emphasizing the role of authentic intellectuals in leading the move toward radical social and political transformation, he describes intellectual responsibility as a "prophetic mission" (*resalat-e payambar-gooneh*) of raising change-oriented

---

[107] Ali Shariati, "Jahatgiri-e tabaghati dar Islam; daftar-e avval" ("Class Orientation in Islam; Book One"), 1356/1977, C.W. 10, *Ali Shariati: The Complete Collection of Works* [CD ROM], Tehran: Shariati Cultural Foundation, 2010.
[108] Shariati, *Ma va Iqbal*, 38.
[109] Ibid., 46, 44.
[110] Ibid., 45.
[111] Ibid., 46, 110–111.
[112] Ibid., 8–9.

consciousness among the masses about the "discordant realities of their society and of their epoch."[113] Intellectual responsibility, for him, also includes developing a revolutionary ideology, which he describes as a prerequisite for raising popular consciousness, mobilizing the masses, and initiating a deep normative change leading to social transformation.[114]

Shariati's emphasis on the leadership role of authentic intellectuals and his thesis of "committed democracy" (*demokrasi-e mota'ahed*), which he lays out in a 1969 lecture at the Hosseinieh Ershad titled "Community and Leadership" (*ommat va imamat*), have been regarded by some as endorsements of a vanguardist vision of top-down change.[115] For critics, the thesis provides clear evidence that Shariati's thought ultimately supports the dictatorship of a Muslim vanguard and the establishment of an Islamic state based on the fusion of spiritual and political authority.[116] Such readings of Shariati's thought, however, neglect the fact that in a number of subsequent lectures and writings Shariati explicitly rejects the idea that intellectuals must undertake political leadership and governance roles, emphasizing instead the prophetic mission of empowering the masses through raising social and political consciousness. Though references to the concept can be found is some of these later works, Shariati nevertheless clarifies that for him "committed democracy" is a transitional model applicable only to tribal societies (such as the Arabian Peninsula during the early Islamic period) that lack the basic requirements of democratic governance.[117]

In *Iqbal and Us*, for instance, he writes, "Even though I see democracy as the most progressive and even most Islamic system of governance, I think that its realization in a tribal society [...] requires a phase of 'committed revolutionary leadership' in order to provide a civilized and democratic social condition."[118] Likewise, in *Return* he is explicit that

---

[113] Ali Shariati, *Bazgasht: majmooeh asar 4 (Return: Collected Works 4)* (Tehran: Entesharat-e Elham, 1373/1994), 95.

[114] Ibid., 144, 311.

[115] The text of this lecture was published and disseminated widely during Shariati's own life and was later included in the twenty-sixth volume of his collected works titled Ali (1982).

[116] Shireen T. Hunter, "Islamic Reformist Discourses in Iran: Proponents and Prospects," in *Reformist Voices of Islam: Mediating Islam and Modernity*, ed. Shireen T. Hunter (Armonk, NY: M. E. Sharpe, 2008), 55. Also see: Saeed Rahnema, "Retreat and Return of the Secular in Iran," *Comparative Studies of South Asia, Africa and the Middle East* 31, no. 1 (2011): 34–45, 41.

[117] Shariati, *Ma va Iqbal*, 48.

[118] Ibid.

the role of intellectuals is not one of taking up "political, executive, and revolutionary leadership." Taking political power, he argues, "is an exclusive right of the people, and when they are absent from the theater of political struggle others cannot claim to exercise this right on their behalf. In fact, in postrevolutionary periods even the best of intellectuals have failed to be good leaders."[119] Shariati's overall orientation in these lectures and essays is one of supporting a bottom-up project of sociocultural and sociopolitical transformation through a modern and radical reformation of local cultural and religious traditions and raising popular consciousness. According to him, "anyone who recognizes that social change requires more than simply political action would agree that the most essential task of committed intellectuals" is to provide the groundwork for "an intellectual-psychological transformation in the consciousness of their nations."[120]

As self-proclaimed heirs to his intellectual legacy, neo-Shariatis often object to the equation of Shariati's thought with the Islamist visions of Maududi, Qutb, Khomeini, and others. Rebuking the claim that Shariati's influence facilitated the ascendancy of Islamism in late-twentieth-century Iran, Reza Alijani, among others, argues that Shariati's modern interpretation of Islamic doctrines must be understood as a radical critique of the very foundations of Islamist thinking.[121] Similarly, Susan Shariati believes that while Islamism regards Muslim identity as an idealized category and as the antithesis of the non-Muslim "Western" other, Shariati fundamentally rejects the view of identity as a fixed and monolithic entity. Though acknowledging Shariati's attentiveness to cultural and civilizational difference, she proposes that Shariati's thought treats identity formation as a dynamic and open-ended process of becoming. Shariati's call for a return to the self, she argues, is informed by his dialogical view of the relationship between the local and global sources of identity.[122] Sara Shariati, too,

---

[119] Shariati, *Bazgasht*, 257.
[120] Ali Shariati, "Moghaddameh" ("Introduction"), in *Kolliat-e Iqbal Lahori (The Poetry Collection of Iqbal Lahori)* (Tehran: Elham, 1384/2005), 8.
[121] Reza Alijani, interview by author (Internet/Skype), November 20, 2012. Alijani points out that Shariati's only direct reference to the notion of a "religious state" is in a piece titled "Toynbee: Civilization-Religion" (CW 22: *Religion vs. Religion*) where he describes it as a particularly oppressive form of social and political tyranny.
[122] Susan Shariati, "Protestantism va fahm-e Shariati az an: goftegooy-e Susan Shariati va Taghi Rahmani" ("Protestantism and Shariati's Understanding of It: A Conversation between Susan Shariati and Taghi Rahmani"), interview with Lotfollah Meisami, *Cheshmandaz Iran* 65, Day-Bahman 1389/January-February 2011, http://drshariati.org/show/?id=472 (accessed September 17, 2012).

dismisses the designation of Shariati's as a discourse of identitarianism along the lines of Islamist calls for a return to an authentic Islamic self. According to her, although Shariati's return to the self discourse is a response to the particular colonial and postcolonial condition of Western hegemony and cultural alienation, his overall project, like Fanon's, places a much greater emphasis on the condition of human emancipation and the challenges of a common humanity.[123]

In probing what they understand to be the intellectual foundations of Shariati's thought, neo-Shariatis often draw attention to the influence of Afghani and Iqbal, among other leading Muslim modernists and reformists.[124] Yet they are also attentive to the ways in which Shariati's particular reformist discourse goes beyond the discourses of his modernist predecessors. Ehsan Shariati, for instance, argues that unlike Afghani, Shariati does not believe that meaningful change could be initiated simply by influencing those in positions of power and through the top-down implementation of reformist measures. He also notes that unlike Iqbal, who is primarily interested in the intellectual and philosophical aspects of religious reform, Shariati attempts to ground his project in social and political activism and in popular movements.[125] Although he recognizes the influence of Afghani's "anticolonialism" and Iqbal's "spiritual interpretation of being" on Shariati's thought, Ehsan Shariati nevertheless believes that Shariati's emphasis on advancing a bottom-up approach to social change and his advocacy of the prophetic mission of authentic intellectuals in raising revolutionary consciousness among the masses effectively set his discourse apart from those of the former two Muslim thinkers.[126] Hossein Mesbahian too points to Shariati's anticapitalist orientation, his emphasis on social justice, and his close engagement with socialist and social democratic intellectual traditions as features that ultimately differentiate his thought and legacy from those of Afghani and Iqbal.[127]

---

[123] Sara Shariati, interview by author (telephone), November 29, 2012.
[124] Hossein Mesbahian, "Jamehe bi arman morde ast" ("A Society without Ideals is a Society without Life"), *Shargh* 1497, 19 Farvardin 1391/April 7, 2012, 26–29, http://old.sharghdaily.ir/pdf/91-01-19/vijeh/29.pdf (accessed August 8, 2012). Also see: Hassan Yousefi Eshkevari, "Ma va miras-e Shariati" ("Us and Shariati's Legacy"), (1385/2006), http://talar.shandel.info/showthread.php?tid=439#post_2222 (accessed October 11, 2011).
[125] Ehsan Shariati, "Pas az seh daheh" ("After Three Decades"), interview with Shariati Cultural Foundation, Ali Shariati Information Center, (no date), http://drshariati.org/show/?id=483 (accessed August 20, 2011).
[126] Ehsan Shariati, "Rah-e Shariati" ("Shariati's Way"), *Jaras*, 10 Tir 1390/July 1, 2011, www.rahesabz.net/story/38930 (accessed November 14, 2011).
[127] Mesbahian, "Jamehe bi arman morde ast."

In its neo-Shariati readings, Shariati's thought also finds important common ground with the contributions of prominent late twentieth century and contemporary Muslim reformists such as Arkoun, Abu Zayd, Soroush, and Gülen. Like these figures, neo-Shariatis reject the mutually exclusive binary of Islam and modernity and instead advocate mutual recognition and synthesis. While accepting the emancipatory function of modernity in freeing the individual from the grip of scripture, tradition, and customs, and giving recognition to human reason, autonomy, and agency, they reject the Eurocentric view of the Enlightenment as the singular manifestation of modernity and instead draw attention to historical interconnections and cross-cultural exchanges that facilitated the emergence of modernity in Europe. Furthermore, neo-Shariatis share the view with other leading Muslim reformists that although Islam's rationalist tradition was influential in the course of the European modernity, there exists an ontological difference between Islamic and Enlightenment reason. Also linking neo-Shariati thought to the discourses of other Muslim reformists is a radical critique of religious and cultural essentialism, an explicit rejection of the religious state and the political rule of the ecclesiastical class, an endorsement of secularism and the democratic principle of popular sovereignty, and a humanist interpretation of Islam. Nevertheless, as the following chapter will discuss, by insisting on the radial nature of Shariati's intellectual project and highlighting his egalitarian interpretation of Islamic thought, neo-Shariatis also seek to distinguish his (and their own) discourse from other contemporary accounts of Islamic reformism, particularly its Islamic liberalism variant.

3

A Postcolonial Discourse of Public Religion

Reworking the Religious/Secular Binary

For much of the twentieth century, the debates on the relationship between religion and the modern processes of social and political development were dominated by various accounts of the secularization thesis.[1] The thesis has its roots in post-Enlightenment thought and the predictions of some of the leading nineteenth-century European sociological theorists about the eventual disappearance of religion from public life in modern industrial societies. In particular, Max Weber's views on the relationship between rationalization and modernity were a major influence on secularization and modernization theories in the latter half of the twentieth century. Weber regarded the rationalization of public life and the replacement of religious reason with secular reason as the particular form of social change that had facilitated the emergence of modernity in Europe.[2] Following a Weberian model, subsequent generations of sociologists came to regard modernity as the product of the structural differentiation of religion from other realms (i.e., politics, economy, science,

---

[1] See: Talcott Parsons, *The Evolution of Societies* (Englewood Cliffs, NJ: Prentice-Hall, 1977); Peter Berger, *The Sacred Canopy: Elements of a Sociological Theory of Religion* (Garden City, NY: Doubleday, 1967); Bryan Wilson, "Secularization: The Inherited Model," in *The Sacred in a Secular Age*, ed. P. E. Hammond (Berkeley: University of California Press, 1985), 9–20; Thomas Luckmann and Karel Dobbelaere, "Secularization: A Multidimensional Concept," *Current Sociology* 29, no. 2 (1981): 1–21; Wolfgang Schluchter, *Rationalism, Religion, and Domination: A Weberian Perspective*, trans. Neil Solomon (Berkeley: University of California Press, 1989).

[2] William H. Swatos, Jr. and Kevin J. Christiano, "Secularization Theory: The Course of a Concept," *Sociology of Religion* 60, no. 3 (Autumn, 1999): 211–212.

aesthetics, etc.), the privatization of religion, and the decline of religion's social functions.³

In the twentieth-century literature on modernity in Muslim societies, however, Islam and Muslim cultures were often regarded as being exceptionally resistant to secularization and to an otherwise universal trajectory of human progress. In his 1958 book, titled *The Passing of Traditional Society: Modernizing the Middle East*, Daniel Lerner argued that the antirationalist and antipositivist characters of the Muslim culture prevented an organic transition to secularism and democracy in Muslim societies. Lerner's "Mecca or mechanization" thesis, hence, favored top-down modernization reforms such as those implemented in Kemalist Turkey and Pahlavist Iran.⁴ Writing a few decades later, British-Czech anthropologist Ernest Gellner asserted that the rise of religious sentiments in Muslim societies in the latter half of the twentieth century represented the singular "exception" to the secularization thesis. Gellner argued that while modernity was the process of rationalization and secularization of the public sphere, its introduction into Muslim contexts had in fact reinforced religion's grip over society.⁵ In his view, the increased "hold of Islam over the minds and hearts of believers" transcended all social, economic, class, gender, and demographic demarcations among Muslims. He thus concluded that if "Christianity has its Bible belt," Islam, in its entirety, "*is* a Qur'an belt."⁶

While for Samuel Huntington Islam was not the only anomaly to an otherwise universal trajectory of secularization, he nevertheless regarded the late twentieth-century "Islamic revival" as a rejection of secularism and democracy and an indication of an inevitable future clash between the West and its antagonists, namely the Islamic and the Confucian civilizations.⁷ In *The Clash of Civilizations and the Remaking of World Order* (1996), Huntington described the "Islamic Resurgence" as a "mainstream" and "pervasive" turn to religious fundamentalism and a popular turn against the separation of church and state that typified the Western

---

³ Talal Asad, "Religion, Nation-State, Secularism," in *Nation and Religion: Perspectives on Europe and Asia*, ed. Peter van der Veer and Hartmut Lehmann (Princeton, NJ: Princeton University Press, 1999), 178–179.
⁴ Daniel Lerner, *The Passing of Traditional Society: Modernizing the Middle East* (New York: Free Press, 1958), 405.
⁵ Ernest Gellner, *Postmodernism, Reason and Religion* (London: Routledge, 1992), 5.
⁶ Ernest Gellner, "Forward," in *Islam, Globalization and Postmodernity*, ed. Akbar S. Ahmed and Hastings Donnan (London: Routledge, 1994), xi.
⁷ Samuel P. Huntington, "The Clash of Civilizations?" *Foreign Affairs* 72, no. 3 (1993): 33.

civilization.[8] According to him, while the Cold War era was characterized by a civil conflict within the West between the competing ideologies of "communism and liberal democracy,"[9] in the post-Cold War era the primary source of global conflict was a clash between the democratic and liberal West and the nondemocratic and illiberal "Confucian-Islamic states."[10]

The thesis of Islamic exceptionalism came to prominence yet again in the post-September 11, 2001 context of the War on Terrorism and the calls for the "imposition or promotion of democracy" in Muslim societies by external powers.[11] In *The Crisis of Islam: Holy War and Unholy Terror* (2003), British-American Orientalist Bernard Lewis, who had coined the phrase "the clash of civilizations" in 1990 to describe the encounter between Muslim societies and the modern West,[12] argued that the socioeconomic and sociopolitical state of Muslim societies indicated an overall failure of modernization and a "rejection of modernity in favor of a return to the sacred past."[13] Elsewhere, echoing Lerner, he contended that in order for them to meet the challenges of modernity Muslims must reject the (postrevolutionary) Iranian model of fundamentalism and return to tradition, and instead embrace the Turkish model of secularism through condemning the past.[14]

Critics of the thesis problematize the ways in which Islamic exceptionalism essentializes both Islam and modernity and undermines their plural manifestations and traditions. According to one critic, the "essentialized conception" of the relationship between religion and politics in Muslim societies presents a picture of these societies as "uniquely resistant to secularism and liberal democracy due to an inner antimodern, religio-cultural dynamic that has few parallels with other religious traditions or civilizations."[15] Another critic argues that the construction of Islam into

---

[8] Samuel P. Huntington, *The Clash of Civilizations and the Remaking of World Order* (New York: Simon and Schuster, 1996), 110.

[9] Ibid., 23.

[10] Ibid., 46.

[11] Sanford Lakoff, "The Reality of Muslim Exceptionalism," *Journal of Democracy* 15, no. 4 (October 2004): 138.

[12] See: Bernard Lewis, "The Roots of Muslim Rage: Why So Many Muslims Deeply Resent the West, and Why Their Bitterness Will Not Be Easily Mollified," *The Atlantic Monthly* 26, no. 3 (September 1990): 47–58.

[13] Bernard Lewis, *The Crisis of Islam: Holy War and Unholy Terror* (New York: Random House, 2004), 120.

[14] See: Bernard Lewis, "What Went Wrong," *Atlantic Monthly*, January 2002, 43–45.

[15] Nader Hashemi, *Islam, Secularism, and Liberal Democracy: Toward a Democratic Theory for Muslim Societies* (New York: Oxford University Press, 2009), xi.

"a uniquely intractable instance of active religion in the modern world" in effect reduces "the rich and diverse history of Muslim societies across three continents and one-and-a-half millennia ... to the essential principles of a distinctive 'religious-civilization'."[16]

The debates around Islamic exceptionalism have been taken into account in some of the contemporary reformulations of the secularization thesis. In *Sacred and Secular: Religion and Politics Worldwide* (2004), Pippa Norris and Ronald Inglehart challenge Huntington's account of an inherent incompatibility between democracy and Muslim cultures. Citing data from World Values Survey (1995–2001), they argue that there are "no significant differences between the publics living in the West and in Muslim religious cultures" with regard to support for democracy and democratic ideals and practices.[17] The rise of religion in Muslim societies, they believe, was not the exception to the secularization thesis, but rather one of various challenges to the thesis's classical accounts. They point to the popular resurgence of religion around the world at the end of the twentieth century and argue that the continued "health and vitality" of religion in contemporary societies constitutes "the most sustained challenge" the secularization theory has faced "in its long history."[18]

Despite their critical reassessment of some of the classical premises of the secularization thesis, Norris and Inglehart are ultimately concerned with saving the metanarrative of modernity as a global trajectory of transition from sacred to secular. Distinguishing between "agrarian," "industrial," and "post-industrial" societies, they argue that while in the agrarian and industrial societies of the global South religion continues to play an important role in social and political life, in postindustrial societies the trajectory of modernity has been one of erosion of religious functions and values in the public sphere. The modern surge of religion around the world, in their view, is primarily a consequence of population growth in poor and agrarian countries that will reverse once these countries transition to modernity and a postindustrial phase.[19] But Norris and Inglehart's conviction about the eventual disappearance of religion from the public sphere in postindustrial societies has already been refuted by the critics of the secularization thesis. There exists a rich body of literature on the

---

[16] Talal Asad, "Europe against Islam: Islam in Europe," *The Muslim World* 87, no. 2 (1997): 188.
[17] Pippa Norris and Ronald Inglehart, *Sacred and Secular: Religion and Politics Worldwide* (New York: Cambridge University Press, 2004), 146.
[18] Ibid., 4, 166.
[19] Ibid., 22–24.

phenomenon of the return of religion, which examines the sustained and rising patterns of public religiosity not only in agrarian and industrial societies of the global South, but also in the postindustrial societies of Western Europe and North America.[20] As Mendieta and VanAntwerpen have pointed out, today, much like the modern public/private binary the religious/secular binary has come to be seriously questioned and needs to be thoroughly reworked.[21]

The attempt to critically revisit and rework the secularization thesis has led, in recent decades, to a sustained effort by a wide range of scholars to develop alternative approaches for conceptualizing the relationship between religion and modern sociopolitical life. Among these approaches, theories of public religion and multiple modernities have received much attention and are being used by an increasing number of Western and non-Western commentators. These frameworks have drawn attention to the continued presence and the plural functions of religion in the public sphere in modern societies and have highlighted the diverse modes of the encounter between local traditions and the modern processes of sociopolitical and socioeconomic development around the world.

According to José Casanova, the metanarratives of modernization and secularization often failed to take into account the historical and ongoing role of religion in the negotiation of contextually grounded patterns of modernity and secularism across various Western and non-Western societies. In *Public Religions in the Modern World* (1994), he draws on Weber's analysis about the relationship between Protestantism and the emergence of capitalism in Europe in order to highlight the role of religious reformation in the historical rise of European modernity.[22] Using case studies from a number of Catholic-majority societies, Casanova argues that in the course of the transition to democracy in these contexts public religion served as the source of a "prophetic commitment

---

[20] See: Christian Smith, *Disruptive Religion: The Force of Faith in Social Movement Activism* (New York: Routledge, 1996); José Casanova, "Public Religions Revisited," in *Religion: Beyond a Concept*, ed. Hent de Vries (New York: Fordham University Press, 2008), 101–119; Kristina Stoeckl, "The Impact of the Return of Religion on Theoretical Approaches to Democracy and Governance in the Social and Political Sciences," *Sociology Compass* 4, 6 (2010): 354–364.

[21] Eduardo Mendieta and Jonathan VanAntwerpen, "Introduction: The Power of Religion in the Public Sphere," in *The Power of Religion in the Public Sphere*, ed. Eduardo Mendieta and Jonathan VanAntwerpen (New York: Columbia University Press, 2011), 1.

[22] José Casanova, *Public Religions in the Modern World* (Chicago and London: University of Chicago Press, 1994), 234.

to the principles of freedom, justice, and solidarity."[23] In his view, the Catholic *aggiornamento* (the transformation of Catholic doctrines in the course of the Second Vatican Council during the early and mid-1960s) played a major role in facilitating the subsequent processes of democratization in Latin America and Eastern Europe during the 1970s and 1980s. This transformation, it is argued, reconciled the religious core of Catholicism with the modern values of democracy and individual rights and freedoms.[24]

In a number of his works over the previous decade, Casanova has sought to examine how the framework of public religion may help to explain the link between religious and sociopolitical change in contemporary Muslim societies.[25] Noting the plural manifestations of public Islam, he argues while it is unlikely that all Islamic revival movements "will be uniformly conducive to democratization," it is safe to stipulate that "democracy is unlikely to grow and thrive in Muslim countries until political actors who are striving for it are also able to 'frame' their discourse in a publicly recognizable Islamic idiom."[26] Casanova's recent work has further challenged the Eurocentric conceptions of modernity and secularism as processes particular to Europe or Western Christianity. In "Public Religions Revisited" (2008), he proposes that any analytical framework that envisions modernity as a total break from "tradition" and/or a unilinear and progressive transition from "sacred" to "secular," is inadequate for understanding the diverse experiences and manifestations of modernity in Western and non-Western societies. According to him, while all "traditions" are radically transformed in their encounter with modernity, "in the process of reformulating their traditions for modern contexts" societies negotiate diverse forms of "religious" and "secular" modernity.[27]

By giving recognition to cultural-historical particularity and difference, theories of multiple modernities such as Casanova's challenge the idea that the modern West constitutes the singular and universal trajectory

---

[23] Ibid., 62.
[24] Ibid., 62, 105, 133.
[25] José Casanova, "Civil Society and Religion: Retrospective Reflections on Catholicism and Prospective Reflections on Islam," *Social Research* 68, no. 4 (Winter 2001): 1051. Also see: José Casanova, "Catholic and Muslim Politics in Comparative Perspective," *Taiwan Journal of Democracy* 1, no. 2 (December 2005): 89–108.
[26] Ibid., 1075–1076.
[27] José Casanova, "Public Religions Revisited," in *Religion: Beyond a Concept*, ed. Hent de Vries (New York: Fordham University Press, 2008), 106.

of development and progress.²⁸ While acknowledging the emancipatory aspects of Enlightenment modernity, these theories also emphasize the cross-cultural and cross-civilizational formations of the modern patterns of change, as well as the multiple manifestations of modern experiences and preferences. According to Armando Salvatore, the development of these theories is rooted in the increased attention of a number of political and historical sociologists including Shmuel N. Eisenstadt and Johann P. Arnason, to the concept of civilization in the early 1970s. This newfound interest in the sociological study of civilizational diversity, argues Salvatore, "marked the beginning of a long trajectory that would make modernity not only more open and plural, but also more adherent to an increasingly complexifying world, and thus more 'tangible'."²⁹ For Eisenstadt, the very idea of "multiple modernities" goes against the long-prevalent assumption "that the cultural program of modernity as it developed in modern Europe and the basic institutional constellations that emerged there would ultimately take over in all modernizing and modern societies."³⁰

In their application to the analysis of the modern patterns of sociopolitical transformation in contemporary Muslim societies, theories of multiple modernities have sought to underscore the complex and nuanced dynamics of lived Muslim experiences. On the one hand, by bringing attention to the capacities of diverse religious and cultural traditions for the "creation and sustenance" of modern civil society, they have challenged the false universalism of Eurocentric and monocivilizational metanarratives of change.³¹ On the other hand, however, by emphasizing the

---

[28] See: Mike Featherstone, Scott Lash, and Roland Robertson, eds., *Global Modernities* (London: Sage, 1995); Scott Lash, *Another Modernity, a Different Rationality* (Oxford: Blackwell, 1999); Dilip P. Gaonkar, ed., *Alternative Modernities* (Durham, NC: Duke University Press, 2001); Charles Taylor, "Two Theories of Modernity," *Public Culture* 11, no. 1 (1999): 153–173; Fred Dallmayr, "Global Modernization: Toward Different Modernities?," in Fred Dallmayr, *Dialogue Among Civilizations: Some Exemplary Voices* (New York: Palgrave Macmillan, 2002), 85–104; S. N. Eisenstadt, ed., *Multiple Modernities* (New Brunswick, NJ: Transaction, 2002); Charles Taylor, *Modern Social Imaginaries* (Durham, NC: Duke University Press, 2004); Modjtaba Sadria, ed., *Multiple Modernities in Muslim Societies: Tangible Elements and Abstract Perspectives* (London: I.B. Tauris 2009).

[29] Armando Salvatore, "From Civilizations to Multiple Modernities: The Issue of the Public Sphere," in *Multiple Modernities in Muslim Societies: Tangible Elements and Abstract Perspectives*, ed. Modjtaba Sadria (London: I.B. Tauris, 2009), 19–20.

[30] S. N. Eisenstadt, "Multiple Modernities," in *Multiple Modernities*, ed. S. N. Eisenstadt (New Brunswick, NJ: Transaction, 2002), 1.

[31] Amyn B. Sajoo, ed., *Civil Society in the Muslim World: Contemporary Perspectives* (London: I.B. Tauris, 2002), 16–17.

universal and cross-civilizational aspects of modernity, they have aimed to distance themselves from tendencies toward cultural essentialism and relativism.[32] For Fred Dallmayr, whose work has made an important contribution to the development of this theoretical framework, multiple modernities is useful for analyzing the ways in which a range of Muslim reformists have gone beyond the dichotomous constructs of Islam/modernity and religious/secular by developing religiously grounded discourses of human dignity, democracy, individual rights and freedoms, and social justice.[33] Dallmayr further draws attention to the efforts of a number of contemporary Islamic reformists to negotiate a third way between the total separation and the total fusion of religion and politics, which he regards as two undemocratic and ultimately unsustainable approaches. In challenging these two extremes, Dallmayr believes Islamic reformists such as Abdullahi Ahmed An-Na'im and Abdolkarim Soroush have revealed the possibility of envisioning and nurturing diverse forms of modernity and democracy. According to Dallmayr, since democracy cannot be separated from "the motivations and aspirations of ordinary citizens," and since these aspirations are themselves reflective of the prevailing religious and cultural traditions, customs, and beliefs, "it follows that democracies cannot be the same everywhere but are bound to vary in accordance with beliefs and customs prevalent in different societies or regions."[34]

"Islamic Protestantism" as a Methodology of Bottom-Up Change

In its descriptive function and its focus on the capacities of religious and cultural traditions in facilitating progressive social and political change Shariati's thought overlaps with the analytical frameworks of public religion and multiple modernities. In its normative turn, however, Shariati's discourse also emphasizes intellectual commitment, social and political engagement, and grassroots activism. Furthermore, even as he believes that the recognition of cultural and civilizational plurality

---

[32] See: Amyn B. Sajoo, "Muslim Modernities and Civic Pluralism," *ISIM Review*, no. 21 (Spring 2008): 28; Nilüfer Göle, "Snapshots of Islamic Modernities," *Daedalus* 129, no. 1, *Multiple Modernities* (Winter, 2000): 91; Mojtaba Mahdavi, "Universalism from Below: Muslims and Democracy in Context," *International Journal of Criminology and Sociological Theory* 2, no. 2 (December 2009): 282.

[33] Fred Dallmayr, "Whither Democracy? Religion, Politics and Islam," *Philosophy and Social Criticism* 37, no. 4 (2011): 442.

[34] Ibid., 445.

allows for the negotiation of diverse experiences of modernity, Shariati is keenly attentive to hegemonic and asymmetrical power structures that have shaped the modern world. As a critic of colonial and neocolonial relations of domination, he challenges the hegemonic expansion of two particular socioeconomic and sociopolitical formations, namely, capitalism and liberal democracy, in the course of the expansion of European modernity.

Shariati's attempt to develop an indigenous vision of progressive change on the basis of a reconstructed and reoriented public religiosity defies the logic of modernization and secularization. By highlighting linkages between religious reformation and the modern processes of sociopolitical transformation, he seeks to unsettle the dominant tradition/modernity binary of his time. Though he makes no direct reference to the Catholic *aggiornamento*, it has been noted that Shariati was well aware of the debates taking place in the Catholic Church during the early 1960s.[35] One of Shariati's mentors during his time in France was Louis Massignon, a leading scholar of Islam as well as a Catholic priest of the Melkite Order whose works are said to have been an important source of influence in the Second Vatican Council.[36] Also during this period, Shariati had learned about Catholic liberation theology through the journal *Esprit* and the writings of its founder Emmanuel Mounier, yet another influential figure in the reform movement within Catholicism.[37] That he opts to advocate a project of Islamic Protestantism instead of an Islamic *aggiornamento* is likely due to his analysis about the role of the Protestant Reformation in the historical rise of Western modernity, as well as his intent to articulate and popularize a "declericalized Islamic theology" (*eslam menhay-e akhund*).[38]

---

[35] Ervand Abrahamian, *Radical Islam: The Iranian Mojahedin* (New Haven, CT: Yale University Press, 1989), 108.
[36] Mahmut Aydin, *Modern Western Christian Theological Understandings of Muslims since the Second Vatican Council* (Washington, DC: The Council for Research in Values and Philosophy, 2002), 16.
[37] Mehrzad Boroujerdi, *Iranian intellectuals and the West: The Tormented Triumph of Nativism* (New York: Syracuse University Press, 1996), 109.
[38] Ali Shariati, "Nameh beh pedar" ("Letter to Father"), 1351/1972, C.W. 1, *Ali Shariati: The Complete Collection of Works* [CD ROM], Tehran: Shariati Cultural Foundation, 2010. In this letter, addressed to his father, Shariati draws parallels between the Protestant reformation and his own religious reform project, and writes: "articulating a declericalized Islamic theology … is an effort to emancipate faith from the narrow frameworks of medieval thinking and from the confines of clerical institutions and stagnant and superstitious worldviews that teach people to be imitators and blind followers."

Shariati describes the Protestant Reformation as the "necessary precursor" to Western modernity, arguing that "had it not been for the efforts of Luther and Calvin in awakening the European masses and challenging the intellectual stagnation of the medieval period ... the occurrence of the Renaissance would have been delayed and its impact would have been restricted to intellectual and elite circles." It was "Protestantism," he continues, "that transformed Christianity from a negative force of individual and social stagnation into a positive and dynamic force of individual and social progress."[39] In his view, the combined forces of the Reformation, the Renaissance, and the Enlightenment facilitated a move toward religious toleration and philosophical and political pluralism in Europe and contributed to the emancipation of the modern individual from the totalitarian domination of the church and medieval traditions. He also argues that European modernity served an emancipatory role by secularizing the state and education system and "by freeing science, philosophy, arts, literature, and finance from the authority of the ecclesiastical class."[40]

Shariati's historical analysis of modernity in Europe is primarily concerned with the processes that, in his view, made possible the recognition of individual autonomy and agency. The rise of modernity, he maintains, enabled the masses of the people to become authors of their own destinies and agents of radical social and political change. It also enhanced the condition for the realization of two universal ideals, namely freedom and equality, which, according to him, have been at the center of all emancipatory struggles throughout history and are manifested in the modern world in the core values of democracy and socialism.[41] Yet for him, in this progressive function, modernity was not a total break from religious traditions but rather a continuation of the message of dignity, freedom, and equality, which had been historically propagated by all monotheistic faiths.[42]

Though attentive to modernity's emancipatory features and the particular context of its historical emergence in Europe, Shariati nevertheless

---

[39] Ali Shariati, "Ommat va imamat" ("Community and Leadership"), 1348/1969, C.W. 26, *Ali Shariati: The Complete Collection of Works* [CD ROM], Tehran: Shariati Cultural Foundation, 2010.

[40] Ali Shariati, "Nameh beh Ehsan" ("Letter to Ehsan") Farvardin-Ordibehesht 1356/ April-May 1977, C.W. 1, *Ali Shariati: The Complete Collection of Works* [CD ROM], Tehran: Shariati Cultural Foundation, 2010.

[41] Ali Shariati, "Arezooha" ("Aspirations") 1355/1976, C.W. 25, *Ali Shariati: The Complete Collection of Works* [CD ROM], Tehran: Shariati Cultural Foundation, 2010.

[42] Ibid.

problematizes Eurocentric narratives that dismiss non-Western cultures and traditions as hostile to the values of modernity and civilization. He argues that while the encounters and interactions between Europe and the Islamic civilization over several centuries served an important role in the rise of the European Renaissance and the Enlightenment, Westerncentric discourses omit from their historiographies of modernity these historical links and the critical contributions of Muslim thinkers and scientists.[43] Critiquing the view that claims modern science, philosophy, and culture as the exclusive products of Western civilization, Shariati maintains that in the course of its expansion European colonialism sought to eliminate civilizational and cultural diversity and to advance the myth of "Europe as the singular trajectory of human culture and progress."[44] He describes "monoculture" as a product of colonialism and points to the "interesting coincidence" that the term explains the processes through which European colonialism obliterated both economic and civilizational-cultural diversity around the world.[45]

Additionally, in diagnosing what he regards as the fundamental crisis of Western modernity, Shariati maintains that the emergence of industrial capitalism, the ascendancy of machinism, the reduction of humans from autonomous agents of change into mere instruments of production, and the rise of a culture of consumerism and profiteering have alienated modern individuals from their true humanity, thus undermining the values of freedom and quality. In his view, these conditions have created a "philosophical-spiritual" crisis in the West, which finds manifestations in a range of social ills including the isolation of individuals and the rising rates of divorce and suicide.[46] Echoing Frantz Fanon in his call for a "new history" and a "new man" [sic] in *The Wretched of the Earth* (1963),[47] Shariati calls for a "new thought," a "new humanity," and a new and more humane modernity that does not seek to turn the Third World into another Europe, another United States, or another Soviet bloc.[48] However, while Fanon's call for reclaiming modern humanism on the basis of the

---

[43] Ali Shariati (1350/1972) "Bazgasht beh khish" ("Return to the Self"), Collected Works 4, *Ali Shariati: The Complete Collection of Works* [CD ROM], Tehran: Shariati Cultural Foundation, 2010.

[44] Ali Shariati, C.W. 2, 67, quoted in Reza Alijani (1388/2009) *Shariati va gharb (Shariati and the West)* (Tehran: Ghalam), 46.

[45] Ali Shariati, C.W. 4, 15, quoted in Alijani, *Shariati va gharb*, 51.

[46] Ali Shariati, C.W. 4, 24–28, quoted in Alijani, *Shariati va gharb*, 47.

[47] Frantz Fanon, *The Wretched of the Earth* (New York: Grove Press, (1963), 315–316.

[48] Ali Shariati, C.W. 1, 110, quoted in Alijani, *Shariat va gharb*, 17.

particular experiences of the colonized is articulated in a secular language and does not engage with religious modes of thought and action, Shariati calls for an alternative to Western modernity precisely by using the social and inspirational capacities of religion.

In making his case for the relevance of religion in advancing a progressive vision of social and political change in Iran and other Muslim societies, Shariati gives simultaneous attention to Islam's social-mobilizational and ontological-inspirational capacities. For him, a project of "Islamic Protestantism" is necessary to end the monopoly of the traditional ulama over religious matters, to turn the Islamic faith from a pacifying and conservative influence into a progressive social force, and to equip the traditionalist and pious Muslim masses with the intellectual-cultural tools to become autonomous agents of change through the exercise of their own reason and free will. He believes that in a society where religious norms and institutions prevail, any sustainable project of social transformation must necessarily begin with a transformation in popular religiosity.[49] At the same time, he holds that a modern restructuring of Islamic thought could contribute to the search for an alternative ontological basis for negotiating a more humane modernity than the hegemonic Western model. In this effort, Shariati builds on Iqbal's project of reconciling modern reason with its others (i.e., emotion, revelation, and intuition) on the basis of a *tawhidi* (monotheistic) spiritual worldview. However, Shariati also expands Iqbal's overwhelmingly philosophical discourse in a sociopolitical direction by proposing a synthesis of spirituality, equality, and freedom as an alternative basis for negotiating an emancipatory and indigenous discourse of modernity for Muslim societies.

Arguably, Shariati's emphasis on Islamic Protestantism as a necessary prerequisite for a bottom-up and sustainable project of sociopolitical change is indicative of a primarily cultural methodological approach. Indeed, according to a leading neo-Shariati figure, for Shariati change in cultural norms must precede structural change and "a cultural revolution must occur before a political and emancipatory revolution."[50] It would, nevertheless, be mistaken to read Shariati's call for religious and cultural reformation in merely culturalist terms. Throughout his works, Shariati

---

[49] Reza Alijani, *Seh Shariati dar ayineh zehn-e ma: eslam-garay-e enghelabi, motefaker-e mosleh, rend-e aref (Three Shariatis in Our Perceptions: Revolutionary Islamist, Reformist Intellectual, Artful Mystic)* (Tehran: Ghalam, 1389/2010), 29.

[50] Ehsan Shariati, "Shariati andishmand-e azadi" ("Shariati, the Thinker of Freedom"), Ali Shariati Information Center (no date). Available at http://drshariati.org/show.asp?id=30, (accessed November 2, 2012).

emphasizes the necessity of social and political engagement, commitment, and activism. According to him, social and political struggles shape the "self-consciousness" of authentic intellectuals and make them aware of "the needs, demands, ideals, strengths, and weaknesses of the masses of people and their capacities for taking action and initiating change."[51] Moreover, Shariati discusses at length a range of noncultural factors such as natural environment, social and historical context, and relations of production in determining the conditions in which individuals and societies find themselves. However, highlighting the role of individual agency in altering the prevailing order, Shariati argues that through the force of their autonomous will humans can overcome these and other structural limitations.[52]

Progressive Public Religion under Islamist Ascendancy

In advancing what they regard to be his unfinished intellectual project, neo-Shariatis have sought to rethink various aspects of Shariati's thoughts and "unthoughts."[53] In contextualizing his corpus in relation to the major social and political developments of his time, they have distinguished between the various phases of Shariati's life, as well as between his intrinsic and contingent ideas.[54] Moreover, in critically rereading these intrinsic and contingent ideas neo-Shariatis have gone beyond Shariati's immediate discourse in a number of ways.[55] Pointing to the political ascendancy of Islamism in Iran and a number of other Muslim societies throughout the 1970s and 1980s, they make a case that while Shariati did not anticipate such developments his intellectual followers

---

[51] Ali Shariati, C.W. 2, 176–177, quoted in Reza Alijani, *Rend-e kham: Shariati-shenasi jeld-e yekom: zamaneh, zendegi, va arman-ha (The Pure Nonconformist: Shariatiology Volume One: Era, Life, and Ideals)* (Tehran: Ghalam 1387), 190.

[52] Ali Shariati, "Khodsazi-e enghelab" ("Revolutionary Self-Preparedness"), 1355/1976, C.W. 2, *Ali Shariati: The Complete Collection of Works* [CD ROM], Tehran: Shariati Cultural Foundation, 2010.

[53] See: Eshsan Shariati, "Nayandishideh mandeh haye falsafi andisheh ye mo'alem Shariati" ("The Philosophical Unthoughts of the Thought of Teacher Shariati"), in *dar hashiyeh matn (On the Margins of the Text)*, ed. Bonyad Shariati (Tehran: Shahr-e Aftab, 1379/2000).

[54] Mojtaba Mahdavi, "Post-Islamist Trends in Post-Revolutionary Iran," *Comparative Studies of South Asia, Africa, and the Middle East* 31, no. 1 (2011): 102.

[55] Ehsan Shariati, "Safar-e bozorg" ("The Big Journey"), *Mehrab* no. 1 special issue Rendezvous with Shariati, 1359/1980: 16–17.

must take account of these events in their engagement with religious and cultural traditions.[56]

Shariati's thesis of committed democracy and his views on intellectual responsibility have also been the subjects of neo-Shariati critique in postrevolutionary Iran. As noted in the previous chapter, in articulating his vision of an indigenous modernity and radical social and political transformation, Shariati often stressed the vital role of committed Muslim intellectuals. Most famously, in "Community and Leadership" he made a case that in the course and the aftermath of a revolutionary uprising and in the absence of enlightened masses authentic intellectuals must take leadership roles and through a system of committed or "guided democracy" (*demokrasi-e hedayat shodeh*) create the necessary conditions for the genuine exercise of popular sovereignty and democratic governance.[57]

Despite their own rejection of the thesis, neo-Shariatis nevertheless repudiate the charge that guided democracy represents the core of Shariati's intellectual project or that it signifies an antidemocratic orientation in his thinking. Instead, they argue that the thesis echoed similar proposals put forth by other Third World intellectuals and leaders at the time (including at the 1955 Bandung Conference), and was informed by Shariati's concern with the challenges of progressive sociopolitical change in the postcolonial context. Thus, Ehsan Shariati argues that Shariati's account of guided democracy must be understood in relation to his overall project of sustainable change from below through the emancipatory force of revolutionary consciousness. Shariati, according to him, believed that the realization of democracy in postcolonial societies was unlikely in the absence of a conscious citizenry and therefore a transitional phase was needed.[58] Neo-Shariatis further point out that in the late phase of his life, disillusioned with the experiences of really existing models of

---

[56] Sara Shariati, "Dar bareh sharaiet-e emkan-e moderniteh dini," ("On the Conditions for the Possibility of Religious Modernity"), in *Dar hashiyeh matn (On the Margins of the Text)*, ed. Bonyad Shariati (Tehran: Shahr-e Aftab, 1379/2000), 162. Also see: "Erfan, barabari, azadi beh masabeh yek projeh" ("Spirituality, Equality, Freedom as a Project"), Ali Shariati Information Center (no date), http://drshariati.org/show/?id=626 (accessed December 22, 2012).

[57] Shariati, "Ommat."

[58] Ehsan Shariati, "Talfigh dar projeh: goftegoo ba Ehsan Shariati dar bareh haghighat va nakami 'demokrasy motahed'" ("Synthesis in Project: Interview with Ehsan Shariati about the Promise and the Failure of 'Guided Democracy'"), interview with Parvin Bakhtiar-Nejad, *Shargh*, 24 Tir 1386/15 July 2007, http://talar.shandel.info/showthread.php?tid=443#post_1997 (accessed May 20, 2012).

guided democracy in postcolonial contexts in Asia and Africa, in the late phase of his life Shariati came to revise his earlier views about intellectual leadership.[59] In Ehsan Shariati's assessment, Shariati's overall views on the question of intellectual responsibility find more in common with the antiauthoritarian discourses of Rosa Luxemburg and Antonio Gramsci than with the vanguardist discourses of Marxist-Leninists.[60]

In their own works neo-Shariatis endorse representative and electoral democracy as a mechanism for bottom-up sociopolitical change. According to Hassan Yousefi Eshkevari, even though the young Shariati was right in diagnosing the challenges of the transition to democracy in postcolonial societies, he was wrong in the prescription that a revolutionary class of intellectuals can facilitate the social and political transformation of a society by occupying positions of power.[61] Similarly, Ehsan Shariati argues, "the problem with the thesis of guided democracy is that democracy cannot be suspended in order to raise a democratic awareness. Practicing democracy is itself a mechanism for having a conscious citizenry."[62] Moreover, in discussing the role of intellectuals in the processes of social and political change, neo-Shariatis often stress

---

[59] Taghi Rahmani, "Azadi dar marhaleh eradeh, shenakht, va ghanoon" ("Freedom in Three Phases: Will, Recognition, and Law"), *Payam-e Hajar*, no. 269 special issue, Shariati and Freedom, 25 Khordad 1378/June 15, 1999: 31.

[60] Ehsan Shariati, "Talfigh dar projeh." Behrooz Ghamari-Tabrizi, too, has described Shariati's cultural approach to social change as "a Gramscian moment in contemporary Iranian politics." He writes, "Similar to Gramsci's assertion that relations of dominance are manifested in the institutions of civil society, Shariati argued that 'an institutionalized movement disappears in the web of the existing social institutions, i.e., state; family; language; banks and insurance; retirement plans; saving accounts; and even lottery tickets' (Shariati, 1971: 39). In this context, Shariati believed that so long as religion remains disengaged with public issues of justice, it would remain as another repressive institution of civil society. Gramsci drew a dialectical relation between 'the ethical-political aspect of politics or theory of hegemony and consent' and 'the aspect of force and economics'. In the same vein, Shariati's 'trinity of oppression' depicted how the institutionalized religion ideologically justified the political order and economic power of dominant classes." See: Behrooz Ghamari-Tabrizi, "Iran: Ali Shariati and Abdolkarim Soroush Contentious Public Religion: Two Conceptions of Islam in Revolutionary," *International Sociology* 19, no. 4 (December 2004): 512.

[61] Hassan Yousefi Eshkevari, "Pasokhi beh pendar-hay-e Akbar Ganji dar mored-e Ali Shariati" ("A Response to Akbar Ganji's Assumptions about Ali Shariati"), Ali Shariati Information Center (no date), http://drshariati.org/show.asp?id=97 (accessed March 3, 2012).

[62] Ehsan Shariati, "Zamaneh Shariati-e pesar sakht-tar ast" ("The Times are Harder for Shariati the Son"), interview with Samina Rastegari, *Etemad* no. 1992, 13 Tir 1388/July 4, 2009, www.etemaad.ir/Released/88-04-13/150.htm (accessed June 7, 2012).

the cultural and civil aspects of intellectual responsibility. According to Taghi Rahmani, in postrevolutionary Iran, Shariati's thought must be expanded in a "civil" direction through grassroots engagement and activism.[63] In Rahmani's view, sociopolitical development from below requires not only the cultural project of restructuring traditional and religious thought, but also the civil project of developing grassroots organizations and facilitating the organic emergence of a pluralistic and participatory civil society.[64] Similarly, Ehsan Shariati argues that in parallel with raising critical consciousness intellectual responsibility requires a sustained commitment to strengthening democratic structures that can protect political pluralism and the genuine exercise of popular sovereignty.[65]

Shariati's historical analysis of the legacy of the Protestant Reformation and its aftereffects in Europe is another aspect of his thought that has been the subject of critique by some of his contemporary intellectual followers. Rahmani, among others, questions whether the thesis of "Islamic Protestantism" should be regarded as a central component of Shariati's discourse of indigenous modernity. According to him, while Shariati saw the Protestant Reformation as a prelude to modernity in Europe, his analysis did not give adequate attention to the link between this historical occurrence and subsequent developments such as the rise of religious fundamentalism and the privatization of religion in modern Western societies.[66] Ehsan Shariati, too, acknowledges that in appealing to the experiences of the Renaissance and the Protestant Reformation, Shariati "overlooked some of the consequences of modernity in the West." He nevertheless points to Shariati's critique of the bourgeois orientation of the Protestant movement and argues that "Shariati was more interested

---

[63] Taghi Rahmani, "Zaban Soroush, zaban-e tanafor" ("The Language of Hate in Soroush's Discourse"), interview with Hossein Sokhanvar, *Etemad* no.1927, 27 Farvardin 1388/April 17, 2009, www.etemaad.ir/Released/88-01-27/256.htm (accessed June 7, 2012).

[64] Taghi Rahmani, "Dar rastay-e moderniteh sharghi" ("Toward an Eastern Modernity"), *Iran-e Farda* 6, no. 34, Tir 1376/July 1997: 26.

[65] Ehsan Shariati, "Bar-e digar enghelab, yad-avar enghelab" ("Once More Revolution, A Reminder of Revolution"), *Shargh*, 18 bahman 1389/February 7, 2011, http://talar.shandel.info/showthread.php?tid=318#post_3691 (accessed May 19, 2011).

[66] Taghi Rahmani, "Protestantism va fahm-e Shariati az an: goftegooy-e Susan Shariati va Taghi Rahmani" ("Protestantism and Shariati's Understanding of It: A Conversation between Susan Shraiati and Taghi Rahmani"), interview with Lotfollah Meisami, *Cheshmandaz Iran* 65, Day-Bahman 1389/January–February 2011, http://drshariati.org/show/?id=472 (accessed September 17, 2012).

in the methodology of Protestant Reformation than in its content and essence."[67]

Further, neo-Shariati thought goes beyond Shariati's immediate discourse by explicitly and vigorously endorsing political values that are generally associated with classical liberalism and described by contemporary political philosophers as negative rights and liberties. This endorsement is not inconsistent with Shariati's thought. Indeed in some of his works, Shariati wrote passionately in opposition to political suppression and in defense of basic democratic rights and freedoms, including the freedom of expression and political activity.[68] Additionally, both in his account of the history of early Islam and in discussing what he understood to be the true message of the Quran, Shariati argued that Islamic thought and tradition contained numerous examples of support for the principles of human freedom, diversity of opinions, and toleration of dissent.[69] Referencing the Quranic verse "There is no compulsion in faith" (2:256), he wrote: "Even though Islam reveals itself as a divine religion and regards its prophet as a messenger of God who was sent to call people to the path of righteousness, it declares that there shall be no coercions in religion ... and that people have the freedom to choose their own paths."[70] Still, in reading Shariati's work and evaluating his critical stance toward "Western liberal democracies" and their "bourgeois freedoms" and "excessive individualism,"[71] it becomes clear that his references to freedom are more frequently and forcefully in relation to positive rather than negative liberties.

---

[67] Ehsan Shariati, interview by Hossein (Mesbahian) Rahyab, no date (unpublished).

[68] Ali Shariati, "Azadi, khojasteh azadi," ("Freedom, Joyous Freedom"), (no date), C.W. 2, *Ali Shariati: The Complete Collection of Works* [CD ROM], Tehran: Shariati Cultural Foundation, 2010.

[69] Ali Shariati, "Yek bar-e digar Abuzar," ("Once Again Abuzar"), (1351/1972), C.W. 3, *Ali Shariati: The Complete Collection of Works* [CD ROM], Tehran: Shariati Cultural Foundation, 2010.

[70] Shariati, "Khodsazi-e enghelab."

[71] Ali Shariati, "Eslam shenasi: dars-e hashtom," ("Islamology: Lesson Eight"), (1351/1972), C.W. 16, *Ali Shariati: The Complete Collection of Works* [CD ROM], Tehran: Shariati Cultural Foundation, 2010; Ali Shariati, "Eslam shenasi: dars-e aval va dovom," ("Islamology: Lessons One and Two"), (1350/1971), C.W. 16, *Ali Shariati: The Complete Collection of Works* [CD ROM], Tehran: Shariati Cultural Foundation, 2010; Ali Shariati, "Ensan, eslam va maktab-hay-e maghreb zamin," ("Human, Islam, and Western Schools"), (no date), C.W. 24, *Ali Shariati: The Complete Collection of Works* [CD ROM], Tehran: Shariati Cultural Foundation, 2010; Ali Shariati, "Haj-e bozorgtar," ("The Greater Haj"), (1350/1971), C.W. 6, *Ali Shariati: The Complete Collection of Works* [CD ROM], Tehran: Shariati Cultural Foundation, 2010.

Though neo-Shariatis repudiate the view that Shariati's critique of Western liberal democracy amounts to a total negation of individual freedoms, their own discourse is much more attentive than Shariati's to negative rights and liberties, and they have also sought to advance a contextually grounded defense of the universality of human rights. Among others, Ehsan Shariati makes a case that commitment to a comprehensive "universal standard" of human rights serves the function of connecting anticolonial struggles to the struggles against domestic forms of despotism and tyranny. Noting that the realization of human rights requires not only legal and political provisions but also public awareness and popular mobilization, he argues that the prophetic mission of intellectuals in the modern world includes advancing "a universal language" of rights that transcends geographical boundaries and brings together various popular struggles from the antiglobalization movements in Europe and North America to the movement against Israeli occupation in Palestine. According to him, at the core of the concept of universal human rights is the idea of innate human dignity (*keramat-e ensani*), which is rooted in the *tawhidi* ontology of Abrahamic religions. He thus concludes that a progressive public religion can reinforce the social commitment of the faithful to the protection and defense of the rights of all.[72]

Similarly, in postrevolutionary Iran some leading neo-Shariati figures have gone beyond Shariati by articulating a religiously grounded discourse of women's rights and gender equality. Neo-Shariatis acknowledge that while Shariati was among the first religious reformers in Iran to explicitly acknowledge the role of women in popular movements and in the processes of social and political change, his discourse fell short of addressing specific issues regarding the status of women in Islamic thought and tradition. According to Susan Shariati, for example, Shariati discusses the question of women not as a distinct and independent issue, but rather in relation to the broader processes of the negotiation of individual subjectivity and social and political agency in Iranian society. As a result, she suggests, Shariati's discourse addresses the general question of the emancipation of women without engaging with concrete concerns such as women's rights in the family, in marriage and divorce, and in the workplace.[73]

---

[72] Ehsan Shariati, "Goftegoo, hoghoogh-e bashar: rahyabi va rahkar" ("Dialogue, Human Rights: Approaches and Methods"), Shariati Discourse Forum (no date), http://talar.shandel.info/pdf/ehsan1003.pdf (accessed August 3, 2012).

[73] Susan Shariati, "Zanan dar projeh Shariati" ("Women in Shariati's Project"), interview with Parvin Bakhtiarnejad, *Etemad*, 15 Aban 1386/November 6, 2007,

In his contributions to the development of an Islamic discourse of gender equality, Reza Alijani draws on Shariati's historical-inspiration approach toward religious thought and doctrines. He argues that while it remains an undeniable reality that various Islamic teachings and several verses in the Quran place women in a lower status than men, a historical-inspirational approach can help to show that first, these teachings are not representative of Islam's general egalitarian and antidomination orientation, and second, that certain religious teachings (including on the question of women) may no longer correspond to the objective realities of contemporary human societies. As such, he calls on religious reformers to distinguish between Islam's historically specific teachings on the question of women and the religion's general orientation within its particular historical context, and to use the latter as a source of inspiration for advancing a new discourse of gender equality in contemporary Muslim societies.[74]

Yousefi Eshkevari is yet another neo-Shariati figure who has addressed, in a number of works, the issue of women's rights and gender equality from an Islamic perspective. Trained as a Shi'i cleric but defrocked in 2002 by the Special Clerical Court due in part to his views on the subject, he calls for a radical reconstruction of Islamic *fiqh* (in both Shi'i and Sunni traditions) in such areas as "family, women's rights, relations between men and women, hijab, inheritance, [and] custody of children."[75] He criticizes theological views that allow polygamy for men, regard the father (or even grandfather)

---

http://drshariati.org/show.asp?id=106 (accessed April 17, 2011). Also see: Susan Shariati, "Chand kalameh harf-e zananeh: beh bahaneye rooz-e jahani-e zan" ("A Few Feminine Words: On the Occasion of the International Women's Day"), in Susan Shariati, *Don kishot dar shahr (Don Quixote in the City)* (Tehran: Rasesh, 1388/2010), 235–238.

[74] See : Reza Alijani, "Din, zan, va donyay-e jadid: goftegoo ba Reza Alijani" ("Religion, Women, and the Modern World: A Conversation with Reza Alijani"), *Cheshmandaz-e Iran* no. 44, Tir-Mordad 1386/July–August 2007: 99–108; Reza Alijani, "Jonbesh zanan: jonbeshi mostaghel ama mortabet" ("Women's Movement: Independence and Interdependence"), *Baztab-e Andisheh* no. 70, Bahman 1384/February 2006: 57–59; Reza Alijani, "Chera zan dar matoon moghadas?" ("Why the Question of Woman in Sacred Texts?"), Shariati Discourse Forum (no date), http://talar.shandel.info/showthread.php?tid=683&pid=3036#post_3035 (accessed July 2, 2011); Reza Alijani, "Motoon-e moghadas va doniaye jaded" ("Sacred Scriptures and the Modern World"), Shariati Discourse Forum (no date), http://talar.shandel.info/showthread.php?tid=683&pid=3036#post_3036 (accessed July 2, 2011).

[75] Hassan Yousefi Eshkevari, "Women's Rights and the Women's Movement," in Ziba Mir-Hosseini and Richard Tapper, *Islam and Democracy in Iran: Eshkevari and the Quest for Reform* (London: I.B. Tauris, 2006), 165. Also see: Hassan Yousefi Eshkevari, "Reformist Islam and Modern Society," in Ziba Mir-Hosseini and Richard Tapper, *Islam and Democracy in Iran: Eshkevari and the Quest for Reform* (London: I.B. Tauris, 2006), 163.

as the guardian or custodian of the child, prevent women from occupying top legal and political positions, and give men a bigger share of inheritance than women.[76] He also rejects the idea that compulsory veiling is sanctioned by Islam and defends the right of women to choose their attire.[77] He argues that all laws regarding the status and rights of women in Muslim traditions, even those that are based directly on Quranic teachings, are "mutable ... by their very nature."[78] Like Alijani, he believes that while religion can provide a general moral orientation in social and political life, laws must be based not on unchanging religious dogma but rather on the prevailing social realities and values.[79] At the same time, he argues, to advance women's rights in Iranian society legislative reform alone is insufficient and a fundamental change in sociocultural attitudes and relations is needed. Like other neo-Shariatis, Yousefi Eshkevari maintains that by rethinking the whole idea of Muslimness religious reformers can pave the path toward a bottom-up negotiation and consolidation of equal gender relations.[80]

The critique of nativism and cultural essentialism has been another common thread and focal point in neo-Shariati thinking in postrevolutionary Iran. In their critical assessments of traditionalist and Islamist discourses, neo-Shariatis emphasize the hybridity of cultural identity and the historical and philosophical unsustainability of identitarian claims.[81] According to Sara Shariati, for example, whether manifested in nationalist, ethnic, or religious terms, identitarian discourses seek to achieve the impossible objective of "restoring a lost past" through compulsion and violence.[82] In her view, these discourses see the global expansion of Western modernity as a threat to local identities and seek to resist this hegemonic force by turning to familiar cultural and national sources of collective identity. Rather than being an authentic representation of tradition, she argues,

---

[76] See: Hassan Yousefi Eshkevari, "Rethinking Men's Authority over Women: 'Qiwāma', 'Wilāya' and Their Underlying Assumptions," trans. Ziba Mir-Hosseini, in *Gender and Equality in Muslim Family Law: Justice and Ethics in the Islamic Legal Tradition*, ed. Ziba Mir-Hosseini, Kari Vogt, Lena Larsen, and Christian Moe (London and New York: I.B. Tauris, 2013), 191–213.

[77] Yousefi Eshkevari, "Women's Rights," 169.

[78] Ibid., 165.

[79] Ibid., 164–165.

[80] Ibid., 171–172.

[81] Sara Shariati, "Chehreh jahani-gar, chehreh jahani-zadeh: siasat jahani kardan va ravand tarikhi jahani shodan" ("The Globalizer Face and the Globalized Face: An Evaluation of Globalizing Policies and the Process of Globalization"), in *Khodkavi-e melli dar asr-e jahani shodan (National Self-Examination in the Age of Globalization)*, ed. Bonyad Shariati (Tehran: Ghasidehsara, 1381/2002), 149–159.

[82] Ibid., 158.

cultural essentialism is "a product of the hegemony of the modern condition."[83] Ehsan Shariati too believes that despite their appeal to tradition, identitarian discourses are in fact creations of the modern world determined to turn religious, national, or ethnic identities into sites of resistance against the universalist claims of Western modernity.[84]

Neo-Shariatis also draw on Shariati's thought to critique the theoretical foundations of the religious state and the theological modes of political legitimation. Though Shariati himself did not live to see the political ascendency of Islamism and the establishment of an Islamic state in post-revolutionary Iran, his writings and lectures contain several references in opposition to theocratic rule and in defense of democratic governance. In *Religion versus Religion*, for instance, he asserts that a "religious state or a regime in which the clerical class occupies positions of power" is the ultimate manifestation of "tyranny," because in it "the ruler sees himself as the shadow and representative of God on earth ..., regards his own will to be the will of God, and therefore commits every injustice and abuse without the slightest hesitation."[85] Moreover, in "What is Islam?" he appeals to the Islamic principles of *ijma* (consensus) and *shura* (consultation), and cites the Quran's call on the faithful to order their affairs through "mutual consultation" (42:38), arguing that Islam's social and political teachings are consistent with the basic principles of democracy.[86]

Expanding on this antitheocratic orientation, Alijani makes a case that contrary to Islamists' rejection of the separation between religious and political power, Shariati's post-theological and humanist interpretation of Islam sits comfortably with the modern notions of secularism and democracy. In his assessment, "a sharia-based religiosity, which seeks a religious state and perceives religious laws to be eternal, deterministic, and absolute," is inevitably irreconcilable with secularism. However, an interpretation of Islamic thought based on opposition to a "juridical, deterministic, and sharia-centered approach" recognizes the modern differentiation between the religious and the political.[87] According

---

[83] Sara Shariati, "Dar bareh sharaiet-e emkan-e moderniteh dini," 133.
[84] Ehsan Shariati, interview by Hossein (Mesbahian) Rahyab.
[85] Ali Shariati, "Mazhab alaih-e mazhab" ("Religion versus Religion"), 1349/1970, C.W. 22, *Ali Shariati: The Complete Collection of Works* [CD ROM], Tehran: Shariati Cultural Foundation, 2010.
[86] Ali Shariati, "Eslam chist?" ("What is Islam?"), 1345/1966, C.W. 30, *Ali Shariati: The Complete Collection of Works* [CD ROM], Tehran: Shariati Cultural Foundation, 2010.
[87] Reza Alijani, "Pre-secular Iranians in a Post-secular Age: The Death of God, the Resurrection of God," trans. Mojtaba Mahdavi and Siavash Saffari, *Comparative Studies of South Asia, Africa and the Middle East* 31, no. 1 (2011): 31.

to Alijani, the "historical-inspirational" understanding of religion that Iqbal and Shariati advocated was and remains a major challenge to the understanding of religion as a comprehensive regulatory system and to the Islamist call for a religious state and the rule of the Islamic sharia.[88]

While the particular postrevolutionary context has had the unquestionable effect of radicalizing their critique of Islamism, Islamic traditionalism, and other discourses of cultural essentialism, neo-Shariatis have not abandoned Shariati's legacy of critical engagement with modernity as a hegemonic condition that offers both emancipatory and oppressive capacities. For Ehsan Shariati, the global expansion of modernity has inevitably affected the processes of social, political, and economic change in societies around the world, and today it is futile to speak of local or national models of modernity without taking into account these transnational developments.[89] "Rapid industrialization," he argues, "along with the integration of local markets into a globalized economy through the movement of capital and technology are realities that have been imposed on all of us, and today no society, not even precapitalist ones, can claim to exist outside of the global condition of modernity."[90]

This understanding of modernity, as a globalized condition, also enables neo-Shariatis to draw on wide range of critical discourses in the modern world including the European Left tradition. Thus, Ehsan Shariati refers to Marx's analysis of economic formations and capitalist relations of production, which in his view, reveals the processes through which the rise and expansion of industrial capitalism undermines individual agency and freedom in modern societies. In his assessment, Marx's foundational "critique of the sociopolitical consequences of modernity" is ultimately a radical call for the democratization of the economic and social spheres through revolutionary action. In this regard, he concludes, the Marxist revolutionary tradition today remains a much more radical critique of really existing Western modernity than the reformist tradition of the European social democratic thought, which aims to introduce an

---

[88] Ibid., 32.
[89] Ehsan Shariati, "Ehsan az Shariati migooyad: dar goftegoo ba ham-mihan" ("Ehsan Talks about Shariati: In Conversation with Ham-Mihan") interview with Mohammad Ghouchani and Mehdi Ghani, *Ham-Mihan*, 29 Khordad 1386/June 19, 2007, http://talar.shandel.info/showthread.php?tid=443#post_3089 (accessed January 11, 2013). Also see: Ehsan Shariati, "Cheh cheshm-andazi bara bahar-e arab?" ("What Prospects for the Arab Spring?"), *Rahnameh* (no date), http://ehsanshariati.org/show/?id=60 (accessed January 4, 2013).
[90] Ehsan Shariati, interview by Hossein (Mesbahian) Rahyab.

egalitarian dimension to liberalism. He, nevertheless, maintains that both Marxism and the European social democracy effectively remain within the rationalist-positivist paradigm of the Enlightenment thought.[91]

For neo-Shariatis, Shariati's attempt to articulate a discourse of indigenous modernity on the basis of a spiritual ontology and a progressive public religiosity represents a poignant challenge and an alternative vision to Enlightenment modernity's positivist and secularist legacy. In this regard, particular attention is given to the trinity of "spirituality, equality, freedom" (*erfan, barabari, azadi*) that Shariati introduced, initially in an essay with the same title.[92] He regarded these triumvirate values as the universal ideals of a collective humanity and the indivisible tenets of all progressive and emancipatory movements in history.[93] In a letter addressed to his son, he wrote:

> The dearest and most glorious ideals of humanity for which millions upon millions have been martyred throughout history include: *monotheism*, which gives birth to spirituality, love, and dignity; *justice*, which replaces bigotry and domination with fairness and equality; and *freedom*, which emancipates humanity from the violence of tyrants and the cruelty of oppressors. A world based on these ideals is one in which all humans are equal, in solidarity, and free from the fear of oppression.[94]

"Humanity's biggest misfortune in the modern age," as Shariati saw it, was that these universal ideals had come to be seen in contradistinction from one another. He argued that "so long as these three ideals are disjointed, they are no more than empty promises; the realization of each one of them requires the concurrent upholding of the other two."[95] The task of revolutionary intellectuals in the modern world, then, was "to wage an emancipatory cultural and intellectual struggle to save *freedom* from the barren wastelands of capitalism and class exploitation, *equality* and justice from the violent and pharaonic dictatorship of Marxism, and *God* from the ghastly and gloomy graveyard of clericalism."[96] Though he believed

---

[91] Ehsan Shariati, interview by Hossein (Mesbahian) Rahyab.
[92] See: Shariati, "Khodsazi-e enghelab."
[93] Ali Shariati, "Erfan, barabari, azadi" ("Spirituality, Equality, Freedom"), 1355/1976, C.W. 2, *Ali Shariati: The Complete Collection of Works* [CD ROM], Tehran: Shariati Cultural Foundation, 2010.
[94] Shariati, "Nameh beh Ehsan" 1355/1967–1968.
[95] Ali Shariati, C.W. 1, 79, quoted in Alijani, *Rend-e kham*, 150.
[96] Ali Shariati, C.W. 1, 97–98, quoted in Masoomeh Aliakbari *Ghera-ati falsafi az yek zed-e filsoof: derang-hayi degar-andishaneh dar matni bi-payan beh nam-e doctor Ali Shariati (A Philosophical Reading of an Anti-Philosopher: Alternative Reflections on an Endless Text Called Dr. Ali Shariati)* (Tehran: Ghalam, 1386/2007), 156.

that the quest for spirituality, freedom, and equality had existed historically in all human societies, Shariati nevertheless saw Islamic thought and its religious worldview as being uniquely positioned to offer a synthesis of these ideals. This, according to Shariati, was due to Islam's simultaneous attention to the material and the spiritual, its recognition of individual reason and autonomy, and its overall egalitarian social orientation.[97]

Acknowledging that his thought does not offer a cohesive and systematic approach for putting into practice the trinity of spirituality, equality, and freedom, neo-Shariatis maintain that advancing Shariati's intellectual legacy in postrevolutionary Iran requires, among other things, clearly defining what it means for spirituality to serve an active role in modern public life.[98] As Ehsan Shariati points out, while European social democratic and social libertarian traditions have already resolved the perceived tension between equality and freedom, it is not yet clear how spirituality can complement and reinforce the other two values and precisely what role it should play in a progressive social and political project.[99] Seeking to define this role, then, neo-Shariatis have focused on aspects of Shariati's religious worldview which they argue can contribute to the negotiation of a more humane modernity than the really existing Western models. Emphasizing Shariati's "spiritual humanism," Alijani for instance, draws parallels between the spiritual ethos of Shariati and Mahatma Gandhi, and argues that for both men spirituality serves as a strong impetus for the recognition of difference, respect for the other, and solidarity with the marginalized and the oppressed.[100] Neo-Shariatis further argue that Shariati's spiritual worldview seeks to cultivate an alternative vision to that of Enlightenment modernity of the relationship between the modern subject and its others. Hence, Susan Shariati contends that in contrast to the Enlightenment's positivist worldview in which human subjectivity is attained through the dominance of the modern subject over the non-modern and nonhuman other, Shariati's spiritual worldview aims to give recognition to both the self and the other and "to make possible the experience of togetherness."[101]

---

[97] See: Shariati, "Erfan, barabari, azadi."
[98] Alijani, *Rend-e kham*, 193.
[99] "Erfan, barabari, azadi beh masabeh yek projeh" ("Spirituality, Equality, Freedom as a Project"), Ali Shariati Information Center (no date), http://drshariati.org/show/?id=626 (accessed December 22, 2012).
[100] Reza Alijani, interview by author.
[101] Susan Shariati, "Paradox-hay-e vojdan-e asheghaneh dar negah-e Shariati" ("The Paradoxes of the Loving Consciousness in Shariati's Thought"), *Madreseh* no. 3, Ordibehesht 1385/ May 2006, http://drshariati.org/show/?id=123 (accessed March 2, 2011).

Neo-Shariatis and Islamic Liberalism

As the representatives of one among several existing religious reform currents in contemporary Iran, neo-Shariatis have focused their efforts on developing an egalitarian and democratic vision of sociopolitical development that draws on both inspirational and mobilizational capacities of religion. In their simultaneous critique of the hegemonic discourses of modernism and secularism, and the essentialist discourses of Islamism and traditionalism, neo-Shariati contributions find common ground with the works of a range of other Muslim reformists in postrevolutionary Iran. While acknowledging some overlaps, neo-Shariatis nevertheless strive to distinguish their discourse from other Islamic reform discourses particularly those associated with the current of Islamic liberalism. Indeed, it may be argued that the neo-Shariati brand of religious and political thought can be (and is often) defined in terms of its differences with the latter current.

The emphasis on politicized public spirituality by neo-Shariatis is seen by many as a direct challenge to the call for *minimal religion* by Abdolkarim Soroush and other leading figures of Islamic liberalism.[102] For neo-Shariatis, this call marks a conservative turn in Islamic reformism aimed at protecting religion from the modern forces of social and political change.[103] As Sara Shariati argues, the sociopolitical implication of this call is that religion can contribute to the process of democratization "not by reforming its historical tradition, but rather by withdrawing

---

[102] Soroush first proposed his theory of minimal religion in a 1998 essay titled "Din-e aghalli va aksari" ("Minimal and Maximal Religion"). In this and a number of subsequent works, he argued that *minimal religion* was an alternative to *ideological religion* championed by Ali Shariati throughout the 1960s and 1970s. According to him, while ideological religion aimed to extract from religion totalizing answers to questions and challenges in all spheres of life, minimal religion sought simply to offer individuals a general direction for living an ethical and spiritual life. See: Abdolkarim Soroush, "Din-e aghalli va aksari" ("Minimal and Maximal Religion"), *Kyan* no. 41 (1377/1998): 2–9; Abdolkarim Soroush, *Bast-e tajrobe-ye nabavi (The Expansion of Prophetic Experience)* (Tehran: Serat, 1378/1999).

[103] Sara Shariati, interview by author (telephone), November 28, 2012; Alijani, interview by author. Also see: Hassan Yousefi Eshkevari, "Reformist Islam and Modern Society," in Ziba Mir-Hosseini and Richard Tapper, *Islam and Democracy in Iran: Eshkevari and the Quest for Reform* (London: I.B. Tauris, 2006), 155–163. Yousefi Eshkevari argues that while Muslim liberals including Soroush and his intellectual followers are more inclined toward "private Islam," the social democratic orientation represented by Shariati's intellectual followers "sees Islam as a social movement and wants to bring about social reforms in Muslim societies by means of a social and reformist Islam" (162–163).

from the social realm."[104] She believes that in a society where religion maintains a monopolizing presence in every aspect of public life, it is not sufficient to attempt to advance a religiously mediated discourse of indigenous modernity through hermeneutical and theological-philosophical debates. Instead, what is needed is to attend to the public presence and social functions of religion and the objective conditions of the religious masses.[105] Similarly, Alijani believes that in contemporary Iran private and minimal modes of religiosity have already proven to be unsustainable. In his view, any attempt to confine religion within the private sphere ultimately undermines the objective of reforming and restructuring its social functions and leads to the rise of fanaticism and conservatism. He also argues that while Shariati's discourse of emancipatory public religion seeks to advance a radical critique of the theologically based interpretations of Islam in all spheres, Soroush's minimal religion effectively leaves theological discourses unchallenged within the private realm.[106]

Despite the neo-Shariati charge and the advocacy of minimal religion by some of its own leading figures, Islamic liberalism as articulated by Soroush, Mohammad Mojtahed Shabestari, or Mostafa Malekian does not call for the total privatization of religion. As discussed in the previous chapter, while Soroush criticizes Shariati for the ideologization of Islamic doctrines he does not dismiss the idea of public religiosity altogether, and indeed differentiates his Islamic liberalism from Western liberal secularism which, in his view, limits and regulates the public presence of religious faith. Nevertheless, a case can be made that critiquing Soroush's liberal Islam in contemporary Iran serves a similar function for neo-Shariatis that critiquing Shariati's radical and Leftist Islam did for Soroush and a number of his fellow Iranian religious intellectuals during the 1990s. In some of his works during this period including *Sturdier than Ideology* (*Farbeh-tar az ideology*) (1993), and *The Theoretical Contraction and Expansion of Religion: The Theory of the Evolution of Religious Knowledge* (*Qabz va bast-e teorik-e shariat: nazarieh-ye takamol-e marefat-e dini*) (1994), Soroush set out to distinguish his particular (minimal) brand of public religiosity from what he saw as a maximal and totalizing public religiosity that had been articulated by Shariati in prerevolution Iran and implemented by Iran's Islamist rulers in the postrevolutionary period. In a somewhat similar fashion, over the

---

[104] Sara Shariati, "Eslah dini beh masabeh eslah ejtemaei?".
[105] Sara Shariati, interview.
[106] Alijani, interview.

course of the last decade, and in a different social and political context, neo-Shariatis have sought to differentiate their own discourse of indigenous modernity from Soroush's precisely by highlighting the emancipatory capacities of politicized and radicalized public religiosity in a bottom-up movement toward democratic reform.

To further probe the distinctions between neo-Shariatis and Muslim liberals two key concerns of the former group ought to be given particular consideration. First, whereas Muslim liberals focus primarily on advancing an interpretation of Islam that is compatible with individual rights and freedoms, neo-Shariatis emphasize both sociopolitical rights and socioeconomic justice. The latter, they insist, is an indispensable component of Shariati's political thought and is evident in his engagement with the European Left tradition as well as in his particular reading of Islam's religious doctrines.[107] According to Alijani, the ideal of equality in Shariati's trinity of spirituality, equality, and freedom signifies economic egalitarianism and a general pro-poor orientation.[108] In his view, by placing egalitarian concerns front and center in his discourse of indigenous modernity, Shariati's project becomes particularly attentive to the problems of the poor and working classes. By contrast, he maintains, while Islamic liberalism has contributed to the negotiation of a contextually grounded discourse of political pluralism and civil and political rights in postrevolutionary Iran, it has neglected the issues of equality and social welfare.[109] Similarly, Rahmani makes a case that while Islamic liberalism has privileged freedom over equality, expanding on the egalitarian and social democratic aspects of Shariati's thought can contribute to progressive movements in Iran by giving simultaneous attention to the grievances of both middle and working classes.[110]

To incorporate the ideal of equality in their vision of progressive sociopolitical development in Iran, some neo-Shariati figures have endorsed the Nordic model of social democracy and welfare state.[111] They,

---

[107] "Shariati va gofteman-e edalat" ("Shariati and the Discourse of Justice"), Ali Shariati Information Center, 23 Azar 1390/December 14, 2011, http://drshariati.org/show/?id=539 (accessed March 5, 2012).

[108] Alijani, *Rend-e kham*, 137.

[109] Reza Alijani, "Tashaio sorkh, ya tashaio seh-rang-e irani" ("Red Shi'ism or Tricolored Iranian Shi'ism"), *Iran-e Farda* no. 34, Tir 1376/July 1997: 31.

[110] "Mizgerd-e nasim-e bidari dar barresi amoozeh-hay-e shariati" ("Nasim-e Bidari's Panel on Shariati's Teachings"), Ali Shariati Information Center (no date) http://drshariati.org/show/?id=212 (accessed July 27, 2012).

[111] Ehsan Shariati, "Edalat zeil-e azadi ast: andisheh-hay-e eghtesadi-e Ali Shariati dar goftegoo ba Ehsan Shariati" ("Equality is a Part of Freedom: Discussing Ali Shariati's

nevertheless, maintain that Shariati's spiritual worldview provides an alternative ontology on the basis of which to theorize and implement a democratic and egalitarian model of economic production and distribution. It is thus that Alijani regards Shariati as "one of the pioneers of a tradition of spiritual social democracy in Iran."[112] Other neo-Shariati figures have sought to add a socioeconomic element with a particularly pro-poor orientation to their engagement with and critique of dominant religion. Among them, Sara Shariati notes that in critiquing traditional and conservative religiosity Islamic reformers must attend both to the ways in which religion has historically served exploitative economic relations, and the conditions under which a particular reading of Islam has come to legitimize neoliberalism and an unjust distribution of wealth in postrevolutionary Iran.[113]

The second characteristic distinguishing the neo-Shariati discourse from Islamic liberalism is the centrality in the former of the critique of colonial and neocolonial relations. As discussed in the previous two chapters, in the context of the mid-twentieth century Iran Shariati emerged as a radical anticolonial thinker with a keen interest in exposing the cultural manifestations of coloniality. Though they acknowledge that the global operations of coloniality have undergone a number of changes in the past half a century, neo-Shariatis nonetheless seek to complement their critique of Islamism, political authoritarianism, and religious-cultural essentialism with a simultaneous problematization of Western hegemony and neocolonialism. Thus, just as Shariati drew attention to the colonial construction of cultural alienation and the Eurocentric visions of modernization, neo-Shariatis focus on the impact of globalization and neocolonial power asymmetries on the global processes of knowledge production and identity formation. The anticolonial orientation of neo-Shariati thought is also manifested in its continued effort to expand on the philosophical critique of Enlightenment modernity by Iqbal and Shariati and to theorize an alternative account of humanism and individual subjectivity through a reformation and reconstruction of the local traditions of knowledge and ontology. This effort, and its philosophical foundations in Shariati's thought, is the focus of the chapter that follows.

Economic Ideas with Ehsan Shariati"), *Ta'adol*, Khordad 1393 /June 2014, http://taadolnewspaper.ir/ (accessed June 19, 2014).

[112] Alijani, *Seh Shariati*, 34.

[113] Sara Shariati, "Faghr, chaleshi barai-e din" ("Poverty, a Challenge for Faith"), Sara Shariati Internet Archives (January 30, 2014), http://sarahshariati.blogspot.com/2014/01/blog-post.html (accessed November 21, 2014).

4

The Enlightenment Subject and a Religiously Mediated Subjectivity

The Philosophical Foundations of an Islamic Discourse

It is only in the last two decades and with the increased interest in examining his encounter with modernity that commentators have begun to pay closer attention to the theoretical and philosophical foundations of Shariati's thought. In these philosophical examinations, commentators have been particularly interested in the relationship between Shariati's religious discourse and a range of modern concepts including human agency, individual freedom, equal rights, and popular sovereignty. Shahrough Akhavi's 1988 essay entitled "Islam, Politics and Society in the Thought of Ayatullah Khomeini, Ayatullah Taliqani and Ali Shariati," appears to be the first systematic effort to examine the ontological and epistemological grounds of Shariati's Islamic discourse. According to Akhavi, Shariati's philosophical thought is founded, on the one hand, on a deep belief in "free will" and human "autonomy," and on the other hand, on an "*tawhidi*" worldview based on the fusion of God, humanity, and nature.[1] Shariati's support for free will, Akhavi argues, is particularly evident in his philosophy of history and his belief that while physical and scientific laws may limit the scope of individual action, individual humans have a "wide latitude" in exercising their autonomous will and shaping the development of

---

[1] Shahrough Akhavi, "Islam, Politics and Society in the Thought of Ayatullah Khomeini, Ayatullah Taliqani and Ali Shariati," *Middle Eastern Studies* 24, no. 4 (October 1988): 406. In this book I have translated *jahanbini-yi tawhidi* as "monotheistic worldview," which I find to be a more accurate equivalence than "integralist worldview."

history.² Akhavi further contends that although his ontology was rooted in metaphysics, Shariati's social and political thought were "firmly rooted in the real world of men" [sic].³

Though Akhavi describes Shariati as one of the prominent "social theorists of the [1979] Iranian revolution," he does not see a link between the postrevolutionary institutionalization of Islamism and Shariati's religiously mediated political discourse. On the contrary, he believes that the inclusion of some democratic provisions in the first draft of the constitution after the revolution may have been due in part to the influence of the humanist Islamic discourses of Muslim reformers such as Shariati and Taliqani.⁴ The antidemocratic structures of the Islamic Republic, he argues, stand in contradiction with Shariati's firm belief in the ability of the common people to rule over their own affairs. He further notes that the existence of radical philosophical and political differences between the Islamic discourses of Shariati and Khomeini led ultimately to "Shariati's virtual 'excommunication' by the [postrevolutionary] regime."⁵

Whereas Akhavi's analysis highlights the humanist, democratic, and egalitarian qualities of Shariati's political philosophy, a number of other commentators have been considerably more skeptical in their readings of the philosophical foundations of Shariati's Islamic discourse. For them, Shariati's revolutionary Islam was an integral part of a broader mid-twentieth century discourse of Islamic authenticity that opposed the philosophical foundations of the Enlightenment, rejected the modern concepts of individual reason and subjectivity, and ultimately set the scene for the ascendency of antidemocratic Islamism in postrevolutionary Iran. This is a charge laid against Shariati by Ali Mirsepassi, who sees Shariati's discourse as having had its roots in a counter-Enlightenment political philosophy. In "Religious Intellectuals and Western Critiques of Secular Modernity" (2006), Mirsepassi argues that Shariati's attempt to develop a nativized vision of modernity in the Iranian context "foundered on a dangerous preoccupation with blinding metaphysical abstractions that, though high sounding and seductive in their language, conceal a narrow and dangerously totalizing understanding."⁶ According to Mirsepassi, within a Heideggerian frame of

---

² Ibid., 412.
³ Ibid., 428.
⁴ Ibid., 420.
⁵ Ibid., 428.
⁶ Ibid., 431.

analysis Shariati's Islamic discourse sought to revive an ontological bond between modern Iranians and their community "as a recovery of the ideal and unified Islamic society."[7] Shariati's authenticist discourse, he posits, constituted an attack on the modern ideas of "democracy," "pluralism," and "secularism," from the vantage point of an ahistorical vision of Islamic authenticity.[8]

In *Political Islam, Iran, and the Enlightenment: Philosophies of Hope and Despair* (2011), Mirsepassi reiterates his case that Shariati's philosophical outlook was grounded on a Heideggerian view about the modern loss of an existential bond between the individual and the community.[9] In attributing this position to Shariati, Mirsepassi only rarely refers directly to Shariati's text, and he does not discuss at any length the extent of Shariati's familiarity or the nature of his engagement with Heidegger. He nevertheless argues that Shariati's Heideggerian outlook was due in part to the influence of Henry Corbin, French scholar of spiritual Islam and one of Shariati's professors at the Sorbonne, who, according to Mirsepassi, was intimately familiar with and had a reputation for espousing Heideggerian ideas. Shariati's Islamic discourse, he concludes, must be discussed and analyzed in light of the influence of Heidegger transmitted through Corbin.[10]

In Mirsepassi's view, the main feature of Heidegger's "anti-Enlightenment" thinking, and one that resonated with Shariati, was its nostalgic appeal to "a 'lost' shared sense of community and social meaning." With this premodern nostalgia at it center, Mirsepassi believes, Shariati's social and philosophical thought sought to restore a fading sense of collective belonging and communal cohesion in the context of the rapid modernization and urbanization of Iranian society.[11] Like Heidegger, it is argued, Shariati wanted to bring an ontological bond back into the everyday life of a modern society by claiming to recover an ideal and unified authentic past.[12] In this reading, the reference to God in Shariati's thought served the extremely important function of "granting singular and ultimate authority" to collective identity and mass movement.[13] Mirsepassi

---

[7] Ibid., 428.
[8] Ali Mirsepassi, "Religious Intellectuals and Western Critiques of Secular Modernity," *Comparative Studies of South Asia, Africa and the Middle East* 26, no. 3 (2006): 416, 428.
[9] Ali Mirsepassi, *Political Islam, Iran, and the Enlightenment: Philosophies of Hope and Despair* (New York: Cambridge University Press, 2011), 126.
[10] Ibid., 1.
[11] Ibid., 2.
[12] Ibid., 127.
[13] Ibid., 126.

further argues that Shariati's collectivist orientation was manifested in his top-down and "statist" approach to social and political change as manifested in his thesis of guided democracy and his emphasis on the leadership role of the committed Muslim intellectuals. Under the influence of a Heideggerian vision of modernity, he argues, Shariati saw the state as the mechanism through which "to elevate the population."[14]

Arguing along much the same lines, though offering a closer reading of Shariati's text, Farzin Vahdat examines Shariati's encounter with the philosophical foundations of Enlightenment modernity in a number of his works.[15] Like Mirsepassi, Vahdat sees a deep contradiction between Shariati's religious ontology and the philosophical foundations of Enlightenment modernity which, in his view, sustain such critical democratic notions as the autonomous individual subject and the rights-bearing individual. Also like Mirsepassi, Vahdat develops his analysis of modernity through a binary distinction between Enlightenment and counter-Enlightenment, with the former category representing the quest for democracy, secularism, and human rights and freedoms, and the latter signifying authoritarianism, totalitarianism, and collectivism. Nevertheless, while Mirsepassi attributes Shariati's "counter-Enlightenment" position to the influence of Heideggerian thought, Vahdat sees it mainly as a function of his Islamic ontology. Drawing heavily on the Hegelian-Habermasian conception of a modern epistemic break between secular and religious reason, Vahdat defines modernity as the rise of the rational, autonomous, and empowered human subject in the course of the European Enlightenment and as a break from pre-Enlightenment metaphysics and the God of revelation and transcendence. By remaining within a religious ontology, Vahdat believes, Shariati's Islamic discourse distorted and rejected the

---

[14] Ibid., 25.
[15] See: Farzin Vahdat, *God and Juggernaut: Iran's Intellectual Encounter with Modernity* (Syracuse, NY: Syracuse University Press, 2002); Farzin Vahdat, "Religious Modernity in Iran: Dilemmas of Islamic Democracy in the Discourse of Mohammad Khatami," *Comparative Studies of South Asia, Africa and the Middle East* 25, no. 3 (2005): 650–664; Farzin Vahdat, "Critical Theory and the Islamic Encounter with Modernity," in *Islam and the West: Critical Perspectives on Modernity*, ed. Michael Thompson (Oxford: Rowman & Littlefield Publishers, 2003): 123–139; Farzin Vahdat, "Metaphysical Foundations of Islamic Revolutionary Discourse in Iran: Vacillations on Human Subjectivity," *Critique: Critical Middle Eastern Studies* 8, no. 14 (1999): 49–73; Farzin Vahdat, "Shariati: bohran-e hoviat-e irani va zehn-bonyadi" ("Shariati: The Crisis of the Iranian Identity and Subjectivity"), trans. Simin Fasihi, in *Khodkavi-e melli dar asr-e jahani shodan (National Self-Examination in the Age of Globalization)*, ed. Bonyad Shariati (Tehran: Ghasidehsara, 1381/2002), 222–237.

autonomous and rights-bearing subject of Enlightenment modernity.[16] Using the theoretical framework of modern subjectivity, Vahdat traces in Shariati's Islamic thought the negotiation of what he regards to be a mediated account of subjectivity that recognizes collective, but not individual, human will and agency. Throughout the 1960s and 1970s, he suggests, Shariati's religiously mediated and collectively oriented account of human subjectivity introduced many Iranians to such modern ideas as revolution and emancipation, thus facilitating their participation in a mass uprising that ultimately led to the overthrow of the Pahlavi regime.[17]

Vahdat's notion of mediated subjectivity provides a useful analytical lens for examining the philosophical foundations of Shariati's social and political thought. As discussed in the previous chapters, in line with the intellectual legacy of Muhammad Iqbal, and in his critical engagement with Western modernity, Shariati sought to theorize an alternative ontology to that of the Enlightenment on the basis of a *tawhidi* religious worldview. Arguably then, by mediating such notions as freedom, popular sovereignty, democracy, socialism, and revolution through a religious or spiritual frame of reference Shariati aimed not only to develop contextually grounded accounts of these modern concepts for his Iranian and Muslim audiences, but also to identify an alternative ontological vantage point to that of Enlightenment modernity for conceiving the modern self in relation to its others. From this perspective Vahdat is quite correct in describing Shariati's views on human freedom and agency as an account of mediated subjectivity. What remains contested, however, is whether a religiously mediated account of subjectivity is necessarily antithetical to the modern notions of individual rights and freedoms or to democratic governance. Another related question is whether a secular language of rights is inherently superior to a religious language of rights. And yet another relevant line of inquiry is whether advancing visions of democracy, secularism, and egalitarianism in contemporary societies inevitably requires remaining within the normative boundaries of the Enlightenment tradition.

---

[16] As I noted in Chapter 1, Vahdat's overall assessment of Shariati's Islamic discourse and his intellectual legacy is less skeptical than Mirsepassi's. He considers the discourse of mediated subjectivity as a transitory discourse which can potentially contribute to the transition of Iranian society to modernity. The full transition, however, requires the negotiation and gradual consolidation of absolute/universal subjectivity.

[17] Farzin Vahdat, *God and Juggernaut: Iran's Intellectual Encounter with Modernity* (Syracuse, NY: Syracuse University Press, 2002), 153.

Modern Subjectivity and the Mediated Subject

Vahdat defines modernity in terms of subjectivity and universality, which he regards to be the twin philosophical pillars of the European Enlightenment. The former is defined as "the property characterizing the autonomous, self-willing, self-defining, and self-conscious individual agent," and the latter as "the mutual recognition among the plurality of subjects of each other's subjectivity."[18] In Vahdat's view, there is a close association between these philosophical pillars of modernity and the ideas of popular sovereignty, democracy, individual and citizenship rights, and equality.[19] The quest for subjectivity and universality, he argues, has shaped the modern "impulse … against objectification and domination," in at least two important ways. In the cultural sphere, it has transformed "primary relations of domination and subordination, prototypically, the relationship between the transcendental God of monotheism and human worshippers," and in the political sphere it has given birth to the rights-bearing citizen and the modern civil society.[20]

Vahdat believes that among the leading figures of the European Enlightenment, Hegel's approach to human subjectivity and religion contains particularly pertinent insights for contemporary Muslim societies. For Hegel, he argues, the modern individual is at once embedded in his/her local cultural context and able to rise above it. To achieve the latter, however, requires treating one's society and culture as objects of conscious and critical reflection. Through the force of critical self-reflection both individuals and nations can rise above the prevailing social and cultural traditions, norms, beliefs, and customs, "even though such phenomena [are] ultimately rooted in the *Geist*."[21] As a premodern phenomenon with fixed concepts and beliefs, religion is ultimately a force against self-conscious and critical reflection, which inevitably arrests the development of genuine subjectivity. Thus, Vahdat believes, Hegel's lesson for contemporary Muslim societies is that the full realization of self-consciousness and the genuine exercise of human freedom would not be possible without a complete break with religious ontology and epistemology.[22] He further argues that the Hegelian conception of the relationship between religion and modernity is advocated today chiefly

---

[18] Vahdat, "Metaphysical Foundations," 51.
[19] Vahdat, *God and Juggernaut*, 2.
[20] Ibid., xiv.
[21] Ibid., 23.
[22] Ibid., 224.

by the philosophical discourse of Jürgen Habermas, and it is primarily through a Hegelian-Habermasian epistemic distinction between religious and nonreligious reason that he analyzes the responses to modernity by Shariati and several other Muslim thinkers.

According to Vahdat, throughout the twentieth century, and in their opposition to Western colonialism and imperialism, a number of radical Muslim thinkers advanced a revolutionary "Islamic discourse" that sought to counter the Western discourse of modernity and instill in the Muslim masses a sense of collective agency in order to mobilize them against Western domination. While this new discourse recognized and encouraged some measure of human agency, by mediating subjectivity through abstract and metaphysical notions, it ultimately distorted one of the main philosophical pillars of modernity.[23] By "mediated subjectivity" Vahdat refers to a distinct, religiously negotiated, conception of subjectivity, advanced through the partial human appropriation of the traditional attributes of the God of monotheism.[24] Hence, it is argued, a particular account of human subjectivity is acknowledged in the Islamic notion of the human vicegerency of God on earth (*khilafate-ilahiah*). According to Vahdat, however, defining human subjectivity as an attribute of divine sovereignty has resulted in a "constant, schizophrenic vacillation" between human and God and between the individual and the collective in Islamic discourse. In his view, the religious mediation and distortion of human subjectivity in the lead-up to the 1979 revolution had the effect of legitimizing restrictions on modern democratic rights and freedoms in the postrevolutionary context.[25]

Shariati is regarded by Vahdat as one of the most influential advocates of the "Islamic discourse" in Iran during the 1960s and 1970s, along with Ruhollah Khomeini and Morteza Motahari.[26] He is also seen as an archetypal Muslim ideologue who developed an indigenous account of collective subjectivity on the basis of a partial human appropriation of the traditional attributes of an absolute and all-powerful deity. According to Vahdat, Shariati reappropriated the traditional religious category of monotheism and used it as "a universal category" based on "consciousness," "will," and "human moral autonomy."[27] Shariati's ontology, he

---

[23] Ibid., 55. Also see: Vahdat, "Metaphysical Foundations," 59.
[24] Vahdat, "Metaphysical Foundations," 53.
[25] Vahdat, *God and Juggernaut*, 134.
[26] Ibid., 131–132.
[27] Ibid., 139.

argues, advanced an account of subjectivity that saw human existence as a journey toward transcendence and ascent from the level of unconscious matter to the level of the conscious and sovereign God of monotheism. Vahdat maintains that although Shariati's mediated subjectivity appealed to self-consciousness, his understanding of the term was radically different from "Hegelian self-consciousness inherent in the subject's freedom." Far from representing a category of critical and reasoned self-reflection, Shariati's notion of consciousness, it is argued, entailed the annihilation of the self in divine sovereignty and the partial appropriation of the latter by a human collectivity.[28]

Vahdat believes that Shariati was at once excited about the modern possibility of a God-like human subject, and alarmed by the crisis of modern subjectivity manifested in philosophical nihilism. He argues that Shariati's encounter with modernity is best described as "bewilderment" (*heyrat*), a term that Shariati himself used frequently to refer to the spiritual-existential angst of the twentieth-century individual. According to Vahdat, Shariati saw the subject of modernity as the lonely wolf, "who, after challenging the Being and nature, was now horrified by the solitude of subjectivity."[29] Shariati, it is argued, feared that his "ontological journey" toward subjectivity might ultimately lead him to the same conclusions as those of Western modernity, namely, diremption from nature and the whole of existence. Vahdat maintains that Shariati found the solution to his modern bewilderment "in submission to the Being, in annihilation of the self in God, and in finding a 'new' self, who, in cooperation with God and Love, would create the universe anew in a utopia of mediated subjectivity."[30]

According to Vahdat, just as Shariati's metaphysical ontology simultaneously accepted and negated human subjectivity, his political philosophy too contained both elements that endorsed, as well as those that opposed, "the notions of popular sovereignty and citizenship rights."[31] For Vahdat, this conflicting position was rooted in a fundamental contradiction in Shariati's Islamic discourse. On the one hand, Shariati's anti-imperialist ideology sought to mobilize the Muslim masses against Western material and cultural domination by giving recognition to a particular form of agency modeled after divine sovereignty and embodied in a human

---

[28] Ibid., 143.
[29] Ibid., 144.
[30] Ibid., 143.
[31] Vahdat, "Metaphysical Foundations," 61.

collectivity. On the other hand, however, suspicious and fearful of the moral and sociopolitical consequences of modern subjectivity, Shariati opposed the individual subject at the center of Enlightenment modernity. Thus, Vahdat argues that while Shariati's discourse acknowledged a measure of human autonomy and subjectivity, in reality this was only an endorsement of "*collective*, not individual agency."[32]

Vahdat acknowledges that in some of his writings Shariati made explicit references to the pivotal role of the "individual" agent.[33] According to Vahdat, Shariati was well aware that "responsibility was meaningless without the individual as the subject" and even argued that the Quran had given recognition to "the individual as the very foundation of the notion of responsibility." At the same time, Vahdat holds that Shariati's approval of "philosophical individualism" did not translate into support for "moral-practical individualism."[34] For Vahdat, Shariati's contention that nature, history, society, and self, constituted the four "prisons" that limited genuine human subjectivity and agency revealed a deep suspicion toward the individual subject and a "profound contempt for the human body."[35] Vahdat believes that Shariati's distrust of the individual subject was also manifested in his critical position toward "liberal democracy" and "individual and civil freedoms."[36] He argues that Shariati's attempt to locate subjectivity in a collective category closely paralleled Marxist views on the relationship between individual and society.[37] Like Mirsepassi, Vahdat holds that Shariati's thesis of guided democracy was reflective of a collectivist ontology and pointed to an antidemocratic crux in Shariati's political philosophy.[38]

Vahdat's analysis of Shariati's religious ontology and positions toward democracy and individual rights presents only a selective reading of Shariati's text and an incomplete depiction of his overall intellectual project. As I have shown in this book, it is entirely possible to demarcate Shariati's thought from Islamist discourses such as Khomeini's, and to have an alternative reading of his text in relation to democracy, secularism, human agency, and individual rights and liberties. In the previous chapter, for example, it was noted that although Shariati was more

---

[32] Vahdat, *God and Juggernaut*, 146 (emphasis in original).
[33] Vahdat, "Metaphysical Foundations," 60.
[34] Vahdat, *God and Juggernaut*, 148.
[35] Ibid., 142.
[36] Ibid., 148.
[37] Ibid., 149.
[38] Ibid., 151–152. Also see: Vahdat, "Metaphysical Foundations," 61.

concerned with the general conditions for the realization of individual freedom than with any specific set of rights and liberties, in some of his writings he explicitly defended democratic freedoms such as freedom of expression and freedom of political association. Similarly, the charge that the thesis of guided democracy represents the core of Shariati's political thought faces a serious challenge once Shariati's own position, namely that the thesis only applies to tribal societies and not to twentieth-century Iran, is taken into account.[39] Furthermore, while Vahdat draws parallels between Shariati's Islamic discourse and Marxist accounts of collective subjectivity, he wholly ignores Shariati's criticism of the suppression of individuality and basic civil rights in the former Eastern bloc countries. Contrary to Vahdat's account, in his critique of really existing socialism, Shariati advanced not only a philosophical but also a moral-practical defense of individual liberties. He even went so far as to argue that despite the violence of capitalism and imperialism, the protection of basic individual rights and liberties made the capitalist West a more desirable place to live for dissident intellectuals and political activists from capitalist and socialist countries alike.[40]

What is more, Vahdat's broader theoretical panorama, his view of the Enlightenment as the singular frame of reference for the negotiation of human subjectivity, and his reliance on the Hegelian-Habermasian epistemic distinction between sacred and secular, between religious reason and nonreligious reason, overlook serious critiques of and ongoing disputes over the Enlightenment tradition both within and without contemporary Western thought. Though he makes references to such critical European thinkers as Theodor Adorno and Max Horkheimer, Vahdat does not offer much in the way of exploring the implications

---

[39] Ali Shariati, *Ma va Iqbal: majmooeh asar 5 (Iqbal and Us: Collected Works 5)* (Aachen, Germany: Hosseinieh Ershad, 1978), 48. It was also mentioned in previous chapters that Shariati changed his position on the role of intellectuals in his later works, including *Iqbal and Us*, and *Return*.

[40] Shariati writes: "How sad that in the name of socialism, and with inhumane violence, [the really existing socialism] denies the freedom of intellect, the freedom to worship, and the freedoms to choose, act, and innovate. And how sad that these barbaric and fascistic ways are justified using lofty and sophisticated philosophical and sociological arguments. There is no bigger catastrophe than the fact that socialism is robbing twentieth century humanity of the gains that were made under Western capitalism, and that today leading anticolonial and even socialist intellectuals from the Third World are forced to seek refuge in capitalist countries." See: Ali Shariati, C.W. 2, 166, quoted in Reza Alijani, *Rend-e kham: Shariati-shenasi jeld-e yekom: zamaneh, zendegi, va arman-ha (The Pure Noncomformist: Shariatiology Volume One: Era, Life, and Ideals)* (Tehran: Ghalam, 1387), 226.

of their critiques for the negotiation of subjectivity and other modern sociopolitical notions in non-Western contexts. Moreover, in identifying Habermas as the leading contemporary representative of the Frankfurt School and European critical theory Vahdat effectively implies that the sacred/secular epistemic divide is part and parcel of the latter tradition. The fact, however, is that such an epistemic distinction has been and remains the subject of much contestation and critique in contemporary political thought and philosophy. Some have dismissed the claim that critiquing Enlightenment modernity and its conception of human subjectivity on the basis of a religious or spiritual ontology necessarily amounts to a rejection of individual autonomy, freedom, and rights. Others have pointed to the capacities of religious discourses and ontologies for making demands for democratic and human rights within the public sphere. Indeed, Habermas's own work in recent years has given recognition to public religion and its potentially progressive capacities in the modern world.

Secularization and the "Myth" of the Enlightenment

Chapter 3 addressed the making and unmaking in contemporary political thought of the secularization thesis, founded on a Weberian conceptualization of modernity as a progressive process of the rationalization and secularization of the public sphere. It is on the foundation of this Weberian view that Habermas develops his conception of modernity and calls for a return to the unfinished project of modernity. Commenting on Weber's *Sociology of Religion* (1920) Habermas writes:

For Weber, the intrinsic (that is, not merely contingent) relationship between modernity and what he called "Occidental rationalism" was still self-evident. He described as "rational" the process of disenchantment which led in Europe to a disintegration of religious worldviews that issued in a secular culture. With the modern empirical sciences, autonomous arts, and theories of morality and law grounded on principles, cultural spheres of value took shape which made possible learning processes in accord with the respective inner logics of theoretical, aesthetic, and moral-practical problems. What Weber depicted was not only the secularization of Western culture, but also and especially the development of modern societies from the viewpoint of rationalization. The new structures of society were marked by the differentiation of the two functionally intermeshing systems that had taken shape around the organizational cores of the capitalist enterprise and the bureaucratic state apparatus. Weber understood this process as the institutionalization of purposive-rational economic and administrative action. To the degree that everyday life was affected by this cultural and societal rationalization, traditional forms of life – which in the early modern period were differentiated primarily according to one's trade – were dissolved.[41]

In line with this Weberian sacred/secular divide, Habermas relegates religion and religious worldviews to a premodern age of the evolution of human societies when mythological-metaphysical views of the world prevailed.[42] In "'The Political': The Rational Meaning of a Questionable Inheritance of Political Theology" (2011), he argues that in traditional societies such as medieval Europe political power was legitimized primarily by religion, whose legitimizing power was "rooted, *independently of politics,* in notions of salvation and calamity (*Heil and Unheil*) and in corresponding practices of coping with redemptive and menacing forces."[43] By challenging the totalizing reign of religion, modernity demythologized and rationalized "the symbolic representation and collective self-understanding" of Europeans.[44] The rise of modern modes of production and bureaucratic administration, and the yearning for religious tolerance and pluralism after Europe's religious wars of the sixteenth and seventeenth centuries contributed to the "dissolution of the amalgamation of religion and politics" and the secularization of the political sphere. The late-eighteenth-century constitutional revolutions marked a major "break with the traditional pattern of legitimation" and further consolidated "the secularization of state authority" in the modern West.[45]

However, as Habermas tells us, the "secularization of the state" has not always meant the concurrent and evenhanded "secularization of society." According to him, the continued presence of religion in public life poses a unique challenge to secular democracies today.[46] While

---

[41] Jürgen Habermas, *The Philosophical Discourse of Modernity: Twelve Lectures,* trans. Frederick G. Lawrence (Cambridge, MA: MIT Press, 1990), 1–2.
[42] See: Jürgen Habermas, *The Theory of Communicative Action. Volume One: Reason and the Rationalization of Society,* trans. Thomas McCarthy (Boston, MA: Beacon Press, 1984); Jürgen Habermas, *Observations of "The Spiritual Situation of the Age,"* trans. Andrew Buchwalter (Cambridge, MA: MIT Press, 1985); Jürgen Habermas, *Religion and Rationality: Essays on Reason, God, and Modernity,* ed. Eduardo Mendieta (Cambridge, MA: MIT Press, 2002); Jürgen Habermas, "Religion in the Public Sphere." *European Journal of Philosophy* 14, no. 1 (2006): 1–25; Jürgen Habermas, *Between Naturalism and Religion,* trans. Ciaran Cronin (Cambridge, UK: Polity, 2008).
[43] Jürgen Habermas, "'The Political': The Rational Meaning of a Questionable Inheritance of Political Theology," in *The Power of Religion in the Public Sphere,* ed. Eduardo Mendieta and Jonathan VanAntwerpen (New York: Columbia University Press, 2011), 17 (emphasis in original).
[44] Ibid., 18.
[45] Ibid., 21.
[46] Ibid., 23.

secularism requires restricting the public influence of religion, political liberalism entails guaranteeing the equal right of all religious and non-religious citizens to influence democratic outcomes. For Habermas, the appropriate response to this condition is not to privatize religion entirely as laicism calls for, but instead to make participation in the collective decision-making process contingent upon the use of "public reason" by all, including religious citizens.[47] Habermas borrows the concept of public reason from American political philosopher John Rawls who saw a similar tension between the use of religious speech or religious reason in the public sphere and the liberal democratic requirements of free speech and religious freedom. In a 1997 essay entitled, "The Idea of Public Reason Revisited," Rawls proposed that religious doctrines and worldviews "may be introduced in public political discussion at any time, provided that in due course proper political reasons – and not reasons given solely by comprehensive doctrines – are presented that are sufficient to support whatever the comprehensive doctrines introduced are said to support."[48]

According to Habermas, however, the Rawlsian proviso that any religious utterance in the public sphere must prove to be translatable into the language of "proper political discourse" faces two important objections. The first objection is that "many citizens *cannot* or are not willing to make the required separation between contributions expressed in religious terms and those expressed in secular language when they take political stances." The second objection is that under a "liberal constitution," which gives recognition to religious freedoms and forms of life, the proviso may impose an "asymmetrical burden" on religious citizens.[49] Seeking to retain Rawls's overall scheme while also addressing these objections, Habermas introduces a modified account of the translation proviso that aims to properly define the scope of the restrictions that may be legitimately imposed on public religious discourse.

For Habermas, though religious citizens are free "to use religious language in the public sphere," they should also accept "that the potential truth contents of religious utterances must be translated into a generally accessible language before they can find their way onto the agenda of parliaments, courts, or administrative bodies and influence their decision." He presents the notion of an "institutional filter"

---

[47] Ibid., 24.
[48] John Rawls, "The Idea of Public Reason Revisited," *University of Chicago Law Review* 64 (Summer 1997): 783, quoted in "'The Political': The Rational Meaning," 25.
[49] Habermas, "'The Political': The Rational Meaning," 25.

that channels potentially relevant religious contributions in the public sphere through to the "formal deliberation of political bodies" by translating them into the "universally accessible language" of public reason.[50] Habermas believes that his modified translation proviso addresses the objections leveled against Rawls by ensuring not only that religious citizens can freely use religious discourse in the public sphere, but also that their contributions are not falling on deaf ears and being rejected or ignored by nonreligious citizens. Thus, he argues that just as religious citizens must adhere to the translation proviso in the public sphere, secular citizens too "are obliged not to publicly dismiss religious contributions to political opinion and will formation as mere noise, or even nonsense, from the start."[51] Moreover, Habermas's translation scheme entails the recognition that "vibrant world religions may be bearers of 'truth contents,' in the sense of suppressed or untapped moral intuition."[52]

Habermas's acknowledgment of the potentially progressive moral and inspirational capacities of religious faith in the public sphere offers a more optimistic view about the role and place of religion in the modern world than that espoused by Vahdat and other critics of Shariati's Islamic discourse. Nevertheless, Habermas's critics have challenged his view of an epistemic divide between secular and religious thought. For some of these commentators, Habermas's epistemic sacred/secular binary is rooted in a Eurocentric framework in which the modern European subject is conceived of as the self of modernity, and the non-European as its subordinate other. In his seminal work, *The Theory of Communicative Action*, Habermas himself describes modernity as a European development and as inseparable from "Occidental rationalism."[53] For one critic, this conception of modernity rests on a "colonial geo-cultural imaginary" in which the Occident represents rationality and philosophy while the Orient represents mythology and spirituality.[54] Robbie Shilliam argues that within a global context of the expansion of European colonialism, a range of modern thinkers – from Kant to Habermas – have advanced a

---

[50] Ibid., 25–26.
[51] Ibid., 26.
[52] Ibid., 27.
[53] Jürgen Habermas, *The Theory of Communicative Action*, vol. 1, *Reason and Rationalization of Society*, trans. Thomas McCarthy (Boston, MA: Beacon Press, 1984), 7.
[54] Robbie Shilliam, "The Perilous but Unavoidable Terrain of the Non-West," in *International Relations and Non-Western Thought: Imperialism, Colonialism and Investigations of Global Modernity*, ed. Robbie Shilliam (New York: Routledge, 2011), 13.

particular discourse of modernity that has "privileged the European being as the teleological truth of human existence" and forwarded "a universal standard of civilization modeled upon an idealized western Europe."[55]

Challenging the monolithic and dichotomistic construction of sacred and secular in Habermas's discourse of modernity, critics have drawn attention to the diverse expressions of the religious matter in the modern world. Judith Butler, for example, points out that the modern public sphere in the West has itself emerged out of certain religious traditions which "help to establish a set of criteria that delimit the public from the private."[56] She argues that in modern societies we are faced not with a singular category of "religion," but rather with "a variety of religious positions on public life and a variety of ways of conceiving of public life within religious terms."[57] In her analysis of the complex nature of the negotiation of three categories, namely "Jewishness," "Judaism," and "Zionism," Butler shows how contemporary Judaic thought has given birth to both "identitarian" and "anti-identitarian" social and political projects.[58]

Charles Taylor also critiques Habermas's treatment of religion as a special case and a unique challenge in modern secular democracies. According to Taylor, the main point of contention in discussions on secularism should not be about "the relation of the state and religion," but rather about the appropriate democratic responses to diversity and difference within the modern public sphere.[59] The principle of state neutrality, he claims, aims precisely to avoid advantaging or disadvantaging any basic position, religious or nonreligious, in the collective decision-making process. Warning against the potentially dangerous and stifling effects of radical secularism or "exclusive humanism" in modern public life, Taylor argues that in a democratic state it should not make a difference what deeper reasons or what ontological and epistemological arguments different groups of citizens (religious or secular) offer in order to gain access to and/or to negotiate and advance the basic tenets of democratic

---

[55] Robbie Shilliam, "Non-Western Thought and International Relations," in *International Relations and Non-Western Thought: Imperialism, Colonialism and Investigations of Global Modernity*, ed. Robbie Shilliam (New York: Routledge, 2011), 2–3.

[56] Judith Butler, "Is Judaism Zionism?," in *The Power of Religion in the Public Sphere*, ed. Eduardo Mendieta and Jonathan VanAntwerpen (New York: Columbia University Press, 2011), 71.

[57] Ibid., 70.

[58] Ibid., 74.

[59] Charles Taylor, "Why We Need a Radical Redefinition of Secularism," in *The Power of Religion in the Public Sphere*, ed. Eduardo Mendieta and Jonathan VanAntwerpen (New York: Columbia University Press, 2011), 36.

governance.⁶⁰ Rejecting the view that democratic public deliberation ought to be necessarily articulated in a secular language, Taylor notes that there is no ground for thinking that a religious discourse of liberation and social justice, such as that of Martin Luther King, Jr., is any less publicly and generally accessible than a secular discourse of rights.⁶¹ Habermas's epistemological sacred/secular distinction, he believes, is rooted in a "myth" of the Enlightenment that sees modernity as the "stepping out of a realm in which Revelation ... counted as a source of insight about human affairs into a realm in which these are now understood in purely this-worldly or human terms." Taylor regards such a view to be historically untenable, and his own account of modernity draws attention to the multiple and multifaceted sources of the modern Western self and the sustained influence of religious traditions in the formation of the public sphere.⁶² His critical engagement with the modern sacred/secular binary also problematizes the unilinear vision of modernity as a trajectory of civilizational "convergence" and cultural homogeneity through an inevitable shift from religious reason to secular reason.⁶³

Habermas's critics have also drawn attention to some of the ways in which contemporary religious discourses such as black liberation theology have been used to challenge the dominating tendencies of Western modernity. Among the leading contemporary representatives of this discourse, Cornel West has acknowledged both the emancipatory and the oppressive manifestations of religion in the modern world by distinguishing between "prophetic" and "dominant" religiosity. Whereas the former is characterized by "an empathetic and imaginative power that confronts hegemonic power," the latter represents a religion that is "well-adjusted to greed and fear and bigotry" and is indifferent toward the condition of poor and working classes. West believes in the power of prophetic religion to initiate "utopian interruptions" against oppression and

---

⁶⁰ Charles Taylor "A Catholic Modernity?," in *A Catholic Modernity?: Charles Taylor's Marianist Award Lecture with Responses by William M. Shea, Rosemary Luling Haughton, George Marsden, Jean Bethke Elshtain*, ed. James L. Heft (New York: Oxford University Press, 1999), 19. Also see: Charles Taylor, *Sources of the Self: The Making of the Modern Identity* (Cambridge, MA: Harvard University Press, 1989), 520.
⁶¹ Charles Taylor, "Dialogue: Jürgen Habermas and Charles Taylor," in *The Power of Religion in the Public Sphere*, ed. Eduardo Mendieta and Jonathan VanAntwerpen (New York: Columbia University Press, 2011), 61.
⁶² Taylor, "Why We Need a Radical Redefinition," 52–53.
⁶³ Charles Taylor, "Two Theories of Modernity," *Public Culture* 11, no. 1 (1999): 161.

hegemony.⁶⁴ Following Émile Durkheim's analysis in *The Elementary Forms of the Religious Life* (1912), he regards "worship and faith" as an "eternal" character of human societies. In his view, whereas in capitalist modernity the worship of God has been replaced with the worship of "the market or its accompaniments and accoutrements," prophetic religion can interrupt this new form of "idolatry" and give the modern subject the courage to love the other and to "sacrifice for justice."⁶⁵ In contemporary American history, he notes, prophetic religion has served as an important "force for democratic good" in a wide range of social and political struggles from the nineteenth-century abolitionist, women's suffrage, and trade unionist movements, to the twentieth-century civil rights movement.⁶⁶

In *Democracy Matters* (2004), as well as elsewhere, West challenges the epistemic sacred/secular binary and criticizes tendencies within political liberalism to police the public sphere by appealing to the concept of secular reason. According to him, even though the radical secularism of such liberal philosophers as John Rawls and Richard Rorty supports "the rights and liberties of religious citizens," it nevertheless "puts up a wall to prevent religious language in the public square, to police religious-based arguments and permit only secular ones."⁶⁷ West finds such "secular policing of public life" to be ultimately dogmatic and authoritarian, and calls for the recognition of the inherent messiness and impurity of public deliberation and democratic practices, and for resistance against both secular and religious impulses to regulate public discourse.⁶⁸ In his view, by marginalizing the deeply religious cultures of "the wretched of the earth," dogmatic secularism depletes the public sphere of potentially emancipatory discourses.⁶⁹ He argues that what is urgently needed in contemporary liberal democracies is not further "secularization", but rather the "democratization of the state" and attention to the condition

---

⁶⁴ Cornel West, "Prophetic Religion and the Future of Capitalist Civilization," in *The Power of Religion in the Public Sphere*, ed. Eduardo Mendieta and Jonathan VanAntwerpen (New York: Columbia University Press, 2011), 99.
⁶⁵ Cornel West, "Dialogue: Judith Butler and Cornel West," in *The Power of Religion in the Public Sphere*, ed. Eduardo Mendieta and Jonathan VanAntwerpen (New York: Columbia University Press, 2011), 105–106.
⁶⁶ Cornel West, *Democracy Matters: Winning the Fight against Imperialism* (New York: The Penguin Press, 2004), 153.
⁶⁷ Ibid., 161.
⁶⁸ Ibid., 162.
⁶⁹ Cornel West, *The American Evasion of Philosophy: A Genealogy of Pragmatism* (Madison: University of Wisconsin Press, 1989), 233.

of the poor.⁷⁰ Noting that Weberian predictions about the decline of "God-talk" were not realized in the modern world, West argues that deepening democracy in contemporary societies is contingent on our "ability to be multicontextual in the various frameworks and reason-giving activities in public spaces." Practicing genuine public multicontextuality for him, requires, among other things, that secular thinkers become more "religiously musical," and religious thinkers more "secularly musical."⁷¹

Also critiquing Habermas's discourse of secular reason, Fred Dallmayr argues that the German philosopher's insistence on the sacred/secular binary marks a departure from the Germanic tradition of critical theory. The latter, he argues, emerged as an attempt to curb the hegemonic tendency of modern reason and to reconcile subjectivity with non-domination. Under the impact of the rise of fascism and anti-Semitism, Dallmayr notes, a range of critical theorists (including Ernst Bloch, Walter Benjamin, Max Horkheimer, and Theodor Adorno) began to draw attention to "the darkly sinister undertow of Western modernity," and to warn against the "ongoing shrinkage of critical reason and self-reflection into a mere instrument of calculation and managerial control."⁷² According to Dallmayr, in their critical analyses of late capitalist modernity, these thinkers often maintained a "sympathetic" position toward emancipatory religious thought and saw religion as a major source of inspiration in the struggle against relations of domination and exploitation. In fact, he argues, in their effort to reconcile the subject of modernity with its others, some German critical theorists turned to the emancipatory and utopian capacities of religious ontologies, including the Jewish tradition of "utopian messianism," which they saw as a radical ontological turn toward the other.⁷³

The critique of Habermas's discourse of modernity by commentators such as Butler, Taylor, West, and Dallmayr shows the limitations of the epistemic sacred/secular binary for understanding the role of religion in modern social and political life. Contrary to Vahdat's claim that Habermas's thought presents a more adequate framework for analyzing the condition of modernity in Muslim societies than that offered

---

⁷⁰ West, "Dialogue," 107.
⁷¹ West, "Prophetic Religion," 93.
⁷² Fred Dallmayr, "The Underside of Modernity: Adorno, Heidegger, and Dussel," *Constellations* 11, no.1 (March 2004): 103.
⁷³ Fred Dallmayr, "Review of Jürgen Habermas, Religion and Rationality: Essays on Reason, God, and Modernity," *Notre Dame Philosophical Reviews* no. 2 (2003), http://ndpr.nd.edu/news/23259/?id=1179 (accessed June 8, 2012).

by classical sociological accounts,[74] the epistemic sacred/secular divide in Habermas's discourse of modernity only perpetuates the very same Weberian religion/modernity binary that underlay the hegemonic twentieth century metanarratives of modernization and secularization. In the context of contemporary Muslim societies, the conceptualization of the modern public sphere as the realm of secular reason does not provide a particularly relevant framework for understanding the complexities and the nuances of the relationship between faith and the modern processes of sociopolitical development. Arriving at an alternative analytical approach in these societies requires simultaneous attention to the ongoing debates on a global scale about the material and normative conditions for the negotiation of human subjectivity and emancipation, as well as to a sustained effort by Muslim thinkers to develop contextually negotiated accounts of progressive change by drawing on the capacities of local cultural and religious traditions. In many ways this also means going beyond the limiting and Eurocentric framework of Enlightenment modernity and delinking the values of human agency, freedom, rights, and equality from this hegemonic tradition. Such a delinking has been an important feature in the works of a wide range of prominent Muslim modernizers and reformers including Iqbal, Shariati, Abu Zayd, Arkun, Gülen, and Soroush. The Islamic humanism of these Muslim thinkers has contributed to the development of indigenous discourses of subjectivity, democracy, and human rights, while at the same time challenging the sacred/secular and reason/non-reason binaries of the Enlightenment thought.

The Descent: A Theistic Narrative of Subjectivity

Shariati's thought and its new readings by neo-Shariatis find shared ground with the thinkings of Butler, Taylor, West, Dallmayr, and a range of other critics of the Hegelian-Habermasian ontological and epistemological juxtaposition of sacred and secular. Like these critics, Shariati and neo-Shariatis reject the conception of modernity as a unidirectional trajectory of the secularization of the public sphere and a total break from religion. They challenge the monolithic construction of the categories of religion, religious reason, and religious discourse by drawing attention to

---

[74] Vahdat, *God and Juggernaut*, 1.

the plural manifestations of the religious matter in modern societies and the role of faith as a perpetual source of individual and collective identity. Thus, pointing to the global phenomenon of the return of religion at the end of the twentieth century and the beginning of the new millennium, one neo-Shariati figure argues that "it is indeed modernity that in the course of its expansion has provided the conditions for the reproduction of the religious matter."[75] Moreover, like some of the Western critics of the Enlightenment's secular rationalism, in their critique of the prevailing sociopolitical and socioeconomic relations of domination, Shariati and neo-Shariatis appeal to the inspirational capacities of religion for human emancipation and for giving recognition to the inherent dignity of the other.

In his critical assessment of European modernity, Shariati argues that by rejecting religious inspiration as an authentic source of insight in the modern world and by reducing humanity to mere rationalism the Enlightenment tradition effectively abandoned the ontological commitment to the other.[76] In maintaining this view, he is influenced primarily by Iqbal and his epistemological distinction between scientific-philosophical and religious-spiritual worldviews. According to Shariati, while the former worldview calls for a total separation between pure reason and its others (i.e., emotion, revelation, and intuition), the latter seeks to reconcile the two. Enlightenment modernity's scientific-philosophical worldview, he contends, defines knowledge exclusively in terms of the relationship between a "rational human subject" and an "objective reality," thus, delinking the individual from community, nature, and existence. By deconstructing the modern juxtaposition of the individual human agent against an outside reality, a spiritual interpretation of being can reunite the modern individual with its others and reconcile the subject of modernity with a multilayered reality.[77]

Despite his critique of the sacred/secular binary, Shariati nevertheless regards the recognition of human reason and autonomy as one of the progressive legacies of Enlightenment modernity, and like Hegel he

---

[75] Sara Shariati, "Dar bareh sharaiet-e emkan-e moderniteh dini," ("On the Conditions for the Possibility of Religious Modernity"), in *Dar hashiyeh matn (On the Margins of the Text)*, ed. Bonyad Shariati (Tehran: Shahr-e Aftab, 1379/2000), 143.

[76] Ali Shariati, "Ba to ei mehrban javdan-e asib napazir" ("With You, O Eternal and Imperishable Kindness"), 1356/1977 C.W. 1, *Ali Shariati: The Complete Collection of Works* [CD ROM], Tehran: Shariati Cultural Foundation, 2010.

[77] Ali Shariati, "Moghaddameh" ("Introduction"), in *Koliat-e Iqbal Lahori (The Poetry Collection of Iqbal Lahori)* (Tehran: Elham, 1384/2005), 14.

sees a direct link between self-consciousness and the rise of the modern subject. Indeed, while Vahdat contends that Shariati's conception of self-consciousness is radically different from Hegel's, the two notions seem to share a fundamental commitment to the critical reassessment of the sources of the self. For Shariati, "consciousness," or "self-consciousness," is achieved through a critical engagement with the world and by gaining an awareness of the relationship between the self and the other. Like the Hegelian concept, Shariati's notion of self-consciousness begins with what he himself calls a "Cartesian doubt" and a radical revolt against the traditional self.[78] As Reza Alijani points out, for Shariati, the first move toward self-consciousness is to step out of one's immediate social and cultural context and to critically engage with the prevailing traditions. Alijani cites Shariati's discussions in the twenty-third volume of his collected works, entitled *Worldview and Ideology* (*jahanbini va ideolojy*), where he argues that arriving at self-consciousness necessitates subjecting "all of our thoughts, beliefs, and norms, and all of our religious, traditional, philosophical, tribal, ethnic, class, or ideological belongings ... to a relentless critique and bringing into question all of their primary claims."[79] As Alijani notes, Shariati even cites English empiricist philosopher, Francis Bacon, to argue that genuine self-consciousness requires breaking down all of the "idols of the mind."[80]

At the same time, Shariati believes that advancing a radical critique of the traditional sources of the self would be impossible without acknowledging the embeddedness of our individual and collective selves. If moving toward self-consciousness begins with a Cartesian doubt, it must inevitably continue with a radical redefinition of the relationship between the self and its others. For Shariati, "it is only in relation with and through knowing the other that one discovers and arrives at the self."[81] From this perspective, there is no contradiction between self-consciousness and a religious ontology, because according to Shariati, religion's call to attend to the transcendental sources of the self is indeed a call to self-consciousness. In his view, by highlighting the "existential condition" of the individual subject, a spiritual-religious worldview can guide humans toward the most complete state

---

[78] Ali Shariati, "Bazgasht beh kodam khish?" ("Return to Which Self?"), 1350/1971, C.W. 4, *Ali Shariati: The Complete Collection of Works* [CD ROM]. Tehran: Shariati Cultural Foundation, 2010.
[79] Ali Shariati, C.W. 23, 131, quoted in Alijani, *Rend-e kham*, 170.
[80] Alijani, *Rend-e kham*, 170.
[81] Ali Shariati, C.W. 24, 19, quoted in Alijani, *Rend-e kham*, 172.

The Descent: *A Theistic Narrative of Subjectivity* 123

of self-consciousness.[82] Moreover, Alijani reminds us that for Shariati faith is ultimately a "personal experience" that begins with a deep philosophical questioning about one's place in the existence and a journey toward existential self-awareness.[83]

Shariati does not see a contradiction between religious faith and human autonomy. Defining the former as a conscious commitment to the other and to a set of transcendental values, he argues that such a commitment necessarily requires free choice and the free exercise of autonomy.[84] Contrary to Vahdat's view that Shariati's thought recognizes freedom only as an attribute of the absolute sovereignty of God, in his writings Shariati makes numerous references to the innate value of human freedom. According to him, "human freedom, dignity, and consciousness are not things to be sacrificed, even in the name of God."[85] Thus, one of Shariati's present-day intellectual followers makes a case that if monotheism constitutes one tenet of Shariati's philosophical thought the other tenet is undoubtedly human freedom.[86] Moreover, while Vahdat believes that Shariati's religious ontology ultimately leads to the rejection of democratic rights and liberties, Shariati himself considers the modern notions of "political, intellectual, artistic, and religious freedoms, and the freedom of making choices and living life from within" as some of the "most glorious achievements of humanity in the course of our evolution." In his view, the suppression of intellectual freedom and pluralism inevitably leads to cultural and civilizational stagnation and decay. Thus, he writes, "if we believe in the possibility of evolution, then we must regard even the slightest deviation from the principles of freedom of conscience and ... intellectual diversity and innovation as nothing short of a tragedy."[87]

Shariati's religious ontology is articulated most conspicuously in his spiritual writings to which he himself refers as *kaviriat* (desert writings). These works are collected primarily in volumes thirteen and thirty three of his collected works, respectively titled *The Descent in the Desert*

---

[82] Ali Shariati, C.W. 24, 22, quoted in Alijani, *Rend-e kham*, 172.
[83] Alijani, Rend-e kham, 170–173.
[84] Ali Shariati, "Khodsazi-e enghelabi" ("Revolutionary Self-Preparedness"), 1355/1976, C.W. 2, *Ali Shariati: The Complete Collection of Works* [CD ROM], Tehran: Shariati Cultural Foundation, 2010.
[85] Ali Shariati, C.W. 35, 549, quoted in Masoomeh Aliakbari, *Ghera-ati falsafi az yek zed-e filsoof: derang-hayi degar-andishaneh dar matni bi-payan beh nam-e doctor Ali Shariati (A Philosophical Reading of an Anti-Philosopher: Alternative Reflections on an Endless Text Called Dr. Ali Shariati)* (Tehran: Ghalam, 1386/2007), 43.
[86] Aliakbari, *Ghera-ati falsafi*, 38.
[87] Shariati, "Khodsazi-e enghelabi."

(*Hoboot dar kavir*), and *Dialogues of Solitude* (*Goftegoo-hay-e tanhayi*). Here I wish to engage with some aspects of Shariati's ontological thought through a reading of a work titled *The Descent (Hoboot)*. In this text, written in 1969, Shariati makes several references to Hegel's conception of self-consciousness and endorses the Hegelian view that what distinguishes modern humans from their traditional predecessors is the former's arrival at a sense of self-awareness, and through it, at individual autonomy and free will. This endorsement, however, does not prevent Shariati from taking a critical position toward Hegel's sacred/secular binary and what he regards as a Eurocentric account of the evolution of human reason and subjectivity. Shariati writes: "Though I accept Hegel's view of history as a gradual shift from objectivity to subjectivity, I do not share his belief that the emergence of self-consciousness can be described in such terms as an evolutionary process that begins with a primitive Eastern mind and culminates with a modern Western mind, or as a shift from religious reason to secular reason."[88]

In *The Descent*, which is an imaginative and free interpretation of the Biblical and Quranic creation stories combined with reflections on various ancient mythologies and references to the author's own life and spiritual journey, Shariati presents an account of self-consciousness and individual subjectivity that remains within a religious worldview. Though he believes that modernity has enhanced the condition for the autonomous exercise of human freedom, Shariati's account of the story of creation suggests that humans have always, since their very creation, possessed the capacity to reason, to have an autonomous will, and to craft their own paths, even to the extent of astonishing God or revolting against divine will.[89] To stress this innate capacity, he appeals to various religious symbolisms. That human life begins when God breathes into clay is interpreted as an act of God embedding in human nature the godly qualities of freedom and ingenuity.[90] A few pages later, in Shariati's account of the story of Satan's rebellion after the creation of the first human, Satan tells God that he is unwilling to bow down before "a creature who disregards God's will ... simply because it

---

[88] Ali Shariati, *Hoboot (The Descent)* (Tehran: Soroush, 1359/1981), 81.

[89] In a passage in *Hoboot*, we read that once the creation of the world and its inhabitants was completed God lined up all creatures and offered them the power of creation which appeared in the form of a flame. The only creature that, to God's own "astonishment" (*shegeft*), stepped forward and took the flame from God's hands was human (Shariati, *Hoboot*, 16).

[90] Ibid., 1.

can."⁹¹ Elsewhere, and repeatedly throughout the text, he refers to the fall of Adam and Eve from the Garden of Eden after eating the fruit of the tree of knowledge as the inauguration of a state of total human autonomy and independence from God.⁹² For him, the religious notion of the fall serves much the same purpose in facilitating human freedom and autonomy as Jean-Paul Sartre's existentialist notion of *délaissement* (abandonment).⁹³

After the fall, self-consciousness is realized gradually through a process of overcoming what Shariati calls the "four prisons of humanity," namely "nature," "history," "society," and the "self." According to Shariati, it is only through self-consciousness that one frees one's being from these prisons and overcomes their deterministic forces.⁹⁴ By overcoming the prison of the self, Shariati means becoming fully aware of the instinctive and unconscious or subconscious aspects of the human mind and body. He writes: "Human is not a 'being'; it is a 'becoming'. In this becoming one gradually frees one's 'being' of God-given qualities and creates new qualities by one's own will until one no longer possesses any unconscious qualities. Whatever one possesses are one's own conscious qualities.... This is the ultimate realization of Hegel's absolute idealism."⁹⁵ Contrary to Vahdat's and Mirsepassi's views about the collectivist orientation of Shariati's ontology, for Shariati it is clear in *The Descent* that for Shariati freedom from the prisons of nature, history, society, and self is tantamount to arrival at individual subjectivity. Contrasting "tribal" and "modern" societies, Shariati asserts that in the former "true individual consciousness does not yet exist" and the very "being of the individual" is made intelligible through a "collective consciousness." In the latter, on the other hand, "collective consciousness or 'we' declines and individual consciousness or 'I' becomes more pronounced."⁹⁶ The birth of "I" is the result of centuries of human evolution and a gradual transition from a state of "natural and instinctual unconsciousness" to "independent consciousness."⁹⁷

For Shariati, while traditional and institutionalized religion serves as a force to inhibit self-consciousness, an emancipated religiosity helps to facilitate self-awareness and individual subjectivity. Thus, he argues

⁹¹ Ibid., 3.
⁹² Ibid., 73.
⁹³ Ibid., 4.
⁹⁴ Ibid., 72.
⁹⁵ Ibid., 70.
⁹⁶ Ibid., 80.
⁹⁷ Ibid., 73.

that "religion more than science, spirituality more than technique, and the worship of God more than the worship of materialism, encourage humans to be self-reflective."[98] A religious worldview also enables the negotiation of a type of subjectivity that does not alienate the individual from other humans, the natural world, and the whole of existence. In this worldview, upon creation, humans are endowed with both absolute freedom as well as a need "to find meaning in the being of the other."[99] Hence, in a first person narrative in *The Descent* told by the first created human, we read: "In this absolute emptiness, beyond the boundaries of the heavens I felt my own self in a way that I am never to experience again.... In that world there was one, and there was no other. I was the only one. God was not there either? ... There was a vast territory whose sovereign was I; a universe whose creator was I."[100] But the innate need to go beyond the self is manifested as the "pain" and "anxiety" of alienation and emptiness; hence the first human embarks on a journey to find its other.[101] In *The Descent* then, much as in the book of Genesis, we are presented with two creation stories: one in which human life begins with a single person created in God's image from clay and divine breath; and another in which humanity is created, still in God's image, but in a pair, a male and a female.[102] In Shariati's inventive interpretation, the Biblical narration of creation in two distinct stories comes to signify the two innate qualities of human nature, namely the desire for total sovereignty and the need for togetherness. Still, for him the two qualities are not mutually exclusive and they do not negate one another. Self-consciousness is the result of the self's awareness of, and is thus impossible without, the other. In the "dialectic of self-discovery" he argues, "the self poses as the thesis, and the other as its antithesis."[103]

Religious Ontology and the Rights-Bearing Subject

It is often noted by his contemporary intellectual followers that Shariati's attempt to reconcile religious ontology and human freedom was informed, in part, by his view of the philosophical crisis of modernity and

---

[98] Ibid., 81.
[99] Ibid., 36. For Shariati, the capacity to be free and the need to be with the other are both divine qualities. In his account, then, God whose freedom and sovereignty are absolute, "creates humans for his own loneliness" (Shariati, *Hoboot*, 61).
[100] Ibid., 22.
[101] Ibid., 17–19.
[102] Ibid., 30.
[103] Ibid., 78.

the ontological abandonment of the other in modern Western philosophical thought. As one neo-Shariati figure puts it, Shariati rightly or wrongly believed that Western philosophy was ultimately unable to resolve the crisis of the diremption of the modern subject, and that even in its socialist and humanist accounts modern Western thought led to "individualism" and a belief in the "futility of sacrifice for the other."[104] Similarly, Shariati's political biographer, Ali Rahnema, argues that even though Shariati was deeply influenced by Sartre's brand of existentialist philosophy, he was nevertheless unsatisfied with the centrality of the concept of *bon sens* (common sense) in Sartre's thought, and argued for the need to locate individual freedom and autonomy within a more transcendental ethical and moral order.[105]

It is in a religiously mediated form of humanism and a religious-spiritual worldview that Shariati and his intellectual followers find a higher moral order that is capable of turning the modern subject toward its others. Thus, Ehsan Shariati makes a case that while there exists some overlap between Shariati's triad of "freedom, equality, spiritually" and the French Revolution's slogan of "Liberté, Égalité, Fraternité," the non-religious ontology of the latter formulation does not go far enough to address the real philosophical crisis of the modern subject. "Fraternité" is a call for "social solidarity" and "coexistence," which attests to a progressive turn in the historical development of Western modernity, but which lacks the necessary philosophical and metaphysical grounding to foster a real sense of existential togetherness. In the absence of these foundations, he argues, the abstract notions of fraternity and solidarity are transmuted into the formalistic concept of "social contract" and a legalistic framework within which a particular set of social policies are imagined and implemented. In his view, while "genuine spirituality" also calls for social solidarity and a commitment to social welfare, it does not reduce humanity to its material needs and instead seeks higher transcendental meaning and a strong ontological bond between the individual and the whole of existence.[106]

Shariati held that in a world characterized by individualism and a prevailing absence of meaning a spiritual worldview was ultimately "a call for the negation of and a rebellion against the self beyond any

---

[104] Hossein Mesbahian, "Shariati va nam-e khoda" ("Shariati and the Name of God"), in *Din va ideolojy* (*Religion and Ideology*), ed. Bonyad Shariati (no publisher/no date), 230.
[105] Ali Rahnema, *An Islamic Utopian: A Political Biography of Ali Shari'ati* (London and New York: I.B. Tauris, 2000), 127.
[106] Ehsan Shariati, interview by Hossein (Mesbahian) Rahyab, no date (unpublished).

rationale and reason …, for a [higher] cause and for the [sake of the] other."[107] While acknowledging that at the core of Shariati's spiritual thought is the love for and a radical ontological turn toward the other, Shariati's intellectual followers nevertheless believe that a spiritually inspired negation of the self does not amount to a rejection of human subjectivity and the surrender of individual agency. Among others, Ehsan Shariati distinguishes Shariati's "humanist" spirituality, which is, according to him, a response to real human needs and social concerns, from "anti-humanist" spirituality, which "essentially sets the social question aside."[108] Likewise, Susan Shariati believes that the spiritual renegotiation of the modern self/other binary in Shariati's thought aims "neither to turn the self into the other nor the other into the self, but instead to give recognition to both and to make possible the experience of togetherness."[109] Similarly, Hossein Mesbahian believes that Shariati's spiritual turn to the other signifies not a negation of subjectivity, but rather an attempt to provoke the possibility of an ethical reimagination of the human subject.[110]

In "Shariati and the Name of God," Mesbahian challenges the reading of Shariati's religious ontology as an antidemocratic theory of collectivist subjectivity. Distinguishing Shariati's unorthodox reinterpretation of the name of God from traditional understandings of deity, he argues that unlike the latter conception Shariati's thought does not conceive humans as the "powerless instruments" of a "powerful God" and as "mere objects in the predetermination of invisible forces."[111] According to him, in developing his religiously mediated account of human autonomy Shariati sought to avoid Enlightenment modernity's normative trap of "reducing the existence to the individual, and reducing the individual to … abstract and barren rationalism."[112] In this regard, Mesbahian finds parallels between Shariati's attempt to curb the destructive tendencies of uninhibited subjectivity by appealing to the ontological possibilities of emancipatory religious thought, and the turn to the name of God by

---

[107] Ali Shariati, C.W. 25, 158, quoted in Mesbahian, "Shariati va nam-e khoda," 231.
[108] Ehsan Shariati, interview by Hossein (Mesbahian) Rahyab.
[109] Susan Shariati, "Paradox-hay-e vojdan-e asheghaneh dar negah-e Shariati" ("The Paradoxes of the Loving Consciousness in Shariati's Thought"), *Madreseh* no. 3, Ordibehesht 1385/May 2006, http://drshariati.org/show/?id=123 (accessed March 2, 2011).
[110] Hossein Mesbahian, interview by author (Internet/Oovoo), April 23, 2013.
[111] Mesbahian, "Shariati va nam-e khoda," 227.
[112] Ibid., 228.

a two prominent twentieth-century Jewish European thinkers, Theodor Adorno and Emmanuel Lévinas.

Drawing on an essay by David Kaufmann entitled "Adorno and the Name of God," Mesbahian points to Adorno's treatment of God's name in the Jewish tradition as a potential ontological basis for an ethical renegotiating of modern subjectivity.[113] According to Kaufmann, Adorno saw the prohibition on speaking God's name in the Jewish tradition as a major step in the direction of rationalizing metaphysics and freeing human beings from the grip of mythology. While traditional metaphysics was characterized by a prevailing belief in the "unavoidability of immanence," Judaism sought to break away from this predeterminism "by making the divine Name transcendent ... as an indication that the world could in fact be different." According to Kaufmann, in his attempt to reconcile the tension between modern subjectivity and universality Adorno hoped "to redeem the ... emancipatory semantic potential of Jewish theology and speculative metaphysics." In the name of God, he argues, Adorno found "a model for and an index of an ontology, of a metaphysical experience of the absolute, in an era of equivalence and ineluctable mediation."[114]

Mesbahian believes that the turn to the name of God in contemporary Western philosophy finds one of its most sophisticated manifestations in the ideas of Lévinas. Citing passages from *Otherwise than Being: Or Beyond Essence* (1974), and *Of God Who Comes to Mind* (1982), he argues that Lévinas attempted to explain the necessary condition for moral responsibility toward the other by appealing to the notion of the moral presence of God. According to Mesbahian, Lévinas sought "to preserve the name of God as the bearing witness to responsibility." By examining alternative understandings of the relationship between God and philosophy, he argues, Lévinas reimagined the modern self/other dichotomy. He distinguishes Lévinas's notion of responsibility toward the other from the "classical liberal" conception of a "rational social contract" binding together "atomized, self-referential, and self-sufficient" individuals. In his view, the kind of ethical responsibility that Lévinas was after strengthens social "solidarity" and "cooperation," while also serving the genuine exercise of individual rights and freedoms.[115]

---

[113] Ibid., 211.
[114] David Kaufmann, "Adorno and the Name of God," *Flashpoint* 1, no. 1 (1996), http://webdelsol.com/FLASHPOINT/adorno.htm (accessed May 2, 2011).
[115] Mesbahian, "Shariati va nam-e khoda," 215.

In Mesbahian's reading, Shariati also believed that a radical reconceptualization of the name of God had the potential "to initiate a different understanding of being; one which necessitates a 'restructuring of the world and the search for a new human.'"[116] He argues that for Shariati, the name symbolized "meaning in existence" and "eternal and uninterrupted love and care for the other." In his view, Shariati's call to return to the transcendental sources of the self served as an ontological basis for negotiating an alternative to uninhibited Cartesian subjectivity. He rejects Vahdat's contention that Shariati's religious ontology ultimately arrived at human submission to God's will and the surrender of individual subjectivity and agency. According to him, Shariati appealed to the religious concept of submission not to negate human subjectivity, but rather to locate subjectivity within a broader existential and ethical framework. In Shariati's thought, he argues, submission is a transcendental union between the individual, nature, and existence. The social and political manifestation of submission to God is not only a moral responsibility toward the other, but also a total rejection of all relations of domination including political authoritarianism, economic exploitation, and religious tyranny.[117]

Increasingly in recent years, and as debates on the philosophical foundations of Shariati's thought continue, a new generation of his intellectual followers in postrevolutionary Iran has come to read Shariati's Islamic ontology and his religious mediation of human subjectivity as the theoretical foundations of an indigenous Iranian discourse of individual agency, autonomy, and rights. For these commentators, Shariati's modern reformulation of religious thought in the Iranian-Islamic tradition represents not a turn away from the modern world, but rather a step toward an "Iranian modernity."[118] They reject the reading of Shariati's thought as an antidemocratic collectivist ontology, and find in his religious discourse the normative basis for an indigenous theory of the rights-bearing individual subject. Distinguishing Shariati's reformist reading of religious doctrines from Islamist and traditionalist conceptions, they argue that the former's emphasis on independent human reason, subjectivity, autonomy, and freedom constitutes a radical departure from the theological,

---

[116] Ibid., 228.
[117] Ibid., 229. Also see: Aliakbari, *Ghera-ati falsafi*, 95.
[118] Faramarz Motamed-Dezfooli, *Kavir: tajrobeh moderniteh irani: tafsir va bazkhani kavir doktor Ali Shariati (The Desert: The Experience of Iranian Modernity: Revisiting and Reinterpreting Dr. Ali Shariati's The Desert)* (Tehran: Ghalam, 1387), 21.

juridical, and mystical understandings of religion in Iranian and Islamic traditions.[119]

Examining Shariati's modern interpretation of traditional Islamic doctrines on the relationship between the God of transcendence and the human subject, Faramarz Motamed-Dezfooli argues that Shariati's Islamic discourse develops an account of "individuated, unmediated, and free" access to transcendence.[120] In *The Desert: The Experience of an Iranian Modernity*, he makes the provocative case that while the possibility of meaning in existence and a God of transcendence remains an important aspect of Shariati's thought, this possibility is itself mediated through and reconciled with a belief in human subjectivity. According to him, in Shariati's thought "it is only with the rise of the individual subject that existence ... comes into being. It is the will of the knowing subject that sheds light on being and carries existence forward.... Without this subject the world and all of existence would remain dark, empty, and behind a veil of unknowability."[121] Although Motamed-Dezfooli sees similarities between Shariati's view and existentialist conceptions of human subjectivity in the ideas of Sartre and Edmund Husserl, he nevertheless argues that in Shariati's thought subjectivity is always negotiated in reference to the other and it is only through this mediation that the subject becomes knowable to itself.[122] In his view, in contemporary Iranian society Shariati's reformist religious discourse has served the development of an indigenous account of the autonomous rights-bearing subject and has presented an example of progressive public religiosity.[123]

Masoumeh Aliakbari too believes that Shariati's reinterpretation of the relationship between God and the human subject has contributed to an ontological shift in contemporary Iranian thought. In *A Philosophical Account of an Anti-Philosopher*, and elsewhere, she argues that in developing his religiously mediated account of human subjectivity Shariati challenges the key characteristic of traditional Iranian thought, namely the assumption of an absolute and predetermined divine will.[124] According to her, in his spiritual writings Shariati articulates an account of

---

[119] Aliakbari, *Ghera-ati falsafi*, 42–45. Also see: Maghsoud Farasatkhah, "Shesh tipe roshanfekre dini" ("Six Types of Religious Intellectualism"), Islah Web, November 15, 2009, www.islahweb.org/node/2879 (accessed November 17, 2012).
[120] Motamed-Dezfooli, *Kavir*, 12.
[121] Ibid., 325.
[122] Ibid., 327.
[123] Ibid., 349.
[124] Aliakbari, *Ghera-ati falsafi*, 94.

divine sovereignty that is in harmony with human subjectivity and which enhances individual agency. In these writings, she argues, divine sovereignty is not treated as the negation of human subjectivity, but instead as the inspirational source that gives the human subject "a God-like confidence to take action in the world."[125] In her reading, Shariati's humanist interpretation of the relationship between the individual and deity in *The Descent* fundamentally challenges the image of an all-powerful God and a "dependent" human subject by suggesting that after the fall humanity has essentially been left to its own device and in charge of its own destiny.[126]

For another commentator, in the context of contemporary Iranian society, Shariati's Islamic discourse has contributed to the negotiation of modern thought by giving recognition to "the self-conscious subject."[127] According to Mohammad-Amin Ghaneirad, whereas in traditional Iranian and Islamic thought the relationship between the individual and deity is based on complete submission and eventual annihilation, modernity introduces an ontological "distance" between the human subject and God, and between "the individual and the collective."[128] Shariati's religious discourse, he argues, redefines the basic relationship "between the individual and God in a way that [makes] possible the emergence of 'human' with innate dignity."[129] In his view, contrary to the traditional Islamic mystical view of the "unity of being" (*vahdat-e vojood*), in Shariati's *tawhidi* worldview "there exists a distance between God and humans and the latter cannot … be annihilated in the former."[130] It is precisely this distance that enables the autonomous subject of Shariati's religious thought to rebel against all sources of authority including God.[131] Ghaneirad further contends that even though Shariati calls for

---

[125] Masoomeh Aliakbari, "Derangi dar zehniat-e ba vaseteh: naghdi bar nazar Farzin Vahdat" ("A Reflection on Mediated Subjectivity: A Critique of Farzin Vahdat's Theory," in *Din va ideolojy (Religion and Ideology)*, ed. Bonyad Shariati (no publisher/no date), 371.

[126] Aliakbari, *Ghera-ati falsafi*, 94.

[127] Mohammad-Amin Ghaneirad, "Panel," in *Shariati dar daneshgah (Shariati in the Academy)*, ed. Bonyad Shariati (Tehran: Bonyad Farhangi-e Doctor Ali Shariati, 1390/2011), 66.

[128] Ibid., 65.

[129] Ibid., 67.

[130] Ibid. Shariati himself makes a distinction between these two worldviews and argues that while from a *tawhidi* can evolve into a God-like being, s/he cannot become or replace God. See: Ali Shariati, "Meraj va Esra" ("Ascension and Isra"), 1355/1977, C.W. 2, *Ali Shariati: The Complete Collection of Works* [CD ROM], Tehran: Shariati Cultural Foundation, 2010).

[131] Ibid.

the "annihilation of the individualistic self" as an ontological reorientation of the self toward the other, such an annihilation is not in the being of a sovereign God, but instead that of a "transcendental humanity."[132]

Though marked by important distinctions in their own religious, philosophical, and political outlooks, the various readings of Shariati's Islamic discourse by his self-proclaimed intellectual followers in post-revolutionary Iran reveal the capacities of emancipatory religious thought, or what West calls prophetic religion, for contributing to the negotiation of contextually grounded conceptions of human emancipation and progressive visions of social and political change in the modern world. In these rereadings, the deconstruction of traditional religious notions such as divine sovereignty by Shariati serves the purpose of advancing a humanist account of the relationship between deity and the human subject. Similarly, Shariati's emphasis on free individual access to transcendence is seen as having served a constructive role in the recognition of philosophical-political pluralism in Iranian society. Furthermore, rejecting the claim that a religious mediation of human agency represents an undemocratic or collectivist challenge to modern individual subjectivity, Shariati's intellectual followers maintain that his religious ontology reconciles the autonomous, willful, and rights-bearing individual self with its (human, natural, and existential) others. For them, by evoking the ontological-inspirational capacities of the Islamic tradition to develop a contextually grounded discourse of individual subjectivity for his Iranian and Muslim audiences, Shariati's thought contributes to an ongoing effort in the postcolonial era to carve out a third way between the hegemonic universalism of the Enlightenment thought and the essentialist particularism of traditionalist and nativist discourses. This is a theme that will be discussed at some length in the following chapter.

---

[132] Ibid., 90–94.

5

Orientalism, Occidentalism, and the Civilizational Framework

Civilization as a Critique of Westernization

It was previously noted that critics often see Shariati's radical Islamic thought and his call for a "return to the self" as part of a broader mid-twentieth century Iranian discourse of authenticity. Drawing parallels between the discourse of authenticity in prerevolutionary Iran and European "counter-Enlightenment" discourses such as German Romanticism and the philosophy of Martin Heidegger, both Vahdat and Mirsepassi describe Shariati's thought as a rejection of the philosophical foundations of the European Enlightenment and a particularistic turn against the universalist ideals of Western modernity. Other commentators, too, have designated Shariati's Islamic discourse as part of a nativist and anti-Western rejection of modernity in Iran during the 1960s and 1970s.[1] They argue that for Shariati the West represents an oppositional binary to an authentic Islamic self, an enemy, and the source of all social, cultural, economic, and political ills in Iranian society. According to one such commentator, Shariati's Islamic ideology properly belongs within a larger Iranian discourse of Occidentalism, or Orientalism in reverse. In *Iranian Intellectuals and the West: The Tormented Triumph of Nativism* (1996), Mehrzad Boroujerdi argues that in its "compulsive tendency to fetishize and celebrate difference," Orientalism in reverse

---

[1] See: B. Hanson, "The 'Westoxication' of Iran: Depictions and Reactions of Behrangi, Al-e Ahmad and Shari'ati," *International Journal of Middle East Studies* 15, no. 1 (1983): 1–23; Ian Buruma and Avishai Margalit, *Occidentalism: The West in the Eyes of Its Enemies* (New York: Penguin Books, 2004); Farhad Khosrokhavar, "The New Intellectuals in Iran," *Social Compass* 51 no. 2 (June 2004): 91–202.

essentially perpetuates Orientalism's monolithic categories of East and West, and defines itself in a total negational opposition to the latter.[2] According to him, the ultimate aim of Shariati's ideological project is to reclaim the authentic existence of his Islamic and Oriental society vis-à-vis such monolithic categories as the modern West or the Christian Occident.[3]

Challenging this reading of Shariati's thought, the previous four chapters made a case that rather than viewing the West and Western modernity as monolithic categories Shariati advocates a selective approach toward both. It was also shown that in advancing a discourse of indigenous modernity in pre and postrevolutionary Iranian society, Shariati and his contemporary intellectual followers have sought to go beyond the hegemonic and totalizing East/West and tradition/modernity binaries that have dominated Iran's intellectual space for over a century. Nevertheless, the critiques of commentators such as Vahdat, Mirsepassi, and Boroujerdi point to an important feature of Shariati's thought which must not be ignored or considered uncritically. As these critics have correctly pointed out, Shariati advances his particular Islamic discourse within a civilizational framework in which the categories of East and West occupy a central place. As with other aspects of Shariati's thought, the civilizational framework of his analysis has been read and interpreted in two major ways. For his critics it is indicative of an Occidentalist and authenticist approach, while for his followers it represents an attempt to unsettle the binary constructs of Islam/modernity and East/West. A close reading of Shariati's text generally supports the latter view while also revealing another important function of the civilizational framework, namely mediating the negotiation of an anticolonial discourse of cosmopolitanism.

In the context of prerevolutionary Iran, Shariati constructs his civilizational discourse as an alternative to the prevailing and state-sponsored discourse of modernization. In a lecture titled "Civilization and Modernization" (*Tamadon va tajadod*), he proposes that genuine development requires not the top-down imposition of the appearances of Western modernity, but instead a radical bottom-up change on the basis of a sustained critical engagement with the cultural-civilizational

---

[2] Mehrzad Boroujerdi, *Iranian Intellectuals and the West: The Tormented Triumph of Nativism* (New York: Syracuse University Press, 1996), 18.
[3] Ibid., 109.

resources of each society.⁴ He distinguishes between two different meanings of the term "civilization." In a particular or specific sense, he believes, civilization signifies "the combination of the experiences and achievements of a particular people or society."⁵ These experiences and achievements reflect historical and geographical differences, and provide the inhabitants of each society with a sense of belonging and the condition for self-consciousness.⁶ In a universal or general sense, on the other hand, civilization means "the combination of all of the spiritual and material experiences and achievements of our common humanity."⁷

Shariati believes that while many civilizations have existed throughout history – each with unique characteristics, norms, and values – all major civilizations also represent collective human achievements and bear the legacies of civilizations that came before them.⁸ To support his claim that all human civilizations have a common source and a universal feature, Shariati refers to studies by French linguist Émile Benvenist (1902–1976) about the cross-cultural commonalities among linguistic structures.⁹ According to him, if we understand civilization as the "accumulated material and spiritual experiences of a collective humanity," then we cannot speak of civilization strictly in "Islamic," "Christian," "Chinese," "Indian," "Eastern," or "Western" terms.¹⁰ Instead, we must recognize that while cultural and scientific productions in a particular geographical zone may go through periods of growth and decline, the ongoing process of human civilization operates in multiple sites and across cultural and geographical boundaries.¹¹

---

⁴ Ali Shariati, "Tamadon va tajadod" ("Civilization and Modernization"), 1348/1969, C.W. 31, *Ali Shariati: The Complete Collection of Works* [CD ROM], Tehran: Shariati Cultural Foundation, 2010.
⁵ Ali Shariati, "Farhang va ideolojy" ("Culture and Ideology"), 1350/1971, C.W. 23, *Ali Shariati: The Complete Collection of Works* [CD ROM], Tehran: Shariati Cultural Foundation, 2010.
⁶ Ali Shariati, "Bahs-e kolli raje beh tamadon va farhang" ("General Discussion about Civilization and Culture"), 1348/1969, C.W. 11, *Ali Shariati: The Complete Collection of Works* [CD ROM], Tehran: Shariati Cultural Foundation, 2010.
⁷ Shariati, "Farhang va ideolojy."
⁸ Ibid.
⁹ Shariati, "Bahs-e kolli raje beh tamadon va farhang."
¹⁰ Ali Shariati, "Tamadon chist?" ("What is Civilization?"), 1349/1970, C.W. 11, *Ali Shariati: The Complete Collection of Works* [CD ROM], Tehran: Shariati Cultural Foundation, 2010.
¹¹ Ibid.

A major characteristic of the modern world, Shariati further contends, is the rise of the West and the decline of non-Western civilizations. He does not offer a systematic analysis about the conditions and mechanisms for the rise and fall of civilizations, or the processes through which civilizational production changes sites from one geographical zone to the next. Nevertheless, like his treatment of modernity, his civilizational thinking entails a critique of Eurocentric metanarratives and a keen attentiveness to diversity and interdependence. In his view, the modern West, like all other civilizations, is the product of cross-cultural and cross-civilizational encounters, and throughout his writings and lectures he makes repeated references to the material and cultural contributions of Islamic, Indian, Chinese, and other civilizations to the rise of modernity in Europe and the formation of the modern Western civilization.

While Shariati sees all civilizations, including the modern West, as manifestations of a universal and shared human civilization, he nevertheless believes that with the rise of European colonialism we are, for the first time in history, faced with a truly globalized civilization that actively seeks to exclude all other cultural traditions and civilizational legacies. According to Shariati: "In the past, we did not have a singular global civilization. That is to say that each nation, each race, each people had its own particular resources in the form of its own culture and civilization ... and all of those diverse cultures are now being destroyed in the assault of industrial European modernity which is fast becoming a globalized entity."[12] In an essay titled "The Characteristics of the Modern Age," under the subtitle The Death and Decline of Diverse Human Cultures and Civilizations and the Formation of a Single Global Civilization, Shariati writes,

> Today, we see on our planet another grave crime, and that is the death of diverse human cultures and civilizations which historically existed and each had different sensitivities, colors, smells, preferences, and directions. In the past, Romans, Iranians, Arabs, Chinese, Africans, and others each had their particular cultures and civilizations. But today, Europe, with its violent robotic civilization is slaughtering all other cultures and replacing them with its own civilization. So now everyone talks the same way, and about the same things. Cities, buildings, attire, relations between men and women and everything else everywhere in the world has been homogenized and a singular global cultural and civilizational model has been imposed. We no longer have inwardly Eastern culture and outwardly Western culture. Chinese ingenuity is today expressed in European forms and

---

[12] Ali Shariati, "Khosoosiat-e ghoroon-e moaser" ("The Characteristics of the Modern Centuries"), 1347/1968, C.W. 12, *Ali Shariati: The Complete Collection of Works* [CD ROM], Tehran: Shariati Cultural Foundation, 2010.

the result cannot be anything other than what has been thought of and imagined once before. This is a major obstacle against the realization of human ingenuity and it is the death of difference and of cultural, spiritual, artistic, intellectual, civilizational, and human evolution.[13]

According to Shariati, by advancing a Eurocentric discourse of civilization, leading Western thinkers since the eighteenth century have played a major role in facilitating European colonialism and imperialism and the formation of a globalized modern order.[14] In his view, failing to recognize that the achievements of the modern West are only the latest manifestations of an ongoing and ever-evolving process of human civilization that carries forth the legacies of civilizations past, contemporary European sociologists, historians, and philosophers have advanced an account of Western modernity as the singular human civilization and the endpoint of evolution and progress. The non-West, Shariati argues, is either regarded as the lesser civilization, as in the case of Asian civilizations (Indian, Chinese, and Islamic), or its civilization and culture is denied altogether, as in the case of black Africa. For European thinkers, he contends, Asian and African societies must either follow in the footsteps of the modern West and join the civilization camp, or forever remain inferior to the West and its civilizational achievements.[15]

Furthermore, Shariati maintains that by erasing all traces of non-Western civilizations and their contributions to modern human achievements the Eurocentric discourses of modernity serve the critical function of convincing Europeans of their own superiority and justifying the imposition of a particular civilizational model on the whole planet.[16] In his view, while European expansionism into Asia and Africa during the nineteenth and twentieth centuries often went hand-in-hand with a civilizational rhetoric, the real aim of Western imperialism was to incorporate non-Western societies into a global system of capitalist modernity and to turn them into consumers of European goods. By undermining the diverse historical characters and traditional cultures of the Third World, imperialism has successfully imposed homogenized patterns of production and consumption on a planetary scale.[17] In this globalized modern

---

[13] Shariati, "Khosoosiat-e ghoroon-e moaser."
[14] Shariati, "Tamadon chist?"
[15] Ali Shariati, "Bazgasht beh khish" ("Return to the Self"), 1350/1972, C.W. 4, *Ali Shariati: The Complete Collection of Works* [CD ROM], Tehran: Shariati Cultural Foundation, 2010.
[16] Ibid.
[17] Ali Shariati, "Cheh bayad kard?" ("What Is To Be Done?"), 1350/1971, C.W. 20, *Ali Shariati: The Complete Collection of Works* [CD ROM], Tehran: Shariati Cultural Foundation, 2010.

civilization, he believes, the individual is a mere laborer and consumer "regardless of whether one lives in Tehran or in ... Paris."[18]

Shariati saves his harshest criticism for those Third World intellectuals who accept the premise of Western supremacy and who call for the Westernization of their societies and the imitation of the Western civilizational model.[19] According to him,

> While in Europe they have come to realize the emptiness and meaninglessness of the modern order, in the Third World many politicians and intellectuals are busy drafting several-year programs to join the civilizational camp. If instead of blindly imitating Europe's robotic civilization the Third World chooses the path of self-awareness, then Third World societies will not only join civilization, they will also create a new and dynamic civilization. Then Fanon's words that we do not want another Europe in Africa will be truly realized, and the Third World can fulfill the humanist promise of European modernity which Europe itself failed to realize.[20]

In Shariati's view, the rhetoric of modernization that many self-alienated Third World intellectuals reproduce in their societies serves only to justify the destruction of non-European cultures and the imposition of new patterns of consumption in the context of a globalized capitalist modernity. He argues that, "If developing countries continue on their current path they will forever remain dependent on Europe both spiritually and materially. But if the intellectuals in these countries arrive at some sense of collective self-consciousness, then they can potentially change the fate of the Third World and humanity."[21]

For Shariati, the rise, in the mid-twentieth century, of anticolonial and anti-imperialist movements, and the increasing disillusionment with Europe's "robotic" civilization, are hopeful signs pointing to alternative civilizational possibilities. He argues that one of the key features of the late phase of "the new civilization" is a deep suspicion and disbelief in the superiority of Western values both in the West and in the non-West. In the West, he believes, this disillusionment has taken the form of a critical reassessment of the foundations of European modernity, while in the Third World it is manifested in a popular rejection of Westernization.[22]

---

[18] Ali Shariati, "Chegooneh mandan" ("How to Stay"), 1355/1976, C.W. 2, *Ali Shariati: The Complete Collection of Works* [CD ROM], Tehran: Shariati Cultural Foundation, 2010.
[19] Shariati, "Bazgasht beh khish."
[20] Shariati, "Khosoosiat-e ghoroon-e moaser."
[21] Ibid.
[22] Ali Shariati, "Vijegihaye tamadon-e emrooz" ("The Characteristics of Today's Civilization"), 1348/1969, C.W. 12, *Ali Shariati: The Complete Collection of Works* [CD ROM], Tehran: Shariati Cultural Foundation, 2010.

According to him, increasingly after the eruption of World War I in Europe, the claim that European modernity represents the highest and most complete form of human civilization has come to be seriously questioned.[23] In the mid-twentieth century world, he argues, Europe no longer has faith in its own civilizational superiority and non-Europe no longer wants to imitate its former colonial master. In Shariati's view, the loss of faith in the modern epistemic regime and its social, scientific, and philosophical tenets is an indication of the decline of the present civilization and the birth of alternative possibilities.[24]

In Shariati's thought, moving beyond Eurocentrism requires giving recognition to a civilizational diversity that has historically shaped different human societies and negotiating alternative and indigenous visions of progressive change on the basis of the particular local determinants and the distinct civilizational and cultural resources of each society.[25] This is the main sentiment captured in Shariati's call for a return to the self. The call, according to Shariati, is informed by the recognition that there is no unilinear, fixed, and predetermined path to development and that "each society must reach its own enlightenment on the basis of its own history and culture, and by relying on its own collective memories, language, and intellectual traditions."[26] The idea, he insists, is not to return to a romanticized vision of an ethnic or racial past, but to renegotiate the progressive accomplishments of the modern civilization on the basis of "a worldview that corresponds to local social and cultural realities."[27] What is more, the thesis of return to the self is seen by Shariati as a radical embrace of cultural-civilizational diversity and difference.[28] It is guided by the assumption that arriving at the ideals of human unity and solidarity cannot be achieved through the forced homogenization of human societies, but only through the recognition of our de facto civilizational cosmopolitanism.[29]

In outlining the cosmopolitan orientation of his vision of return to the self, Shariati problematizes what he sees as misguided, backward, and

---

[23] Ibid.
[24] Ibid.
[25] Ibid.
[26] Shariati, "Bazgasht beh khish."
[27] Shariati, "Vijegihaye tamadon-e emrooz."
[28] Ali Shariati, "Estekhraj va tasfieh manabe farhangi" ("Extraction and Refinement of Cultural Resources"), 1348/1969, C.W. 20, *Ali Shariati: The Complete Collection of Works* [CD ROM], Tehran: Shariati Cultural Foundation, 2010.
[29] Shariati, "Vijegihaye tamadon-e emrooz."

fascistic discourses of return that reproduce the hegemonic universalism of colonial modernity by denying or relegating to a lower status all other human experiences and achievements. The point of attending to the local sources of the Iranian self, he contends, is not to perpetuate the colonial myth of a singular and superior civilization. Instead, the goal is to show that Iranians, too, have possessed a civilization and they, too, have contributed to the advancement of a common humanity.[30] While maintaining this overall cosmopolitan frame of reference, in his critical engagement with the cultural and civilizational sources of the Iranian self Shariati is far more attentive to Iran's Islamic-Shi'i past than its extra-religious sources of identity or its pre-Islamic heritage.[31] He acknowledges that the latter is an unassailable part of the Iranian self, but insists that the dominant component of Iranian identity in the twentieth century is its Islamic-Shi'i tradition. From this vantage point, he advances his vision of an indigenous modernity in Iranian society primarily through a critical engagement with and reconstruction of the prevailing Islamic and Shi'i traditions.[32]

Despite his repeated references to the categories of East and West, throughout his writings and lectures Shariati persistently challenges what he regards to be a Eurocentric conceptualization of the East/West binary. In particular, he is critical of discourses that regard rationalism and scientific thought to be inherently Occidental and spirituality and metaphysics to be inherently Oriental. He argues that such a binary is rooted in a colonial framework that sees Europe as having an exclusive monopoly over modernity and the modern civilization.[33] He describes this Eurocentric construction of the East/West binary as a form of "racialized essentialism,"[34] and criticizes a wide range of European intellectuals for reproducing the myth of the superior West and the inferior East.[35] Furthermore, he is harshly critical of a number of his intellectual peers in Iran who, in calling for a return to the Iranian and Islamic self, perpetuate the colonial myth of the East as the representation of tradition and spirituality

---

[30] Shariati, "Bazgasht beh khish."
[31] Despite his emphasis on the Islamic-Shi'i sources of the Iranian identity, Shariati also discusses Iran's pre-Islamic civilizational/cultural heritage in a number of his works including in articles and lectures collected in the twenty-seventh volume of his collected works, entitled, *Rediscovering the Iranian-Islamic Identity* (*Bazshenasi-e hoviat-e irani-eslami*).
[32] Shariati, "Bazgasht beh khish."
[33] Shariati, "Tamadon chist?"
[34] Shariati, "Bazgasht beh khish."
[35] Shariati, "Estekhraj va tasfieh manabe farhangi."

and the West as the flag bearer of modernity and reason. In Shariati's view, far from advancing a progressive postcolonial position, the discourses of these intellectuals constitute a new form of "traditionalism and fundamentalism." For him, those who simply reproduce the assertions of European Orientalists about the inherent differences between East and West fail to recognize that the relationship between these two entities is the relationship of "colonizer and colonized" and "exploiter and exploited."[36]

In his attempt to go beyond the prevailing East/West civilizational binary of his time, Shariati draws attention to the simultaneous existence of science and spirituality in both Eastern and Western civilizational contexts. He believes that rationalist traditions have had a long history in the East and makes a case that contrary to the conventional wisdom "naturalism" did not begin in the West, but rather in the East and in ancient Chinese philosophies.[37] He also points to the contributions of ancient Eastern civilizations (Sumerian, Babylonian, Assyrian) to mathematics, astronomy, and naval exploration,[38] as well as Indian and Muslim contributions to algebra and physics.[39] He argues that if the East appears more spiritual, it is mainly because it has had a longer history of civilization than the West. Defining spirituality as the product of a civilized consciousness, he argues that since the East is the historical birthplace of major civilizations and religions it is only inevitable that spiritually finds a firm ground there. Nevertheless, he also believes that like naturalism, spirituality too has travelled from East to West and has played a major role in human evolution in both contexts.[40]

The Civilizational Framework Revisited

It may be argued that by appealing to civilizational categories such as East and West Shariati aims to highlight the contextual particularities of Iranian society and to problematize Westerncentric metanarratives of progress. As noted previously, Shariati frequently faults Iranian intellectuals with failing to sufficiently attend to local histories and cultural

---

[36] Shariati, "Bazgasht beh khish."
[37] Shariati, "Tamadon chist?"
[38] Shariati, "Bahs-e kolli raje beh tamadon va farhang."
[39] Shariati, "Estekhraj va tasfieh manabe farhangi."
[40] Ali Shariati, "Erfan, barabari, azadi" ("Spirituality, Equality, Freedom"), 1355/1976, C.W. 2, *Ali Shariati: The Complete Collection of Works* [CD ROM], Tehran: Shariati Cultural Foundation, 2010.

nuances, and he calls on progressive social and cultural reformers to pay closer attention to the contextual determinants of Iranian society and its Eastern and Islamic civilizational heritage.[41] In this regard Shariati's concerns echo the similar preoccupations of a range of leading twentieth-century postcolonial thinkers who in challenging Western domination and Eurocentric modes of knowledge production drew attention to a precolonial state of civilizational diversity and appealed to civilizational categories such as East and West. Yet it is possible, in a critical rereading of these pioneering postcolonial contributions, to carefully consider some of the limitations of the civilizational framework and its associated categories.

Edward Said's celebrated 1978 book, *Orientalism*, is perhaps the best known systematic deconstruction of civilizational thinking and the East/West binary. In this book and elsewhere, Said presents a critical analysis of the European intellectual discipline of Orientalism and its function in the broader configuration of European colonialism in Muslim societies. According to Said, since its very beginning, European colonialism in Asia and Africa went hand-in-hand with the construction and advancement of an intellectual discourse (ultimately a discourse of power) that drew a continental and civilizational line between a powerful and superior Europe with its universal values and modes of thought, and a weak and defeated East that only became comprehensible when examined and articulated by Europe itself. In this particular civilizational construction, the West came to represent the standard of human evolution and progress, and the Orient its oppositional other.[42] In Said's view, the line which separated the Occident from the Orient in this newly manufactured civilizational discourse was less a fact of nature than of "human production" and "imaginative geography."[43]

Said believes that as categories of representation the Orient and the Occident inevitably perpetuate a kind of determinism that reduces multifaceted human dynamics to simplistic and fixed categories. His detailed analysis reveals how a wide range of European Orientalists framed not only their historiographies, but also their analyses of contemporary social and political challenges, in terms of an East/West civilizational binary.[44]

---

[41] Shariati, "Bazgasht beh kodam khish?"
[42] Edward W. Said, "Orientalism," *The Georgia Review* 31, no. 1 (Spring 1977): 170.
[43] Edward W. Said, "Orientalism Reconsidered," *Cultural Critique*, no. 1 (Autumn, 1985), 90. Also see: Edward W. Said, *Orientalism*: 25th Anniversary Edition (New York: Vintage Books, 1994), 259.
[44] Said, *Orientalism*, 270.

Said's analysis radically questions the assumption of an enduring and unchanging view of an Oriental or Occidental essence, type, or mentality, which in his view only undermines and distorts the heterogeneity, dynamism, and complexities of human realities. He shows how throughout the nineteenth and twentieth centuries a range of European Orientalists advanced a view of an inherent "ontological difference between Eastern and Western" religious, social, and economic "mentalities."[45] While the Occidental mind was defined as being rational and entrepreneurial, the Oriental mind was regarded as being antimodern and incapable of "economic rationality."[46] Moreover, in these productions the Occidental mind came to represent the maturity of human civilization and culture, and the Oriental mind its infancy. Thus, Said notes that Orientalism saw civilization as a "westwards [movement] away from Asia and towards Europe."[47]

In his critical analysis of Orientalism as a colonial discourse of power, Said makes a case for abandoning the categories of Orient and Occident and the civilizational framework in which they have been constructed.[48] The Orient and Occident, he believes, are products of a colonial geography which distorts and suppresses the plurality of lived experiences in diverse societies. Similarly, he argues that the very concept of Western civilization is essentially meaningless "except as ... an ideological fiction, implying a sort of detached superiority for a handful of values and ideas none of which has much meaning outside of the history of conquest, immigration, travel, and the mingling of peoples" that have shaped the diverse social formations and mixed identities of European societies.[49] It nevertheless appears that Said's analysis retains aspects of the civilizational framework that he himself persuasively deconstructs. As Fred Dallmayr has pointed out, throughout his study, Said juxtaposes and contrasts "the Orient as constructed by Orientalist discourses with something else elusively called the 'real Orient,' the 'true Orient,' or the 'Orient itself.'"[50] Said also makes many references to millennia-old cultural, material, and intellectual relations between the Orient and the Occident and describes the rise of European colonialism as the West's move "upon the East."[51]

[45] Ibid., 330.
[46] Ibid., 259.
[47] Said, "Orientalism Reconsidered," 94.
[48] Ibid., 95.
[49] Said, *Orientalism*, 347.
[50] Fred Dallmayr, *Beyond Orientalism: Essays on Cross-Cultural Encounter* (Albany, NY: State University of New York Press, 1996), xvi.
[51] Said, "Orientalism," 187.

In a 1985 essay titled, "Orientalism Reconsidered," Said explains that his critique of the discourse of European Orientalism should not imply that "the division between Orient and Occident ... is simply fictional." Instead, he argues, his analysis seeks to demonstrate that both entities are produced by human beings in the context of the prevailing power relations, and thus, "must be studied as integral components of the social, and not the divine or natural, world."[52]

Notwithstanding his own implicit reliance on aspects of this framework, an important feature of Said's deconstruction of civilizational thinking is his critique of the reappropriation of colonially constructed civilizational and national identities in the course of anticolonial struggles. In *Culture and Imperialism* (1993) and elsewhere, Said makes a case that resistance to colonialism and imperialism during the nineteenth and twentieth centuries has given rise to ethnic nationalism and cultural nativism around the world. For Said, these identitarian tendencies have characterized a range of responses to colonialism, from the discourse of *négritude* in Africa to the call for return to a precolonial Islamic essence in Muslim societies.[53] He argues that Eurocentrism and nativism are binary forces that "feed off each other."[54] While the latter emerges in response to the former and its colonial consequences, it nevertheless accepts and assumes "the consequences of imperialism, the racial, religious, and political divisions imposed by imperialism itself."[55] Said's analysis reveals that in nativist reappropriations of colonially imposed units of identity, the West, as a monolithic category, forever remains the singular reference point, the interlocutor, in the negotiation of local identity, in identifying and analyzing historical and ongoing challenges, and in outlining future prospects and possibilities. Though he is critical of this hostile fixation or *ressentiment* toward the West and of the nativist reproductions of colonial binaries in much of postcolonial thought, Said nevertheless remains more optimistic about the more "imaginative" liberation discourses of Aimé Césaire and Frantz Fanon and their call for a new soul and a new humanity.[56] He argues that today it is possible to negotiate "a more generous and pluralistic vision of the world," while acknowledging the existing

---

[52] Said, "Orientalism Reconsidered," 90.
[53] See: Edward W. Said, *Culture and Imperialism* (New York: Alfred A. Knopf, 1993), xxiv; Edward Said, *Orientalism*, 337–338.
[54] Said, *Culture and Imperialism*, xxiv.
[55] Ibid., 228.
[56] Ibid., 242, 307.

polarities and asymmetries of power. Drawing on Fanon, Said calls for "a transformation of social consciousness beyond national consciousness."[57]

Said is certainly not alone in calling for a departure from the categories of civilization and civilizational analysis. Critics have pointed out that in the context of nineteenth- and twentieth-century European imperialism in Africa and Asia the discourse of civilization was used to facilitate and justify imperial violence and expansionism.[58] Critics have also drawn attention to a close link between the discourse of civilization and the values of Enlightenment modernity.[59] For commentators such as Prasenjit Duara, in post-Enlightenment European thought civilization came to represent not simply a category for differentiation between distinct formations of value systems and sociopolitical and socioeconomic structures, but instead a signifier to distinguish the European self from its others through the juxtaposition of different, and sometimes clashing, communities of values.[60] According to Duara, in modern Europe "civilization" was used as a category "to identify a transnational group of Enlightened civilized nations in opposition to their colonies. The latter were seen as lacking civilization – in the sense of Enlightenment values – and hence, not worthy of sovereignty." But Duara also identifies an alternative notion of civilization that emerged in the colonized world and which challenged the Eurocentric conception of the category. According to him, the new conception, formulated in the aftermath of the disillusionment with the civilizational claims of European modernity, defined civilization in terms of cultural and historical particularities and differences. While the "civilizational discourse" of European

---

[57] Ibid., 230.
[58] See: Dipesh Chakrabarty, "From Civilization to Globalization: The 'West' as a Shifting Signifier in Indian Modernity," *Inter-Asia Cultural Studies* 13, no. 1 (2012): 138–152; Brett Bowden, *The Empire of Civilization: The Evolution of an Imperial Idea* (Chicago and London: University of Chicago Press, 2009). For other contemporary perspectives and discussions on the categories of civilization and civilizational analysis see: Harry Redner, *Beyond Civilization: Society, Culture, and the Individual in the Age of Globalization* (New Brunswick, NJ: Transaction, 2013); Peter J. Katzenstein, ed., *Civilizations in World Politics: Plural and Pluralist Perspectives* (New York: Routledge, 2010); Peter Baofu, *Beyond Civilization to Post-Civilization: Conceiving a Better Model of Life Settlement to Supersede Civilization* (New York: Peter Lang, 2006); Said Arjomand and Edward A Tiryakian, ed., *Rethinking Civilizational Analysis* (London: SAGE, 2004).
[59] See: Walter D. Mignolo, *Local Histories/Global Designs: Coloniality, Subaltern Knowledges, and Border Thinking* (Princeton, NJ: Princeton University Press, 2012), 38; Prasenjit Duara, "The Discourse of Civilization and Decolonization," *Journal of World History* 15, no. 1 (March 2004): 2.
[60] Duara, "The Discourse of Civilization," 1.

imperialism advanced a singular vision of a universal civilization, a range of non-European thinkers including Okakura Kakuzo, Gu Hongming, Liang Qichao, Rabindranath Tagore, and Mahatma Gandhi advocated the idea of "multiple civilizations." Nevertheless, Duara ultimately argues that even though these non-Western discourses of civilization served an "emancipatory" function in the course of anticolonial struggles in the postcolonial period they also gave birth to militant forms of nationalism and identitarianism.[61]

Also stressing the colonial disposition and the imperial operations of the civilizational framework, Hamid Dabashi has called for abandoning the language of civilization altogether. Expanding on Said's analysis, Dabashi argues that the non-West and particularly the Orient served an important role in the construction of the category of Western civilization. In "For the Last Time: Civilizations" (2001), Dabashi argues that European Orientalism "concocted" the categories of Islamic, Indian, and Chinese civilizations as the Oriental others of an Occidental self and as the "civilizational mirrors" of a superior West. Defined in juxtaposition with the modern West, these civilizational categories were invented "to raise the Western Civilization as the normative achievement of world history and lower all others as its abnormal antecedents."[62] In Dabashi's view, in the context of the "emerging globality" of capitalist modernity such a "metaphoric division of the world into civilizational boundaries and center and periphery no longer are valid."[63] Not only civilizational boundaries, but also the boundaries and the very legitimacy of the modern nation-state are now in question. According to Dabashi,

> At the threshold of the 21st century, the self-same capital has evolved in the global logic of its operation and the unitary basis of national economies and their colonial consequences can no longer serve as the currency of its operation. The circular spiral of capital and labor has now so ferociously destroyed the artificial national boundaries of its own making not more than 200 years ago that it is no longer possible for any claim to national economy to have a legitimate claim on operation. The result is the aggressive acculturation of individuals from their national economies and national cultures, as they are being thrown into an entirely new configuration of capital and its ever-changing cultures.[64]

---

[61] Duara, "The Discourse of Civilization," 3.
[62] Hamid Dabashi, "For the Last Time: Civilizations," *International Sociology* 16, no. 3 (September 2001): 365.
[63] Ibid., 366.
[64] Ibid., 366–367.

The appropriate response to this condition, for Dabashi, is not to resort to constructed and colonially imposed identities or to attempt to reappropriate the civilizational discourse from its colonial end. Instead, what is need is an understanding of "the new configuration of global capital and labor" as the material basis for the emergence of a culture that is "at once post-national and as a result post-civilizational."[65]

Problematizing the reproduction of modern civilizational binaries by a range of contemporary Muslim thinkers, Dabashi describes the category of "Islamic civilization" as a colonial invention which, like other civilizational categories, has been debased with the decentralization of capital. According to Dabashi, prior to the expansion of capitalist modernity in the Middle East and North Africa, "what we know of Islam as an historical practice is the simultaneous polyvocality of its discourse, polylocality of its geographical manifestations, and the polyfocality of its visions." In the course of the expansion of capitalist modernity, and as the intellectual arm of European colonialism, "Orientalism successfully suppressed [Islam's] cacophonous configuration and collectively theorized it as one particularly poignant civilizational other of 'The West.' "[66] Today, however, we can no longer speak of the Islamic civilization because the very categories of the West and Western civilization against which other civilizational categories were constructed have lost their meaning within the current configuration of global power relations. Thus, in *Islamic Liberation Theology: Resisting the Empire* (2008), Dabashi writes, "Islam can no longer speak. It has no particular interlocutor. Its once 'Western' interlocutor has now imploded, vaporized into the thin air of globalization. The world has no center, no periphery. In the absence of a civilizational other, Islam has become mute."[67] In Dabashi's view, contemporary Muslim thinkers must abandon "any intellectual engagement with Islam that is conversant with the very centrality of the notion of 'Europe,' or more specifically with the European colonial modernity,"[68] and rediscover what he calls Islam's "cosmopolitan worldliness."[69]

---

[65] Ibid., 367.
[66] Hamid Dabashi, "For the Last Time: Civilizations", in *Hegemony and Multiculturalism: Texts and Subsidies, ed.* Candido Mendes (Rio de Janeiro and Paris: Academia de la Latinidad, 2004), 138.
[67] Hamid Dabashi, *Islamic Liberation Theology: Resisting the Empire* (New York: Routledge, 2008), 111.
[68] Ibid., 100.
[69] Ibid., 99.

In a number of his works, Dabashi examines the limitations and capacities of the discourses of a number of Muslim thinkers including Shariati for contributing to the revival of Islam's "cosmopolitan worldliness" in the twenty-first century. For Dabashi, Shariati's life and intellectual productions are reflective of a constant effort to transcend the nativist and identitarian traps that characterized the discourses of many other Muslim thinkers and activists during the twentieth century and continue to do so today. Pointing to Shariati's active solidarity with Cuban and Algerian revolutionaries, his interest in Latin American Catholic liberation theology movement, and his correspondence with Frantz Fanon about the conditions for advancing anticolonial struggles in Iran and Algeria, Dabashi argues that in his "critical and creative conversation" with a diverse range of global emancipatory discourses, Shariati abandoned "nativism, regionalism, and tribalism" in favor of "a globality of learning and action."[70] By combining his strong Shi'i faith with socialism and "Sartrian existentialism," Shariati navigated "the topography of a liberation theology beyond any particular domain or denomination."[71]

In *Islamic Liberation Theology*, Dabashi draws parallels between Shariati and another prominent twentieth-century Muslim revolutionary thinker and activist, American civil rights leader Malcolm X. According to Dabashi, though they belonged to two different contexts, the Islamic liberation theologies of both Malcolm X and Shariati cultivated "cosmopolitan and transnational solidarities" which transcended the "outdated, divisive, and disabling [East/West] axis."[72] Furthermore, in the liberation discourses of these two Muslim revolutionaries Dabashi finds commonalities with the emancipatory discourses of two other leading mid-twentieth-century revolutionary thinkers and activists, Frantz Fanon and Ernesto Che Guevara. In *Post-Orientalism: Knowledge and Power in Time of Terror* (2009), he argues that despite their differences, the common denominator that connects the ideas of these exemplary twentieth century revolutionaries is "a universalized parlance sublating the particulars of their revolutionary message."[73] According to him, the "defiant hybridity and cultural inauthenticity" of Shariati, Malcolm X, Fanon,

---

[70] Ibid., 114.
[71] Hamid Dabashi, *Post-Orientalism: Knowledge and Power in Time of Terror* (New Brunswick, NJ: Transaction Publishers, 2009), 201.
[72] Dabashi, *Islamic Liberation Theology*, 115.
[73] Dabashi, *Post-Orientalism*, 201.

and Guevara "expose the colonial manufacturing of civilizational divides and cultural authenticity."[74] Nevertheless, in his final analysis Dabashi believes that in comparison with the radically transnational and transracial orientation of Malcolm X's thought after his post-pilgrimage transformation, Shariati's discourse seems to get somewhat bogged down by a "delusional configuration called 'the West.'"[75] He argues that while Malcolm X's "unfinished" liberation theology found a truly "cosmopolitan disposition" after his 1964 pilgrimage, Shariati's revolutionary anti-colonialism was "incarcerated, normatively severed, and framed – held tightly in pigeonholes like 'Iran,' 'the Middle East,' or even 'Islam.'"[76] In his view, for Shariati's revolutionary discourse to achieve its cosmopolitan potential it must avoid the trap of incarceration within the colonially manufactured and no-longer-applicable civilizational categories and binaries. A genuine conversation between diverse modes of resistance against "globalized tyranny," he maintains, requires "visualizing the normative emergence of a new geography of liberation that can no longer be bogged down on a debilitating [East/West] axis or framed and incarcerated within specific nation-states that have hitherto distorted the far more global potentials of such revolutionary Muslim liberation activists as Ali Shariati or Malcolm X."[77]

Whereas Said and Dabashi call for a total departure from the civilizational discourse and frame of analysis, a number of other commentators have articulated their simultaneous critiques of Eurocentrism and nativism without fully rejecting the category of civilization and the representational categories of East and West. Among others, Fred Dallmayr has, in numerous books and essays over the last two decades, presented an alternative account of the civilizational framework that in some ways finds common ground with Shariati's search for civilizational diversity. Though he draws on Said's deconstruction of the colonial discourse of Orientalism, Dallmayr nevertheless seeks to explore the possibilities and conditions of cross-cultural encounters "beyond Eurocentric arrogance and ... 'beyond Orientalism'."[78] As a political theorist who sees himself as being firmly grounded in the Western intellectual tradition, Dallmayr attempts to identify and revive

[74] Ibid., 195.
[75] Dabashi, *Islamic Liberation Theology*, 99.
[76] Ibid., 140.
[77] Ibid., 114.
[78] Ibid. xi.

the dialogical capacities of Western political and philosophical thought in order to make a case as well as a theoretical space for engaging in genuine dialogue with non-Western traditions of political thought and philosophy.[79]

Dallmayr acknowledges that in the context of the expansion of European colonialism the discourse of civilization has served as a discourse of power. As he puts it, "the claim of civilizational benevolence ('white man's burden') backed up by the asserted need to control backward peoples" was used as the primary justification offered in support of empires building both historically and in the contemporary period.[80] For Dallmayr then the civilizational discourse of colonialism represents a hegemonic universalism that is inherently opposed to the universal values of diversity and heterogeneity. This homogenizing tendency of hegemonic universalism, he contends, has informed the way in which the West has approached the non-West at least since the sixteenth-century Spanish colonialism in the Americas.[81] In the postcolonial context, he continues, Western economic and military hegemony has persisted, albeit in "subtler forms." In this context, he believes, the dominant discourses of civilization, universalism, and globalization have served only as smokescreens "for neocolonial forms of domination."[82]

While Dallmayr is attentive to the new global configuration of power and the decentralization of capitalism as a consequence of the globalization of markets, technology, and communication, he does not believe that the present condition has meant the end of the West or other civilizational categories. For him, the "steady advance of globalization" in the post-World War II context along with "the internal self-questioning or self-decentering of European or Western thought," which is particularly evident in contemporary Continental philosophy and its turn toward "difference" or "otherness," have contributed to the formation of a global discursive space that makes possible a different type of engagement between West and non-West.[83] According to him, the present global context is increasingly shaped by the rise of two opposing

---

[79] Ibid., iv-xix.
[80] Fred Dallmayr, "Empire or Cosmopolis? Civilization at the Crossroads," *Globalizations* 2, no. 1 (2005): 14.
[81] Dallmayr, *Beyond Orientalism*, xv.
[82] Ibid., xi.
[83] Ibid., ix.

forces or tendencies. On the one hand, he argues, there is a push to move toward "empire" and "world dictatorship," while on the other hand there is an ongoing fight to keep alive the hope of "global cooperation" and "an interdependent community of peoples (which can loosely be called 'cosmopolis')."[84] The former tendency is manifested today in the forceful expansion of the "pax-Americana" empire and neoliberal economics, which are inherently homogenizing and antidemocratic, while the latter tendency is captured by discourses that call for preserving the innate hybridity of the global arena.[85] Dallmayr believes that cultivating genuine cosmopolitanism requires moving beyond the Westerncentric and civilizational-cultural arrogance that has largely informed the interactions between West and non-West for roughly five centuries. Moreover, he maintains that true cosmopolitanism is achieved not through a "tightly unified or blandly homogeneous cosmopolis," but instead through some form of global interdependence "nurtured by local and regional centers of political agency."[86]

In making a case for a new kind of encounter between West and non-West, Dallmayr advances two distinct but interrelated lines of argumentation. On the one hand, he believes that the rejection of homogenizing universalism should not imply the assumption of "an 'essential' or unbridgeable difference between West and non-West." For him, to assume such an "essential" division is not only inaccurate in a globalized world, but also "equally misguided when applied to earlier periods." While cultural diversity is an integral component of our human society, differences in cultural norms and practices are not representations of antithetical essences, but rather the results of historical and contextual particularities. Nevertheless, he argues, the formation of all human cultures involves "a certain measure of cross-cultural learning." On the other hand, however, Dallmayr insists that "the denial of essential or invariant differences between cultures does not amount to an endorsement of essential sameness or non-distinction." In other words, for Dallmayr, the critique of essentialism should not lead to the reproduction of homogenizing universalism and unilinear and Westerncentric visions of the past, present, and future of humanity. He therefore asserts that the "ideology of sameness," articulated by Fukuyama and other defenders of the neoliberal order, "flies in the face

---

[84] Dallmayr, "Empire or Cosmopolis?," 15.
[85] Ibid., 14–16.
[86] Ibid., 14.

of diverse historical-cultural trajectories and also of profound asymmetries in the distribution of global wealth and power."[87]

Dallmayr argues that the only viable alternative to both hegemonic universalism and cultural-civilizational essentialism is to move toward a dialogical ethos of mutual recognition, which in his view is the true manifestation of the innate diversity and plurality of human cultures and civilizations. In making a case for civilizational dialogue and dialogical cross-cultural encounters, Dallmayr draws on the ideas of German philosopher Hans-Georg Gadamer, whose work, Dallmayr argues, has "shunned the telos of consensual convergence in favor of a nonassimilative stance of 'letting-be.'"[88] For Gadamer, the idea of "human solidarity" is not realized through "global uniformity" but instead, through "unity in diversity." According to him, "We must learn to appreciate and tolerate pluralities, multiplicities, cultural differences. The hegemony or unchallenged power of any single nation ... is dangerous for humanity.... Every culture, every people has something distinctive to offer for the solidarity and welfare of humanity."[89]

Building on Gadamer's discourse of civilizational dialogue, Dallmayr's work has problematized the singular conception of a world civilization, and particularly the Eurocentric notion that Western civilization represents the standard of civility. Thus, in a number of his works, including *Dialogue among Civilizations: Some Exemplary Voices* (2002), Dallmayr has made a case for a "civilizational dialogue" that gives recognition to the inherent dignity of the other. According to him, "If civilization is a frame of significance allowing members to articulate their self-understanding, then civilizational dialogue must be properly 'civilized' by considering participants in their intrinsic worth."[90] While highlighting the emancipatory capacities of this Gadamerian dialogical framework, Dallmayr's analysis is nevertheless attentive to the hegemonic and exploitative power relations that pose a challenge to the ideal of dialogue. He argues that the advocacy of "dialogue and hermeneutical interrogation" would be

---

[87] Fred Dallmayr, "Introduction: Toward a Comparative Political Theory," *The Review of Politics* 59, no. 3, Non-Western Political Thought (Summer, 1997): 423.

[88] Dallmayr, *Beyond Orientalism*, xii.

[89] Hans-Georg Gadamer quoted in Fred Dallmayr, *Beyond Orientalism*, xiii. See: Thomas Pantham, "Some Dimensions of the Universality of Philosophical Hermeneutics: A Conversation with Hans-Georg Gadamer," *Journal of Indian Council of Philosophical Research* 9 (1992): 132.

[90] Fred Dallmayr, *Dialogue among Civilizations: Some Exemplary Voices* (New York: Palgrave MacMillan, 2002), 67. Also see: Fred Dallmayr, "Globalization and Inequality: A Plea for Cosmopolitan Justice," *Comparative Studies of South Asia, Africa and the Middle East* 26, no. 1 (2006): 63.

incomplete without a close attention to "political and economic asymmetries shaping the respective status of West and non-West, of Northern and Southern hemispheres, and of 'developed' and 'developing' societies."[91]

Dallmayr's call for dialogue and the recognition of difference is echoed by a range of other contemporary commentators. In a 2002 book, titled *The Dignity of Difference: How to Avoid the Clash of Civilization*, Jonathan Sacks, whom Dallmayr quotes frequently in a number of his works, makes a case for sustained dialogue among members of all faiths in order to cultivate mutual respect and to avoid a civilizational clash. The genuine coexistence of diverse human societies, he argues, requires something beyond the formalism of "rights" or even "mere tolerance." Instead, what is needed is the recognition that "just as the natural environment depends on biodiversity, so the human environment depends on cultural diversity, because no one civilization encompasses all the spiritual, ethical and artistic expressions of mankind."[92]

Borrowing Sacks' concept of "dignity of difference," Mojtaba Mahdavi and W. Andy Knight also endorse civilizational dialogue as an alternative to discourses that view diversity and difference as a source of unending tension and conflict. Initially in an essay titled "On the 'Dignity of Difference': Neither the 'End of History' nor the 'Clash of Civilizations'" (2008) and later in an edited volume, titled *Towards the Dignity of Difference?: Neither End of History nor Clash of Civilizations* (2012), they deconstruct the hegemonic discourses of end of history and clash of civilizations, which they see as the most influential contemporary articulations of a Westerncentric vision in which the West is the superior civilization and the singular representation of the universal values of modernity, progress, and civility.[93] In critiquing the Westerncentric civilizational framework in which Huntington and Fukuyama advance their accounts, Mahdavi and Knight reject the essentialist constructions of diverse human cultures and argue for the negotiation of a third way between the extremes of universalism and particularism by presenting an alternative conception of the civilizational discourse on the basis of "self-respect and respect for the others."[94]

---

[91] Dallmayr, *Beyond Orientalism*, xvii.
[92] Jonathan Sacks, *The Dignity of Difference: How to Avoid the Clash of Civilizations* (London and New York: Continuum, 2002), 62.
[93] Mojtaba Mahdavi and Andy Knight, "On the 'Dignity of Difference': Neither the 'End of History' nor the 'Clash of Civilizations,'" *Journal for the Study of Peace and Conflict* (Winter 2008): 35.
[94] Ibid., 28.

In their view, we live in a world of "irreducible" cultural and civilizational diversity, and it is possible "to frame the issue of self/other in a manner that is representative of humanity as a whole rather than of those bent on some paternalistic civilizing mission." Furthermore, they argue that in a world shaped by the reality of de facto cultural pluralism and hybridity the categories of "Western" or "Islamic" civilization do not exist in any "coherent" way.[95] Civilizations, they assert, "are not static and impermeable." Instead, they are "malleable forms of collective consciousness always in a state of flux and evolution."[96] No civilization is a "shut-down, sealed-off" unit and no civilizational analysis can be inattentive to the internal dynamism and pluralism of distinct civilizational categories.[97] For Mahdavi and Knight, then, civilizational categories, Western or otherwise, do not exist in any monolithic or unitary way. Thus, they assert that there is "no single West" and that the category of "Western civilization" has historically been, and continues to be, "an amalgam of liberalism and fascism, democracy and dictatorship, development and underdevelopment, equality and inequality, and emancipation and racism."[98] It also follows that there is "no single Rest," and that all non-Western civilizations (African, Asian, Islamic, etc.) are themselves combinations of "differences and contradictions."[99]

While they problematize the essentialist and monolithic construction of civilizational categories, Mahdavi and Knight nevertheless see "civilizational differences" as a reality in our contemporary world. However, like Dallmayr, rather than seeing difference and diversity as a source of tension and clash, they see them as opportunities to cultivate a global cosmopolitan consciousness. They note historical interactions between different civilizations and cite as an example some of the ways in which the "Islamic civilization" and the scholarship of the likes of Al-Kindi, Al-Razi, Al-Farabi, Ibn Sina, Al-Ghazali, and Ibn Rushd contributed to the rise of "modern Western civilization."[100] Echoing Dallmayr's warning

---

[95] Mojtaba Mahdavi and Andy Knight, "Preface," in *Towards the Dignity of Difference?: Neither End of History nor Clash of Civilizations*, ed. Mojtaba Mahdavi and W. Andy Knight (London, UK: Ashgate, 2012), xxiii.

[96] Ibid., xxiv.

[97] Mojtaba Mahdavi and Andy Knight, "Introduction," in *Towards the Dignity of Difference?: Neither End of History nor Clash of Civilizations*, ed. Mojtaba Mahdavi and W. Andy Knight (London, UK: Ashgate, 2012), 5.

[98] Ibid., 5.

[99] Ibid., 6.

[100] Ibid., 8.

about the "ideology of sameness," Mahdavi and Knight problematize "the dominant tendency of seeing the future as a globalizing merger of all civilizations into one" and emphasize the possibility as well as the desirability of dialogue "among coexisting cultures in a plural world."[101] Drawing on Shariati's view about the progressive potential of revisiting and restructuring cultural-civilizational resources, they make a case that the ideal of recognition of difference requires that every culture enters "in critical dialogue with its own traditions" and articulates the universal values of a common humanity (i.e., freedom, equality, justice, democracy) "in a local language" in order to facilitate their implementation through local and homegrown institutions.[102]

Civilizational Analysis in Neo-Shariati Thought

As the previous chapters argued, neo-Shariatis reject the reading of Shariati's thought as a nativist discourse of Occidentalism. Their rereading of Shariati stresses, on the one hand, his repudiation of the view of Western modernity as the universal standard of human civilization, and on the other hand, his critique of identitarian discourses that call for a total rejection of modernity and the revival of an authentic cultural and civilizational past. While they acknowledge that the civilizational categories of East and West occupy a central place in Shariati's thought, neo-Shariatis dismiss the charge that the categories represent binary opposites or fixed and clashing essences. In their view, Shariati's particular articulation of the civilizational frame of analysis reveals an effort to transcend the dichotomous discourses of Orientalism and Occidentalism, and to advance a vision of civilizational dialogue. In its neo-Shariati reading, then, Shariati's civilizational discourse finds overlaps with the civilizational discourses of Gadamer and Dallmayr and their calls for the recognition of difference and cooperative coexistence. Nevertheless, it may be argued that in their attempt to go beyond Shariati's immediate discourse neo-Shariatis also find common ground with the critical discourses of Said, Dabashi, and other critics of civilizational thinking.

According to Sara Shariati, though Shariati uses the categories to highlight the contextual particularities of Iranian society and the inadequacy of the Eurocentric frames of analysis, he nevertheless goes beyond the

[101] Ibid., 17.
[102] Ibid., 14.

essentialist construction of East and West in Orientalist and Occidentalist discourses. She draws parallels between Shariati's treatment of East and West and the ideas of a range of twentieth-century Western scholars of Islamic thought including Louis Massignon, Henry Corbin, Henri Laoust, William Montgomery Watt, Jacques Berque, and Maxime Rodinson, who all emphasized the existence of historical and sustained interconnections and interactions between the eastern and western sides of the Mediterranean region and rejected the view of East and West as essentially dissimilar civilizational categories characterized by irreconcilable differences. In her view, without denying that civilizational categories represent certain historical, social, and political particularities, Shariati is convinced that the realization of the promise of a new humanity and a new civilization necessitates a simultaneous reclaiming of East and West and the unveiling of their historical coconstitution and their mutual influences on one another.[103]

Similarly, Ehsan Shariati believes that while Shariati's thought is attentive to the particularities of the historical formations of East and West, it does not accept the essentialist and deterministic conceptions of the two categories.[104] Shariati, he argues, offers a third way between an uncritical embrace of the East in the name of local religious and cultural traditions (i.e., fundamentalism), and a blind embrace of the West in the name of modernity, progress, and civilization (i.e., Westerncentrism).[105] Susan Shariati also holds that in Shariati's thought East and West are neither polar opposites nor reducible to any singular and predetermined historical process or fixed cultural essence.[106] She makes a case that by rejecting the essentialist construction of the East/West binary, "Shariati seeks to avoid a deterministic view of civilizational difference and to provide a dialogical space for mutual engagement and exchange."[107] She also points

[103] Sara Shariati, interview by author (telephone), November 28, 2012.
[104] "Mizgerd-e dovom nashrieh nasim-e bidar. dar bar-rasi shenakht shakhsiat Shariati," ("Nasim-e Bidariy's Second Panel on Examining Shariati's Character"), Ali Shariati Information Center (no date), http://drshariati.org/show/?id=213 (accessed December 11, 2012).
[105] Ehsan Shariati, interview by Hossein (Mesbahian) Rahyab, no date (unpublished).
[106] Susan Shariati, "Moghadameh: tafakor dar taghato" ("Introduction: Thinking at Crossroads"), in Faramarz Motamed-Dezfooli, *Kavir: tajrobeh moderniteh irani: tafsir va bazkhani kavir doktor ali shariati (The Desert: The Experience of Iranian Modernity: Revisiting and Reinterpreting Dr. Ali Shariati's The Desert)* (Tehran: Ghalam, 1387), 13.
[107] Susan Shariati, "Dar mian-e do-ganeh-hay-e terajik: shariati olgoo ya ravesh" ("Between Tragic Binaries: Shariati, Model or Method?"), *Shargh*, 29 Khordad 1386/June 19, 2007, http://drshariati.org/show/?id=36 (accessed April 13, 2011).

out that for Shariati the prerequisite for such a dialogue is a radical and concurrent critique of "Westernism" and "Easternism." In her reading, rather than embracing one and rejecting the other Shariati sees himself as standing between East and West and "refusing the binary choice."[108] Quoting Shariati that "to be a human is to be in a state of suspense between one's own East and West," she argues that for Shariati more than representing two separate geographical entities, East and West represent two "unfinished projects" and "existential orientations" that complement one another.[109]

In articulating their own account of indigenous modernity, neo-Shariatis often refer to Shariati's idea of the 'extraction and refinement' of local civilizational resources as the basis for the negotiation of an alternative to Enlightenment modernity. At the same time, for neo-Shariatis any engagement with local cultures and traditions must be paired with an attentiveness to the global imposition of the condition of modernity, the interdependence between local and global patterns of change, and the reality of cultural hybridity and flux. Thus, Ehsan Shariati maintains while there exist differences in worldview (*Weltanschauung*) between Western and non-Western thought, addressing common human challenges, from environmental degradation to human alienation and atomization, require cooperation and engagement beyond national and cultural boundaries.[110] For Sara Shariati, too, the project of returning to and reorienting local identity must be advanced with a view to the interconnection between the local and the global. In her view, as a consequence of the globalization of capital and technology and the rise of various forms of resistance against this movement in recent decades, homogenization and fragmentation have become the two dominant orientations of the modern world. The former orientation is manifested in Fukuyama's end of history thesis and the metanarratives of modernization and secularization, while the latter orientation is evident in Huntington's clash thesis and a wide range of identitarian movements and discourses around the world.[111]

---

[108] Susan Shariati, "Moghadameh," 13.
[109] Ali Shariati, quote in Susan Shariati, "Moghadameh," 12.
[110] Ehsan Shariati, interview by Hossein (Mesbahian) Rahyab, no date (unpublished).
[111] Sara Shariati, "Chehreh jahani-gar, chehreh jahani-zadeh: siasat jahani kardan va ravand tarikhi jahani shodan" ("The Globalizer Face and the Globalized Face: An Evaluation of Globalizing Policies and the Process of Globalization"), in *Khodkavi-e melli dar asr-e jahani shodan (National Self-Examination in the Age of Globalization)*, ed. Bonyad Shariati (Tehran: Ghasidehsara, 1381/2002), 147–148.

For neo-Shariatis, responding to the postcolonial calls of Fanon and Shariati for developing an alternative to Europe and the United States in the Third World requires, on the one hand, attending to the universal values and the global concerns of a common humanity, and on the other hand, giving recognition to and critically engaging with the cultural-civilizational particularities of each society.[112] As Hossein Mesbahian puts it, without a "universalist" vantage point, "particularism" only serves "to undermine the broader demand for equality and becomes a form of self-imposed segregation limiting the local culture's prospects for reinvention and eventually leading to its demise."[113] Particularist approaches, in his view, are incapable of addressing common human challenges which are the products of the globalization of certain sociopolitical and socioeconomic formations. At the same time, however, he argues that taken to its extreme, universalism becomes a form of forceful homogenization of the world which only reinforces the relations of domination and exploitation that European colonialism initially introduced. Thus, in his view, a project of indigenous modernity is simultaneously a radical critique of essentialism and nativism, and a call for the recognition of difference. For Mesbahian, while difference is informed by the distinct modes of civilizational and cultural particularity, the mutual recognition of difference requires articulating particularity and difference in universally negotiated terms.[114]

In much the same way as their engagement with other aspects of his thought, in rereading Shariati's civilizational discourse neo-Shariatis seek to go beyond Shariati by identifying his limitations, blind spots, and unthoughts. As discussed in previous chapters, though neo-Shariatis embrace the call for a return to the local sources of the self and the indigenous epistemological and ontological resources of the Iranian-Islamic civilizational heritage, they nevertheless believe that Shariati's project must be critically revisited in light of the emergence of Islamism and other nativist articulations of postcoloniality in the latter half of the twentieth century. Neo-Shariati figures such as Sara Shariati and Reza Alijani also point out that the acceleration of the processes of globalization in recent decades has brought important changes to the global configurations of

---

[112] Ibid., 170–174.
[113] Hossein (Mesbahian) Rahyab, "Mahiat, mavane' va emkanat-e no-sazi-e hoviat-e irani" (Nature, Possibilities and Challenges of the Restructuring of Iranian Identity), in *Khodkavi-e melli dar asr-e jahani shodan (National Self-Examination in the Age of Globalization)*, ed. Bonyad Shariati (Tehran: Ghasidehsara, 1381/2002), 7.
[114] Hossein Mesbahian, interview by author (Internet/ooVoo), April 23, 2013.

power. Noting that Shariati developed his discourse in a context where the East/West binary was widely used by various commentators, they suggest that the framework may no longer provide an accurate picture of the prevailing global power asymmetries. Sara Shariati, for example, believes that although in his own era Shariati sought to critically reconceptualize the categories of East and West, the realities of the modern world necessitate questioning and moving beyond the logic of civilizational thinking. She acknowledges that while for Shariati and many of his contemporaries the categories of East and West served as the symbolic representations of Islam and Europe, in today's world neither Islam nor Europe exist in any coherent, uniform, and monolithic forms.[115] Alijani also believes that in many ways the civilizational framework may be outmoded and in need of serious reconsideration. According to him, whereas in the colonial context the categories of East and West sought to highlight cultural, philosophical, and historical differences between Europe and non-Europe, in the postcolonial world the North/South framework provides a new and more useful lens through which to analyze economic, political, and military relations between developed and underdeveloped societies. Alijani notes that even though the North/South binary is itself contested, its analytical lens and its focus on the economic relations of domination and exploitation may provide a wider space in which to expand on Shariati's transnational solidarities with the struggles of the marginalized and oppressed groups around the world.[116]

Reworking the Framework

Though Shariati uses the categories of "civilizational rise" and "civilizational decline" to explain the emergence of Western modernity and the expansion of European colonialism in Asia and Africa, his analysis is also attentive to the centrality of colonial and imperial domination in shaping relations between the West and its civilizational others. Shariati's close attention to the cultural, social, political, and economic aspects of colonialism and imperialism, his emphasis on civilizational diversity, and his call for the reclaiming of local cultural-civilizational resources, find common ground with the discourses of many other postcolonial thinkers in the mid-twentieth century. As Ashis Nandy points out, in the course of national liberation struggles during this period, the revival

---

[115] Sara Shariati, interview.
[116] Reza Alijani, interview by author (Internet/Skype), November 20, 2012.

and reaffirmation of cultural traditions came to be seen as the heart and soul of authentic anticolonialism.[117] In his writings and lectures, Shariati himself makes numerous references to what he sees as the emancipatory postcolonialism of Gandhi, Nyerere, César, Fanon, and others. The concurrent emergence of these discourses across the Third World, he argues, reveals on the one hand the decline of Western hegemony and its corresponding colonial modernity, and on the other hand the possibility of reviving a civilizational diversity that colonialism sought to eliminate.

Critics may rightly charge that Shariati's advocacy of a postcolonial reclaiming of indigenous sources of identity was not always attentive to the often oppressive social and political consequences of such projects. As the analyses of Said, Duara, Dabashi, and a number of other contemporary scholars have revealed, in various parts of the global South postcoloniality took the form of militant nativism and anti-Westernism. In postrevolutionary Iran, to take one relevant example, the discourses of indigeneity and return to the self were effectively hijacked by the country's Islamist rulers and turned into discourses of power and oppression. However, if Shariati himself was not alive to see this nativist turn in his homeland and elsewhere, in their radical critique of Islamism and other forms of identitarianism, his present-day followers in Iran have sought to draw a clear demarcation between his emancipatory vision for a postcolonial world and the oppressive and nativist articulations of postcoloniality.

For neo-Shariatis, Shariati's idea of an indigenous modernity, with its overall civilizational framework, represents neither a total rejection of Western modernity nor a total embrace of the native self. Instead, they argue, by calling for a critical and selective approach toward both the local sources of identity and the global condition of modernity, one based on the recognition of cultural flux and hybridity, Shariati seeks to transcend the prevailing oppositional binaries of tradition/modernity, Islam/modernity, Islam/West, and East/West. In revisiting what they see as his unfinished project, neo-Shariatis also reject the reading of Shariati's civilizational discourse as a discourse of Occidentalism. They maintain that by critiquing the monolithic and essentialist constructions of the categories of East and West, Shariati tries to establish a new (dialogical) relationship between these two hegemonic categories and to transcend

---

[117] Ashis Nandy, "Cultural Frames for Social Transformation: A Credo," in *Between Tradition and Modernity: India's Search for Identity: A Twentieth Century Anthology*, ed. Fred Dallmayr, G. N. Devy (Delhi: Altamira Press, 1998), 251.

the dichotomous discourses of Orientalism and Occidentalism. In their view, Shariati's discourse of religious and cultural reform provides a general outline not only for negotiating contextually grounded projects of sociocultural and sociopolitical development in the particular context of Iranian society, but also for moving toward a postcolonial discourse of cosmopolitanism and civilizational dialogue.

Shariati's and neo-Shariatis' vision of postcolonial cosmopolitanism finds shared ground with the discourses of a number of contemporary Western and non-Western scholars who call for cultural and civilizational dialogue as a way out of the destructive dichotomy between the extremes of universalism and particularism. In this regard, the contributions of Fred Dallmayr may be particularly relevant. While advancing a radical critique of Orientalism and Occidentalism, Dallmayr's work nevertheless highlights the possibility of non-monolithic, nonhierarchical, and antiessentialist modes of differentiation in dealing with diverse social, cultural, and traditional entities. Using Dallmayr's argument about the possibility of and the conditions for cross-cultural interactions beyond Orientalism and Occidentalism, a case may be made that Shariati's proposal for return to the self represents not a Laclauian notion of "self-apartheid,"[118] but rather a contextually negotiated entry point into a broader global space of resistance against and emancipation from all relations of domination and exploitation. In this view, Shariati's extraction and refinement of the pertinent and progressive capacities of local cultural and religious traditions for advancing radical social and political change on the basis of universal values of freedom, equality, and spirituality signifies not an unmitigated rejection of universalism, but rather a move from the particular to the universal. It is precisely this feature of Shariati's thought which gives it a transnational and global quality, while simultaneously making it context-specific and locally grounded.

While Dallmayr's contributions may be particularly useful for identifying the progressive capacities of the civilizational framework in which Shariati and neo-Shariatis outline their project of indigenous modernity, attentiveness to the radical critique of the East/West binary and the category of civilization by Said and others may help to highlight some of the limitations of this framework. I have shown in this book that for Shariati's present-day followers the project of indigenous modernity aims not only

---

[118] Ernesto Laclau, *Emancipation(s)* (New York: Verso, 1996), 32, quoted in Mojtaba Mahdavi, "Beyond Culturalism and Monism: The Iranian Path to Democracy," *Iran Analysis Quarterly* 2, no. 3 (Winter 2005): 3.

to advance a contextually grounded (Iranian) discourse of modernity, but also to identify an alternative (Islamic) ontology to that of Enlightenment thought on the basis of which to negotiate a more humane vision of modernity. Still, as I discussed before, in critiquing the hegemonic conceptualization of the categories of East and West, Said and others challenge the very claim of an inherent ontological difference between Western and Oriental or Islamic cultures and societies. Moreover, Dabashi's salient reminder about the historical "polyvocality," "polylocality," and "polyfocality" of Muslim discourses, geographies, and visions questions whether it is at all possible to speak of the categories of Islam, Islamic civilization, or Islamic thought in any clear and coherent sense. This doubt, as mentioned earlier, is also shared by other scholars such as Mahdavi and Knight, as well as by some neo-Shariatis including Sara Shariati.

A key question that emerges upon the acknowledgment of the limitations of civilizational thinking, and one which neo-Shariatis are yet to adequately answer, is whether it is possible to continue to speak of a particular Islamic ontology as the potential basis for negotiating an alternative to Enlightenment modernity. Or is it perhaps more appropriate to speak of diverse (even contesting) Islamic ontologies and worldviews, the same way that today we speak of Islams and modernities? Another, and somewhat related, question that arises here is whether the search for an alternative or indigenous ontology for developing contextually negotiated sociopolitical and socioeconomic visions of progressive change in Iran and other Muslim societies must be confined only to the religious traditions of these societies? Arguably, neo-Shariatis have been more attentive than Shariati himself to the non-Islamic sources of Iranian identity, and in their new readings of Shariati's discourse of return to the self they have sought to advance a critical engagement with pre-Islamic Iranian history as well as the modern sources of the contemporary Iranian self. However, as the discussion in the present chapter illustrates, the very claim that Islam constitutes the primary component of a collective Iranian identity remains a contested notion that cannot be simply assumed, and which demands careful observation and critical reflection.

Finally, one may ask, as Dabashi does, whether Shariati's civilizational framework and the centrality of the categories of Islam and West in his thought distort or undermine the far more global potential of his revolutionary discourse. It was already noted that for neo-Shariatis, Shariati's critique of colonial modernity and his engagement with other postcolonial and anticolonial discourses of emancipation from a particularly Eastern, Islamic, and Iranian vantage point represent an attempt to avoid the trap of false universalism, or what Dallmayr calls the ideology of sameness. Nevertheless, it may also be suggested that expanding on Shariati's transnational solidarities and cosmopolitan engagements necessitates entering into and broadening the sites of dialogue with a wide range of global emancipatory and progressive discourses that are today contributing to the negotiation of pluralistic visions of the world beyond any constructed civilizational, cultural, religious, and national boundaries.

Conclusion
Toward a Postcolonial Cosmopolitanism

A Postcolonial Reclaiming of Islam and Modernity

In their revisiting of Ali Shariati's thought and legacy in postrevolutionary Iran, neo-Shariatis have contributed to the critical deconstruction of the Islam/modernity, tradition/modernity, and East/West binaries that have framed debates about the patterns of sociopolitical and sociocultural change in Muslim societies since the late nineteenth century. In this revisiting, neo-Shariatis have also advanced an account of Shariati's thought as an alternative, anticolonial, and indigenous conception of modernity in Persianate and Islamicate contexts. As I have shown in the preceding pages, Shariati's critical engagement with colonial modernity was itself shaped in cross-cultural dialogues with other global emancipatory discourses advocating pluralistic visions of the world beyond the clashing yearnings for hegemony and essentialism. These cross-cultural dialogues and alternative visions have harbingered a paradigm shift in the historiography and genealogy of modernity in the global South which has unsettled the universalistic claims of European modernity and its Enlightenment project.

The view of incompatibility between Islam and modernity (or clash between East and West) that continues to resurface in contemporary debates works against the logic of interconnectedness, pluralism, and dialogue. Such binary thinking is predicated on a particular Eurocentric narrative of modernity that has been dominant in much of the post-Enlightenment Western thought. In this view, modernity is an exclusively Occidental phenomenon and the modern West represents the height of human civilizational, cultural, artistic, philosophical, social, political, scientific, and economic achievements. It was this Eurocentric narrative of modernity that informed Hegel's conception of the modern West as the maturation of human reason and the exclusive site of human self-consciousness.[1] A similar view was also held by Weber, for whom, even though non-Western civilizations (particularly those in India, China, Babylonia, and Egypt) had historically contributed to the production of knowledge, it was only Western thought and science that could be considered as truly universal. In particular, Weber believed that what set modern Europe apart from all other civilizations was the former's rational organization of sociopolitical and socioeconomic relations, which was itself rooted in the "specific and peculiar rationalism of Western culture."[2] Throughout the twentieth century, this Eurocentric narrative of modernity was reproduced in various disciplines of humanities and social sciences, and it continues to be reproduced today by a range of prominent scholars and commentators. For Francis Fukuyama, for instance, the modern West and its liberal democratic norms and institutions represent nothing short of the final and universal model of human civilization.[3] And for Jürgen Habermas, modernity remains an essentially European development and inseparable from "Occidental rationalism."[4]

While Eurocentric conceptions of modernity continue to resurface in some of the contemporary scholarly and mainstream debates, there has also existed a sustained attempt by various Western and non-Western commentators to move away from this hegemonic framework and to identify alternative visions of (as well as to) modernity. As a result of this persistent effort, we have in recent years and decades witnessed, in Immanuel Wallerstein's words, an ongoing "paradigmatic shift ... in the basic historiography of modernity."[5] In their contributions, prominent scholars like Wallerstein himself, Enrique Dussel, and others have drawn attention to the colonial underside or the dark side of modernity.

---

[1] Enrique Dussel, "World-System and 'Trans'-Modernity," in *Nepantla: Views from South* 3, no. 2 (2002): 222.
[2] Max Weber, *The Protestant Ethics and the Spirit of Capitalism: The Relationship between Religion and the Economic and Social life in Modern Culture*, trans. Talcott Parsons (New York: Charles Scribner's Sons, 1958), 26.
[3] Francis Fukuyama, "The End of History," *The National Interest* no. 16, (Summer 1989): 4
[4] Jürgen Habermas, *The Theory of Communicative Action*, vol. 1, *Reason and Rationalization of Society*, trans. Thomas McCarthy (Boston, MA: Beacon Press, 1984), 7.
[5] Immanuel Wallerstein, "*Eurocentrism and its Avatars: The Dilemmas of Social Science*," *New Left Review* 226, (1997): 96.

A Postcolonial Reclaiming of Islam and Modernity 167

For Dussel, the discourse of modernity is intimately connected to the European colonial project that began in the fifteenth century and that in the course of its expansion dominated and subsumed all other world cultures and civilizations.[6] Without taking into account this colonial history, he argues, the Eurocentric historiography of modernity sees the modern West as the product of internal processes of change within Europe that originate in ancient Greece and Rome and continue in the various stages of Europe's history. According to Dussel, this Eurocentric framework reduces all of world history into the course of the "becoming" of Europe, as if "Europe had been chosen by Destiny as the final meaning of universal history."[7]

Other scholars, such as Sanjay Subrahmanyam, have challenged the Eurocentric construction of the discourse of modernity by advancing an account of modernity as a global condition with diverse histories and a multiplicity of normative and structural constellations.[8] By drawing attention to precolonial experiences of what we know today as the modern patterns of sociopolitical and socioeconomic change in various parts of Eurasia and other civilizational zones Subrahmanyam's conception of modernity as a "global shift" and other alternative conceptions such as the newly emerged framework of multiple modernities seek to delink modernity from the particular trajectory of modern Europe. Others yet, have challenged the Eurocentric discourses of modernity by problematizing the claim that European colonialism was responsible for introducing modernity to non-Westerners. Hamid Dabashi, for instance, has done this by distinguishing between "colonial" and "anti-colonial" conceptions of modernity.[9] According to Dabashi, in the non-Western world modernity, defined in such terms as individual and collective sociopolitical agency, civil society, and notions of historical progress, has not been achieved through the violent and destructive force of colonialism or by "aping or mimicking Europe," but in the course of the resistance against Europe's colonial modernity.[10]

---

[6] Enrique Dussel, *The Underside of Modernity: Apel, Ricoeur, Rorty, Taylor, and the Philosophy of Liberation*, trans. Eduardo Mendieta (Atlantic Highland, NJ: Humanities Press, 1996), 131.
[7] Dussel, "World-System and 'Trans'-Modernity," 222.
[8] Sanjay Subrahmanyam, "Connected Histories: Notes towards a Reconfiguration of Early Modern Eurasia," *Modern Asian Studies* 31, no. 3 (1997): 737.
[9] Hamid Dabashi, *Iran: A People Interrupted* (New York: New Press, 2007), 217–218, 253.
[10] Hamid Dabashi, "An Interview with Hamid Dabashi," ZNet, September 22, 2009, www.zcommunications.org/an-interview-with-hamid-dabashi-by-hamid-dabashi (accessed February 21, 2013). In more recent works including in *The World of Persian Literary*

Like many other critics of European modernity Shariati makes a normative distinction between the legacies of the Reformation, the Renaissance, and the Enlightenment, and the trajectory and consequences of European colonialism and globalized capitalism. Thus, even as he critiques the devastating impact of the latter two on the people of the global South, Shariati seeks to identify the progressive aspects of the diverse experiences of European modernity. In particular he is attentive to historical processes that facilitated the rise of modern humanism and the recognition of human subjectivity in Europe, and the implications of such processes in a global context shaped by the hegemonic expansion of the Western colonial and capitalist order. Still, in identifying what he regards as the emancipatory or lofty consequences of modernity, Shariati dismisses the suggestion that such developments were Western civilizational achievements and the exclusive products of an Occidental rationalism. To this end, he draws attention to non-European traditions of rationalism and humanism and to the cross-cultural makeup of the accumulated knowledges and processes of change that have come to be associated monolithically with the category of Western modernity. On the basis of this analysis he concludes that negotiating a postcolonial or indigenous vision of modernity requires working against the colonial logic of homogenizing universalism, giving recognition to cultural and civilizational diversity and heterogeneity, and engaging critically with local knowledges, practices, and sensibilities. For Shariati, the refinement and restructuring of local traditions and knowledge sources is the basis not only for a sustained project of modernity and development from within, but also for arriving at a postcolonial vision of cosmopolitanism.

If, as Wallerstein argues, we have in fact entered a new phase in the historiography of modernity, then Shariati must certainly be recognized on as one of the pioneers of this paradigmatic shift in the Muslim world. As I have argued in this book, however, Shariati's postcolonial reclaiming

---

Humanism (2012) Dabashi proposes a total departure from the discourse of modernity and for the negotiation not of alternative modernities but of alternatives to modernity. Despite this discursive shift, there remains in Dabashi's work a dialogical convergence with Shariati's thought, particularly as Dabashi appeals to the category of humanism and examines the differential modes of the construction of human subjectivity in Persian literary tradition and European philosophy. In fact, Dabashi's notion of a "contingent subject" in Persian literary humanism (one which at once asserts and withholds its subjectivity) finds affinity with Shariati's mediated subjectivity which was discussed in Chapter 4. See: Hamid Dabashi, *The World of Persian Literary Humanism* (Cambridge, MA: Harvard University Press, 2012), 187, 306.

of Islam and modernity is itself part of a historical and ongoing effort by Muslim modernists and reformists to advance contextually grounded discourses of modern sociocultural and sociopolitical change. In this effort, Muslim modernists and reformists from Afghani, Abduh, and Iqbal to Arkoun, Abu Zayd, Gülen, and Soroush have rejected the mutually exclusive binary of Islam and modernity and called for reciprocal recognition and synthesis. In developing their discourses of indigenous modernity, these modernists and reformists have also launched an effort to simultaneously reclaim modernity from the monopoly of Europe and Eurocentric modernists, and Islam from the monopoly of traditional Muslim ulama and agents of nativism and culturalism.

Indigenous Modernity and the Post-Islamist Turn

In the late 2000s and early 2010s, the Middle East and North Africa region witnessed the emergence of a host of popular uprisings with predominantly democratic demands. These included the Green Movement in Iran, a wave of revolutions across the Arab world known in the West as the Arab Spring, and a popular protest movement in Turkey dubbed the Gezi Revolt or the Turkish Spring. The rise of these movements was regarded by some as the beginning of the latest or the fourth wave of democratization in the modern world.[11] Drawing parallels between the Arab revolutions of the second decade of the twenty-first century and the Latin American social movements of the century's first decade, prominent political theorists Michael Hardt and Antonio Negri described the developments in the Middle East and North Africa as the opening of a new chapter in democratic experiences with potential implications far beyond the region.[12] Others noted that such developments are indicative of a much broader change in the prevailing social and cultural attitudes of the people of the region and a deep and ongoing ontological and epistemological shift that will continue to shape social and political life in Muslim

---

[11] See: Stephen R Grand, "Starting in Egypt: The Fourth Wave of Democratization?," Washington, DC: Brookings Institution, February 10, 2011, www.brookings.edu/research/opinions/2011/02/10-egypt-democracy-grand (accessed January 7, 2013); Philip N. Howard and Muzammil M. Hussain, *Democracy's Fourth Wave? Digital Media and the Arab Spring* (New York: Oxford University Press, 2013).

[12] Michael Hardt and Antonio Negri, "Arabs are Democracy's New Pioneers," The Guardian – Comment is Free, February 24, 2011, www.guardian.co.uk/commentisfree/2011/feb/24/arabs-democracy-latin-america (accessed April 11, 2013).

societies in the years to come. Thus, one observer described the emergence of the Green Movement and the Arab Spring as nothing short of a "discursive paradigm shift" and as "the most important historical [development] in the region in the postcolonial era."[13] But what do these experiences (some by now effectively suppressed, others still ongoing) tell us about the relationship between religion and modernity in contemporary Muslim societies? And what insights are offered by Shariati's thought and its new readings for making sense of the ongoing changes and identifying their challenges and prospects? To fully answer these questions requires a detailed analysis of the ongoing events in the region, and is thus beyond the scope of this conclusion. What I wish to do here is to simply offer some preliminary observations along the lines of the arguments made earlier.

For some commentators, the recent developments confirm once again the inadequacy of normative frameworks that assume an inherent tension and clash between Islam and modernity. They point out that the emergence of popular uprisings with democratic demands debunks the thesis of Islamic exceptionalism, which posits that Muslim cultures and societies are exceptionally resistant to modernity and the ideas of secularism, democracy, and human rights and freedoms. These developments, it is argued, also reject the view that democratic changes in Muslim societies are unlikely to occur organically and without Western support or intervention. Moreover, the rise of the Green Movement and the Arab Spring is interpreted as an indication of the decline of Islamism as a sociopolitical condition as well as a mode of social and political mobilization.[14] What we are witnessing, it is suggested, is a shift away from Islamism as the dominant condition and mode of action in various Muslim societies throughout the 1970s and 1980s and toward an era of "post-Islamism."[15] What is meant by post-Islamism, of course, is not the end of the public role of religion in the social and political life of Muslim societies. On the contrary, post-Islamism refers to a condition in which religion maintains an active presence within the public sphere.[16] At the same time, however,

---

[13] Mojtaba Mahdavi, "Middle East has Truly Reached Turning Point," *Edmonton Journal*, 12, March 12, 2011, www2.canada.com/edmontonjournal/news/ideas/story.html?id=824ac4a2-5a7e-4974-a8d4-a5bc049e145f (accessed March 28, 2013).

[14] See: Hamid Dabashi, *The Arab Spring: The End of Postcolonialism* (London and New York: Zed Books, 2012).

[15] Asef Bayat, "The Post-Islamist Revolutions: What the Revolts in the Arab World Mean?" *Foreign Affairs* – Snapshots, 26, April 26, 2011, www.foreignaffairs.com/articles/67812/asef-bayat/the-post-islamist-revolutions (accessed April 9, 2013).

[16] Ibid.

post-Islamism implies moving away from Islamism's binary construction of Islam and modernity and its attempt to find Islamic alternatives to all things modern. Thus, for Asef Bayat, who is often credited with coining the phrase, post-Islamism constitutes not a shift from Islamic faith toward ontological and epistemological secularism, but instead, "a complex process of breaking from an Islamist ideological package by adhering to a different, more inclusive, kind of religious project in which Islam nevertheless continues to remain important both as faith and as a player in the public sphere."[17] In the new post-Islamist framework, Bayat argues, Muslims can confidently remain Muslim while also demanding citizenship rights within a "democratic state" and a "pious society."[18]

In the context of the ongoing shift to post-Islamism, the brand of indigenous modernity that Shariati and neo-Shariatis advocate appears to be particularly well-positioned for addressing some of the pressing issues which Muslim societies are faced with today. One of these issues is the relationship between religion and state, and the precise nature of the public role of religion. As Bayat and others have noted, the emergence of post-Islamist visions does not automatically mean a harmonious and tension-free relationship between religion and politics. On the one hand, it is a fact that the demands of the Green Movement and the Arab uprisings were predominantly secular and democratic. One of the major demands of these movements, which found clear articulations in the main slogans of the Green Movement, *ray-e man kojast?* (where is my vote?), and of the Arab Spring, *al sha'b yurid isqat al-nizam* (the people want the system to fall), was the recognition of the democratic principle of popular sovereignty. And unlike the Islamist movements of the 1970s and 1980s, these recent movements did not call for the establishment of Islamic states.[19] On the other hand, however, religion remains a vital political force in post-Green Movement Iran and in post-Arab Spring Tunisia, Egypt, Libya, and elsewhere. Islamic parties were the major winners of the immediate postrevolution elections in Tunisia and Egypt (though they eventually conceded power to secular parties, in Tunisia through a democratic election and in Egypt through a military coup), and in both countries

---

[17] Asef Bayat, "Post-Islamism at Large," in *Post-Islamism: The Many Faces of Political Islam*, ed. Asef Bayat (New York: Oxford University Press, 2013), 25–26.
[18] Bayat, "The Post-Islamist Revolutions."
[19] It was quite telling when after the 2010–2011 Tunisian uprising which ousted the country's long-time dictator Zine El Abidine Ben Ali, Rachid al-Ghannouchi, the leader of Tunisia's main Islamist party, Islamic Nahda, explicitly rejected the Iranian model of the Islamic state and declined to run for president.

the question of sharia law and its compatibility or incompatibility with secular law was a contentious issue in the aftermath of the formation of new, democratically elected governments.[20] Furthermore, as Bayat notes, the recent rise of the conservative Salafi movements in several countries in the region suggests that "the possibility of a renewed fundamentalism" remains a realistic issue in various Muslim societies.[21]

Given the historical experiences of many Muslim societies with colonial modernity and authoritarian secularism, it is quite likely that even with a post-Islamist turn many Muslims will continue to articulate their religious and political discourses in opposition to a host of modern concepts including secularism and democracy. Like the discourses of other leading contemporary Muslim reformists such as Arkoun, Abu Zayd, Gülen, Soroush, and others, the neo-Shariati discourse has sought to advance contextually grounded and religiously mediated conceptions of popular sovereignty, secularism, democracy, and equal citizenship, and in doing so it has contributed to the ongoing shift from Islamism to post-Islamism in the particular context of postrevolutionary Iran. To the extent that in today's Muslim societies religion remains one of the primary sources of individual and collective identity and a major sociocultural factor in ongoing social and political processes of change, the continuation of the Islamic reform projects of indigenous modernity by neo-Shariatis and other Muslim reformers appears to be an indispensable component of any progressive vision of sociopolitical development.

In some ways, however, the neo-Shariati discourse may be argued to have an advantage over other, competing, discourses of indigenous

---

[20] The 2013 toppling of Muhammad Morsi's government in Egypt in the aftermath of a popular uprising and the clashes between the opponents and the supporters of the Muslim Brotherhood following the July 3 military takeover revealed both the prospects and the challenges of the transition to democracy in the post-Islamist context. On the one hand, the participation of an unprecedented number of Egyptians in the anti-Morsi demonstrations across the country was indicative of the disillusionment of many religious and secular Egyptians with Islamist discourses and politics. On the other hand, however, the events served as a reminder that despite this crisis Islamist parties and organizations remain important forces in the social and political life of Egypt and other Muslim societies. It remains to be seen what role the Muslim Brotherhood and other Islamic parties (from the more moderate Al-Wasat to the more conservative Al-Watan, or Al-Raya) may potentially play in future social and political changes in Egypt. However, to the extent that the historical experiences of Egypt and other Muslim countries in the region may be any indication, the suppression of Islamic parties and the imposition of restrictions on their activities in the public sphere often lead to their further radicalization and create additional challenges in the path toward progressive social and political change.

[21] Bayat, "The Post-Islamist Revolutions."

modernity in contemporary Islamicate contexts. For one thing, following Shariati's example, in developing their religiously mediated and contextually grounded accounts of secularism and democracy neo-Shariatis maintain a critical position vis-à-vis Western-style liberal democracy, which is distrusted by many in Muslim societies and equated with the projects of imperialism and Western hegemony. Another advantage of the neo-Shariati discourse is its close attention to the public manifestations and social functions of religious faith and its rejection of the call for the privatization of religion. As discussed in Chapters 2 and 3, for Shariati and neo-Shariatis religious and social matters are inseparable from one another. Thus, contrary to some of their fellow contemporary Muslim reformers who emphasize private piety and individual spirituality, neo-Shariatis draw attention to religion's oppressive and emancipatory functions in private and public spheres and insist on disseminating a thin progressive conception of the Islamic faith in both realms. Cautioning that privatization undermines the attempt to reform and reinterpret traditional religious doctrines and dogmas that are manifested publicly in everyday life, they argue that private religiosity ultimately feeds religious conservatism and fundamentalism. Furthermore, in its neo-Shariati articulation the project of indigenous modernity is advanced not only through developing modern and democratic interpretations of religious thought, but also through sustained civil engagement and popular mobilization and action. This social orientation further differentiates the neo-Shariati discourse from those reformist discourses whose primary modes of engagement are religious hermeneutics and theological and jurisprudential reform.[22]

In addition to the ongoing debates about the relationship between religion and the processes of democratization and secularization, a number of other issues have come to prominence in the context of the recent developments. Let me end this section by commenting briefly on two of these and examining some of the ways in which the neo-Shariati approach toward them may differ from the approaches of other advocates of Islamic-indigenous modernity. The first is the question of social welfare and socioeconomic development. As a number of commentators have pointed out, socioeconomic factors have played a major role in the emergence of recent uprisings and the framing of their demands. Despite the participation of various social groups in these movements, many

---

[22] See: Saba Mahmood, "Secularism, Hermeneutics, Empire: The Politics of Islamic Reformation," *Public Culture* 18, no. 2 (2006): 339.

of the protesters are said to belong to a new class of young, educated, urban poor, faced with the prospects of unemployment and economic and political disenfranchisement.[23] In analyzing the Arab uprisings, commentators have pointed to the consequences of neoliberal policies that were implemented in various countries in the Middle East and North Africa during the 1980s and 1990s. As in much of the rest of the global South, neoliberalism in these countries resulted in the deterioration of the public sector and social services, as well as in major changes in the labor market including the skyrocketing of unemployment rates among the youth.[24] Furthermore, the incorporation of the national economies of these countries into the global financial system increased their vulnerability vis-à-vis the failures of larger and more powerful economies. As one observer notes, it is no accident that the Arab Spring initially began in the context of the North American and European economic crisis. According to Valentine Moghadam, the impact of the 2008 financial meltdown was felt immediately in many Arab states, causing a sharp increase in the prices of food and other basic commodities and resulting in street protests and workers strikes.[25] The question of economic justice and social welfare continues to be a major issue in postrevolution Arab states and is likely to remain a pressing matter in the near future.[26] In the Iranian case too concern with economic welfare is becoming an increasingly pressing issue for various social sectors, particularly as the state, under the presidency of Hassan Rouhani, continues apace with its neoliberal turn and the implementation of policies that further disadvantage working and low-income classes.[27]

Arguably, in a context where the demand for social welfare and economic democratization is becoming an important site of social mobilization and popular action, one of the advantages of the neo-Shariati discourse over other Islamic discourses of indigenous modernity is the

---

[23] Bayat, "The Post-Islamist Revolutions."
[24] Valentine M Moghadam, "What is Democracy? Promises and Perils of the Arab Spring," *Current Sociology* published online (April 17, 2013), 6, http://csi.sagepub.com/content/early/2013/04/16/0011392113479739 (accessed April 21, 2013).
[25] Ibid., 6.
[26] Both the governments of Morsi and Abdel Fattah el-Sisi supported the continuation of much of Mubarak-era neoliberal policies. In Tunisia, too, the Islamic Nahda party, which came to power after the 2011 revolution, was generally supportive of the "free market" economic policies of the ousted regime. See: Moghadam, "What is Democracy?," 11.
[27] Ismael Hossein-zadeh, "Neoliberal Economics Comes to Iran," *CounterPunch* (October 17, 2014), www.counterpunch.org/2014/10/17/neoliberal-economics-comes-to-iran (accessed February 17, 2016).

former's attentiveness to the issues of social and economic justice. While some of the leading advocates of Islamic reformism have been either inattentive to socioeconomic issues or supportive of capitalism and free market economics, the critique of neoliberalism and emphasis on economic egalitarianism by neo-Shariatis can contribute to the negotiation of a new language of indigenous modernity that corresponds to the everyday challenges of an increasingly growing sector of the economically vulnerable and disenfranchised. At the same time it must be noted that while the neo-Shariati discourse advocates an egalitarian and socialistic economic orientation, it falls short of offering specific models of economic production and distribution that correspond to Iran's particular socioeconomic condition and the country's place in the existing structures of a globalized capitalist economy.

Of the leading neo-Shariatis whose ideas I have discussed in this book, Reza Alijani has taken greater interest in the question of economic development and has attempted to expand Shariati's triad of spirituality, equality, and freedom in a socioeconomic direction. According to him, while Shariati's thought does not include a specific economic theory its egalitarian orientation lends support to a "pro-poor development agenda" and a "social democratic" or "welfare state" model of economic policy-making.[28] Though Alijani's position undoubtedly inserts a necessary element of economic egalitarianism into the discourse of indigenous modernity, in the current context of the global hegemony of neoliberal economics, and the weakening of the nation-state vis-à-vis powerful international financial institutions (i.e., International Monetary Fund, the World Bank, the World Trade Organization, etc.) and multinational and transnational corporations, his endorsement of the social democratic and welfare state models of economic distribution seems at best insufficient for moving toward a bottom-up and equitable model of economic development in Iran. Neo-Shariatis like Alijani may thus benefit from attending to the ongoing discussions in the global South about the prospects of economic development through increased South-South cooperation and through a fundamental rethinking of the growth and industrialization models of neoclassical economics.[29]

---

[28] Reza Alijani, *Rend-e kham: Shariati-shenasi jeld-e yekom: zamaneh, zendegi, va armanha (The Pure Noncomformist: Shariatiology Volume One: Era, Life, and Ideals)* (Tehran: Ghalam, 1387), 6.

[29] In her critical assessment of the discourse of globalization, Sara Shariati addresses some of the limitations of the growth and industrialization models of socioeconomic development. See: Sara Shariati, "Chehreh jahani-gar, chehreh jahani-zadeh: siasat jahani kardan

The other major issue that has been put on the front burner in recent years is that of women's rights and gender equality.[30] A rich body of literature is beginning to emerge on topics such as the participation of women in popular uprisings, women's sociopolitical rights and socioeconomic conditions, the status of women in Islamic law, and the social dynamics of sexual harassment and other forms of sexual exploitation. In recent years, there has also been much interest in the question of the status of women in Muslim societies within the Western academy and particularly in works dealing with the relationship between Islam and modernity. Within contemporary Islamic thought, however, the question of women's rights and status has remained a largely neglected issue. There has, of course, existed a sustained effort by a number of contemporary Muslim feminists including Fatima Mernissi, Leila Ahmed, Amina Wadud, Azam Taliqani, Ziba Mir-Hosseini and others to develop contextually grounded discourses of gender equality on the basis of modern interpretations of Islamic law and religious doctrines. Nevertheless, these efforts have not yet brought a shift in the mainstream of modern Islamic thought, including its reformist current, toward greater attentiveness to gender issues.

Among the prominent Muslim reformists of the twentieth century, Shariati appears to be one of the first to explicitly address the issue of gender equality and to argue that Islam's principle of egalitarianism recognizes the equality of men and women.[31] He also defends women's education and their active participation in social, political, and economic

---

va ravand tarikhi jahani shodan" ("The Globalizer Face and the Globalized Face: An Evaluation of Globalizing Policies and the Process of Globalization"), in *Khodkavi-e melli dar asr-e jahani shodan (National Self-Examination in the Age of Globalization)*, ed. Bonyad Shariati (Tehran: Ghasidehsara, 1381/2002): 127–174. Susan Shariati also notes that in the context of non-Western societies industrialization and urbanization-centered development policies often result in uneven socioeconomic development, rise of urban slums, concentration of poverty and wealth within certain social sectors, the deterioration of traditional social networks that enable a sense of solidarity and interdependence, the crisis of political legitimacy, and the rise of populism. See: Susan Shariati, "Popolism: khizeshi baray-e tashakhos" ("Populism: A Movement for Recognition"), in Susan Shariati, *Don kishot dar shahr (Don Quixote in the City)* (Tehran: Rasesh, 1388/2010): 103–108.

[30] See: Moghadam, "What is Democracy?," 5–6.
[31] Ali Shariati, "Eslam shenasi: dars-e haftom" ("Islamology: Lesson Seven"), (1351/1972), C.W. 16, *Ali Shariati: The Complete Collection of Works* [CD ROM], Tehran: Shariati Cultural Foundation, 2010; Ali Shariati, "Ensan va Islam" ("Humanity and Islam"), (1347/1968), C.W. 24, *Ali Shariati: The Complete Collection of Works* [CD ROM], Tehran: Shariati Cultural Foundation, 2010; Ali Shariati, "Eslam Chist?" ("What is Islam?"), (1345/1966), C.W. 30, *Ali Shariati: The Complete Collection of Works* [CD ROM], Tehran: Shariati Cultural Foundation, 2010.

spheres.³² Even though, as neo-Shariatis themselves have acknowledged, Shariati's thought does not offer a systematic analysis about the status of women and gendered relations of domination and subordination, his thought and its new readings by neo-Shariatis seem to offer pertinent insights about the conditions for advancing contextually negotiated accounts of women's rights and gender equality. Here again the contributions of Reza Alijani and other leading neo-Shariati figures such as Susan Shariati and Hassan Yousefi Eshkevari seem to be particularly relevant. While placing the question of the status of women at the center of their analysis, these contributions have nevertheless expanded on Shariati's broader revolutionary framework by addressing the challenges and prospects of strengthening the links between the projects of women's liberation and social emancipation.³³

Indigenization and the Quest for Universalism from Below

As discussed in Chapters 4 and 5, Shariati's critical position toward Enlightenment modernity and his attempt to develop a contextually

---

³² Ali Shariati, "Fatemeh Fatemeh ast" ("Fatemeh Is Fatemeh"), (1350/1971), C.W. 21, *Ali Shariati: The Complete Collection of Works* [CD ROM], Tehran: Shariati Cultural Foundation, 2010.

³³ For Reza Alijani's discussions on the topic, see: Reza Alijani, "Din, zan, va donyay-e jadid: goftegoo ba Reza Alijani" ("Religion, Women, and the Modern World: A Conversation with Reza Alijani"), *Cheshmandaz-e Iran* no. 44 (Tir-Mordad 1386/July-August 2007): 99–108; Reza Alijani, "Jonbesh zanan: jonbeshi mostaghel ama mortabet" ("Women's Movement: Independence and Interdependence"), *Baztab-e Andisheh* no. 70, Bahman 1384/February 2006, 57–59; Reza Alijani, "Chera zan dar matoon moghadas?" ("Why the Question of Woman in Sacred Texts?"), Shariati Discourse Forum (no date), http://talar.shandel.info/showthread.php?tid=683&pid=3036#post_3035 (accessed July 2, 2011); Reza Alijani, "Motoon-e moghadas va doniaye jadid" ("Sacred Scriptures and the Modern World"), Shariati Discourse Forum (no date), http://talar.shandel.info/showthread.php?tid=683&pid=3036#post_3036 (accessed July 2, 2011). For Susan Shariati's discussions on the topic see: Susan Shariati, "Zanan dar projeh shariati" ("Women in Shariati's Project"), interview with Parvin Bakhtiarnejad, *Etemad*, 15 Aban 1386/November 6, 2007, http://drshariati.org/show.asp?id=106 (accessed April 17, 2011); Susan Shariati, "Chand kalameh harf-e zananeh: beh bahaneye rooz-e jahani-e zan" ("A Few Feminine Words: On the Occasion of the International Women's Day"), in Susan Shariati, *Don kishot dar shahr (Don Quixote in the City)* (Tehran: Rasesh, 1388/2010): 235–238. For Hassan Yousefi Eshkevari's work on the topic see: Hassan Yousefi Eshkevari, "Women's Rights and the Women's Movement," in Ziba Mir-Hosseini and Richard Tapper, *Islam and Democracy in Iran: Eshkevari and the Quest for Reform* (London: I.B. Tauris, 2006), 163–173; Hassan Yousefi Eshkevari, "Reformist Islam and Modern Society," in Ziba Mir-Hosseini and Richard Tapper, *Islam and Democracy in Iran: Eshkevari and the Quest for Reform* (London: I.B. Tauris, 2006), 155–163.

grounded discourse of revolutionary social and political change on the basis of a modern reinterpretation of Islamic thought has been read in two radically different ways. According to his critics, in the context of mid-twentieth century Iran Shariati's Islamic discourse was part of a broader anti-Western discourse of nativism and Orientalism in reverse that emphasized an inherent dichotomy between Islam and modernity and between the Orient and the Occident. Shariati's attempt to advance a localized conception of an anticolonial modernity is interpreted by these critics as an antidemocratic and anti-secular embrace of traditional authenticity which ultimately paved the way for a radical Islamist turn and the establishment of the Islamic Republic. Critics also draw links between Shariati's critique of Westernization and the postrevolution project of the top-down Islamization of Iranian society and of various academic disciplines. Thus, some commentators have suggested that Shariati's call to return to the authentic self and his emphasis on the reaffirmation and reappropriation of the indigenous culture helped to justify in postrevolutionary Iran such oppressive policies as the imposition of the veil on Iranian women and the gendered segregation of public spaces.[34] Others yet have argued that Shariati's insistence on developing a modern account of Islamic ontology and epistemology was a major precursor to the postrevolutionary discourse of Islamization of social sciences and humanities.[35]

For neo-Shariatis as well as for a number of other contemporary Iranian commentators, however, Shariati's emphasis on the necessity of reappropriating and critically engaging with local cultural resources was informed by his analysis about the conditions for advancing a bottom-up and sustainable project of social and political change in the particular context of Iranian society. These commentators reject the reading of Shariati's thought as an endorsement of or a precursor to the postrevolutionary calls for Islamization of knowledge and of cultural, social, political, and economic realms. They do, however, argue that Shariati's thought was an attempt toward indigenizing modern social science and humanities analysis in a creative and critical dialogue with the contributions of

---

[34] See: Nayereh Tohidi, "Modernity, Islamization, and Women in Iran," in *Gender and National Identity: Women and Politics in Muslim Societies*, ed. Valentine M Moghadam (London: Zed Books, 1994), 123. Also see: Roksana Bahramitash, "Revolution, Islamization, and Women's Employment in Iran," *The Brown Journal of World Affairs* ix, no. 2 (Winter/Spring 2003): 232.

[35] See: Sohrab Behdad, "Islamization of Economics in Iranian Universities," *International Journal of Middle East Studies* 27, no. 2 (1995): 193–217, 198.

a wide range of Western and non-Western thinkers. Increasingly in recent years, a number of non-Iranian commentators too have begun developing a similar reading of Shariati's thought as an exercise in indigenous social theory and as part of a broader effort in the global South to break away from the hegemony of Eurocentric metanarratives of social and political change. It is precisely from this lens that Raewyn Connell analyzes Shariati's thought in her 2007 book entitled *Southern Theory: The Global Dynamics of Knowledge in Social Science*.[36] For Walter Mignolo too, who discusses Shariati in some of his recent works on coloniality and modernity, Shariati's significance is primarily in his contribution to the postcolonial struggles to delink from the colonial modes of knowledge and understanding and to give recognition to indigenous knowledges and epistemologies.[37]

The critical deconstruction of the colonially mitigated modes of knowledge and the search for alternative ontologies and epistemologies on the basis of which to negotiate alternative future possibilities place Shariati's thought in conversation with a wide range of progressive and emancipatory discourses in the global North and the global South. Nevertheless, if the experiences of postcolonialism in various parts of the global South and the experience of Islamism in postrevolutionary Iran are any indication, engagement with the discourse of indigeneity and the search for alternative or indigenous ontologies and epistemologies run the risk of falling in the trap of the West/rest binary and of producing or at least bolstering new forms of parochialism and ethnocentrism. To avoid these potential dangers, the project of indigenization must be clearly discerned from the projects of nativism and Orientalism in reverse. This means that indigenization or decolonization ought to be defined not as a turn against universalism but rather as a move toward cosmopolitanism and universalism from below. In this regard, by grouping together Shariati with Islamists such as Qutb and Khomeini as part of an overall Islamic project of "de-coloniality," commentators like Mignolo effectively undermine this major distinction and overlook the dynamic heterogeneity of Islamic responses to modernity and coloniality.[38]

---

[36] See: Raewyn Connell, *Southern Theory: The Global Dynamics of Knowledge in Social Science* (Cambridge: Polity Press, 2007), 125–134.
[37] See: Walter D. Mignolo, "Prophets Facing Sidewise: The Geopolitics of Knowledge and the Colonial Difference," *Social Epistemology: A Journal of Knowledge, Culture and Policy* 19, no. 1 (2005): 117.
[38] See: Walter Mignolo, "Delinking: The Rhetoric of Modernity, the Logic of Coloniality and the Grammar of De-Coloniality," *Cultural Studies* 21, no. 2 (2007): 457.

By distinguishing between the discourses of indigenization and Islamization, a number of Muslim scholars have drawn attention to precisely the kind of ontological, epistemological, and methodological differences within Islamic thought that have produced two entirely different social and intellectual projects in contemporary Muslim societies. According to Syed Farid Alatas, for instance, while Islamization entails a nativist rejection of all Western knowledge, indigenization calls for moving away from the hegemonic universalism of Eurocentric modes of knowledge production and moving toward an inclusive universalism from below by giving recognition to differential histories and contextual particularities.[39] Shariati's project, argues Alatas, is a contribution to the indigenization of social science analysis in Muslim societies and is entirely different from the project of Islamization of knowledge and the discourses of Qutb and other Islamist thinkers.[40] As I have argued in this book, it is essentially along the lines of a vision of universalism from below that neo-Shariatis have read Shariati's unfinished intellectual project in postrevolutionary Iran. As suggested in Chapter 5, however, by going beyond the limiting contours of the civilizational framework of his Islamic discourse, Shariati's contemporary intellectual followers can further distinguish his thought from nativist and identitarian Islamic discourses and cultivate what Dabashi aptly terms Shariati's "cosmopolitan and transnational solidarities."[41]

---

[39] Syed Farid Alatas, "The Sacralization of the Social Sciences: A Critique of an Emerging Theme in Academic Discourse," *Archives des sciences sociales des religions*, 91, no. 91 (1995): 91.

[40] Syed Farid Alatas, "Interview," in *Shariati dar daneshgah (Shariati at the University)*, ed. Bonyad Shariati (Tehran: Bonyad Farhangi-e Doctor Ali Shariati, 1390): 109–130, 112–119.

[41] Hamid Dabashi, *Islamic Liberation Theology: Resisting the Empire* (New York: Routledge, 2008), 115.

Select Bibliography

English Sources

Abduh, Muhammad. "The True Reform and its Necessity for Al-Azhar," *al-Manar* 10, no. 28 (February 1906), trans. Kamran Talattof. In *Contemporary Debates in Islam: An Anthology of Modernist and Fundamentalist Thought*, edited by Mansoor Moaddel and Kamran Talattof, 45–52. New York: St. Martin's Press, 2000.

Abedi, Mehbi. "Ali Shariati: The Architect of the 1979 Islamic Revolution of Iran." *Iranian Studies* 19, no. 3–4 (1936): 229–234.

Abrahamian, Ervand. "Ali Shari'ati: Ideologue of the Iranian Revolution." *MERIP Reports*, no. 102, *Islam and Politics* (January, 1982): 24–28.

——— *Iran between Two Revolutions*. Princeton, NJ: Princeton University Press, 1982.

——— *Radical Islam: The Iranian Mojahedin*. New Haven, CT: Yale University Press, 1989.

Abu-Rabi, Ibrahim M. "Editor's Introduction." In Nevval Sevindi, *Contemporary Islamic Conversations: M. Fethullah Gulen on Turkey, Islam, and the West*, edited by Ibrahim M. Abu-Rabi, translated by Abdulah T. Antepli, vii–xiv. New York: State University of New York, 2008.

——— "Editor's Introduction: Contemporary Islamic Thought: One or Many?" In *The Blackwell Companion to Contemporary Islamic Thought*, edited by Ibrahim M. Abu-Rabi, 1–20. Malden, MA: Blackwell Publishing, 2006.

——— "Editor's Introduction: Islamism from the Standpoint of Critical Theory." In *Contemporary Arab Reader on Political Islam* edited by Ibrahim M. Abu-Rabi. London and Edmonton: Pluto Press and University of Alberta Press, 2010.

——— *Intellectual Origins of Islamic Resurgence in the Modern Arab World*. Albany: State University of New York Press, 1996.

Abu Zayd, Nasr Hamid. "The Modernization of Islam or the Islamization of Modernity." In *Cosmopolitanism, Identity and Authenticity in the Middle East*, edited by Roel Meijer, 71–86. London: Routledge Curzon Press, 1999.

"The Other as Mirror of Selfunderstanding. Comparing Two Traditions." Reset DOC: Dialogues on Civilizations, July 18, 2011, www.resetdoc.org/story/00000021674 (accessed August 4, 2012).

Adib-Moghaddam, Arshin. "The Pluralistic Momentum in Iran and the Future of the Reform Movement." *Third World Quarterly* 27, no. 4 (2006): 665–674.

Afary, Janet, and Kevin Anderson. *Foucault and the Iranian Revolution: Gender and the Seductions of Islamism*. Chicago: University of Chicago Press, 2005.

Ahmed, Akbar S. *Postmodernism and Islam: Predicament and Promise*. London: Routledge, 1992.

Akhavi, Shahrough. "Islam, Politics and Society in the Thought of Ayatullah Khomeini, Ayatullah Taliqani and Ali Shariati." *Middle Eastern Studies* 24, no. 4 (October 1988): 404–431.

Al-Azmeh, Aziz. *Islams and Modernities*. London and New York: Verso, 1993.

Alatas, Syed Farid. *Alternative Discourses in Asian Social Science: Responses to Eurocentrism*. London and California: Sage Publications, 2006.

"The Sacralization of the Social Sciences: A Critique of an Emerging Theme in Academic Discourse." *Archives des sciences sociales des religions* 91, no.91 (1995): 89–111.

Algar, Hamid. *The Roots of the Islamic Revolution*. Areekode, Kerala: Islamic Foundation Press, 1988.

Alijani, Reza. "Pre-secular Iranians in a Post-secular Age: The Death of God, the Resurrection of God," translated by Mojtaba Mahdavi and Siavash Saffari, *Comparative Studies of South Asia, Africa and the Middle East* 31, no. 1 (2011): 27–33.

An-Na'im, Abdullahi Ahmed. "The Islamic Law of Apostasy and Its Modern Applicability: A Case from the Sudan." *Religion* 16, no. 3 (1986): 197–224.

Arkoun, Mohammed. "Positivism and Tradition in an Islamic Perspective: Kemalism." *Diogenes* 32, no. 127 (1984): 82–100.

The Unthoughts in Contemporary Islamic Thought. London: Saqi Books, 2002.

Asad, Talal. "Europe against Islam: Islam in Europe." *The Muslim World* 87, no. 2 (1997): 183–195.

Formations of the Secular: Christianity, Islam, modernity. Stanford University Press, 2003.

"Religion, Nation-State, Secularism." In *Nation and Religion: Perspectives on Europe and Asia*, edited by Peter van der Veer and Hartmut Lehmann, 178–196. Princeton, NJ: Princeton University Press, 1999.

Aydin, Mahmut. *Modern Western Christian Theological Understandings of Muslims since the Second Vatican Council*. Washington, DC: The Council for Research in Values and Philosophy, 2002.

Ayoob, Mohammed. "The Revolutionary Thrust of Islamic Political Tradition," *Third World Quarterly* 3 no. 2 (1981): 269–276.

Ayoub, Mahmoud M. "Forward." In Ibrahim M. Abu-Rabi, *Intellectual Origins of Islamic Resurgence in the Modern Arab World*. ix-x. Albany: State University of New York Press, 1996.

Bahramitash, Roksana. "Revolution, Islamization, and Women's Employment in Iran." *The Brown Journal of World Affairs* ix, no. 2 (Winter/Spring 2003): 229–241.

Bayat, Asef. "Is there a Future for Islamist Revolutions?: Religion, Revolt, and Middle Eastern Modernity." In *Revolution in the Making of the Modern World: Social Identities, Globalization, and Modernity*, edited by John Foran, David Lane, Andreja Zivkovic, 96–112. New York: Routledge, 2008.
"Islamism and Social Movement Theory." *Third World Quarterly* 26, no. 6 (2005): 891–908.
"Post-Islamism at Large." In *Post-Islamism: The Many Faces of Political Islam*, edited by Asef Bayat, 3–34. New York: Oxford University Press, 2013.
"The Post-Islamist Revolutions: What the Revolts in the Arab World Mean?" *Foreign Affairs*– Snapshots, April 26, 2011, www.foreignaffairs.com/articles/67812/asef-bayat/the-post-islamist-revolutions (accessed April 9, 2013).
Behdad, Sohrab. "Islamization of Economics in Iranian Universities." *International Journal of Middle East Studies* 27, no. 2 (1995): 193–217.
Boroujerdi, Mehrzad, *Iranian Intellectuals and the West: The Tormented Triumph of Nativism*. Syracuse, NY: Syracuse University Press, 1996.
Burgess, Andrew. "Forward: On Drawing a Line." In Ali Shariati, *Religion vs. Religion*, translated By Laleh Bakhtiar, 5–9. Chicago: Kazi Publications, 1993.
Butler, Judith. "Is Judaism Zionism?" In *The Power of Religion in the Public Sphere*, edited by Eduardo Mendieta and Jonathan VanAntwerpen, 70–91. New York: Columbia University Press, 2011.
Casanova, José. "Catholic and Muslim Politics in Comparative Perspective," *Taiwan Journal of Democracy* 1, no 2 (December 2005): 89–108.
"Civil Society and Religion: Retrospective Reflections on Catholicism and Prospective Reflections on Islam," *Social Research* 68, no. 4 (Winter 2001): 1041–1080.
Public Religions in the Modern World. Chicago and London: University of Chicago Press, 1994.
"Public Religions Revisited," in *Religion: Beyond a Concept*, edited by Hent de Vries, 101–119. New York: Fordham University Press, 2008.
Connell, Raewyn. *Southern Theory: The Global Dynamics of Knowledge in Social Science*. Cambridge: Polity Press, 2007.
Dabashi, Hamid. "An Interview with Hamid Dabashi," ZNet, September 22, 2009, www.zcommunications.org/an-interview-with-hamid-dabashi-by-hamid-dabashi (accessed February 21, 2013).
"For the Last Time: Civilizations." In *Hegemony and Multiculturalism: Texts and Subsidies*, edited by Candido Mendes, 109–145. Rio de Janeiro and Paris: Academia de la Latinidad, 2004.
"For the Last Time: Civilizations." *International Sociology* 16, no. 3 (September 2001): 361–368.
Iran: A People Interrupted. New York: New Press, 2007.
Islamic Liberation Theology: Resisting the Empire. New York: Routledge, 2008.
Post-Orientalism: Knowledge and Power in Time of Terror. New Brunswick, NJ: Transaction Publishers, 2009.
The Arab Spring: The End of Postcolonialism. London and New York: Zed Books, 2012.
The World of Persian Literary Humanism. Cambridge, MA: Harvard University Press, 2012.

Theology of Discontent: The Ideological Foundation of the Islamic Revolution in Iran. New York and London: New York University Press, 1993.

Dallmayr, Fred. *Alternative Visions: Paths in the Global Village*. Lanham, MD: Rowman & Littlefield Publishers, 1998.

"Beyond Monologue: For a Comparative Political Theory." *Perspectives on Politics* 2, no. 2 (June 2004): 249–257.

Beyond Orientalism: Essays on Cross-Cultural Encounter. Albany, NY: State University of New York Press, 1996.

(ed.). *Border Crossings: Toward a Comparative Political Theory*. Lanham, MD: Lexington, 1999.

Dialogue among Civilizations: Some Exemplary Voices. New York: Palgrave Macmillan, 2002.

"Empire or Cosmopolis? Civilization at the Crossroads." *Globalizations* 2, no. 1 (2005): 14–30.

"Globalization and Inequality: A Plea for Cosmopolitan Justice." *Comparative Studies of South Asia, Africa and the Middle East* 26, no. 1 (2006): 63–74.

"Habermas and Rationality." *Political Theory* 16, no. 4 (1988): 553–579.

"Introduction: Toward a Comparative Political Theory," *The Review of Politics* 59, no. 3, Non-Western Political Thought (Summer, 1997): 421–427.

"The Underside of Modernity: Adorno, Heidegger, and Dussel." *Constellations* 11, no 1 (2004): 102–120.

"Whither Democracy? Religion, Politics and Islam." *Philosophy and Social Criticism* 37, no. 4 (2011): 437–448.

Dallmayr, Fred, and G. N. Devy (eds.). *Between Tradition and Modernity: India's Search for Identity: A Twentieth Century Anthology*. Walnut Creek, CA: Altamira Press, 1998.

"Introduction." In *Between Tradition and Modernity: India's Search for Identity: A Twentieth Century Anthology*, edited by Fred Dallmayr and G. N. Devy, 15–52. Walnut Creek, CA: Altamira Press, 1998.

Dobbelaere, Karel. "Secularization: A Multidimensional Concept," *Current Sociology* 29, no. 2 (1981): 1–216.

Duara, Prasenjit. "The Discourse of Civilization and Decolonization." *Journal of World History* 15, no. 1 (March 2004): 1–5.

Dussel, Enrique. *The Underside of Modernity: Apel, Ricoeur, Rorty, Taylor, and the Philosophy of Liberation*, translated by Eduardo Mendieta. Atlantic Highland, NJ: Humanities Press, 1996.

"World-System and 'Trans'-Modernity." *Nepantla: Views from South* 3, no. 2 (2002): 221–244.

Eickelman, Dale F. "Islam and the Languages of Modernity." *Daedalus* 129, no. 1, Multiple Modernities (Winter, 2000): 119–135.

Eisenstadt, S. N. "Multiple Modernities." *Daedalus* 129, no. 1 (Winter 2000): 1–30.

"Multiple Modernities." In *Multiple Modernities*, edited by S. N. Eisenstadt, 1–29. New Brunswick, NJ: Transaction, 2002.

Enayat, Hamid. *Modern Islamic Political Thought: The Response of the Shi'i and Sunni Muslims to the Twentieth Century* – New Edition. New York: I.B. Tauris, 2005.

Esposito, John. *Islam and Politics*. Syracuse, NY: Syracuse University Press, 1984.

The Islamic Threat: Myth or Reality? – Third Edition. New York: Oxford University Press, 1999.

Euben, Roxanne L. "Contingent Borders, Syncretic Perspectives: Globalization, Political Theory, and Islamizing Knowledge." *International Studies Review* 4, no. 1 (2002): 23–48.

Enemy in the Mirror: Islamic Fundamentalism and the Limits of Modern Rationalism: A Work of Comparative Political Theory. Princeton, NJ: Princeton University Press, 1999.

"Mapping Modernities, 'Islamic' and 'Western'." In *Border Crossings: Toward a Comparative Political Theory*, edited by Fred Dallmayr, 11–37. New York: Lexington Books, 1999.

Euben, Roxanne L., and Muhammad Qasim Zaman. "Ayatollah Ruhollah Khomeini." In *Princeton Readings in Islamist Thought: Texts and Contexts from al-Banna to Bin Laden*, edited by Roxanne L. Euben and Muhammad Qasim Zaman, 155–162. Princeton, NJ: Princeton University Press, 2009.

"Introduction." In *Princeton Readings in Islamist Thought: Texts and Contexts from al- Banna to Bin Laden*, edited by Roxanne L. Euben and Muhammad Qasim Zaman, 1–48. Princeton, NJ: Princeton University Press, 2009.

"Sayyid Abu'l-A'la Mawdudi." In *Princeton Readings in Islamist Thought: Texts and Contexts from al-Banna to Bin Laden*, edited by Roxanne L. Euben and Muhammad Qasim Zaman, 79–85. Princeton, NJ: Princeton University Press, 2009.

"Sayyid Qutb." In *Princeton Readings in Islamist Thought: Texts and Contexts from al- Banna to Bin Laden*, edited by Roxanne L. Euben and Muhammad Qasim Zaman, 129–135. Princeton, NJ: Princeton University Press, 2009.

Fanon, Frantz. *Black Skin, White Masks*, translated by Charles Lam Markmann. London: Pluto Press, 1986.

The Wretched of the Earth. New York: Grove Press, 1963.

Farhang, Mansour. "Resisting the Pharaohs: Ali Shariati on Oppression." *Race & Class* 21, no. 1 (July 1979): 31–33.

Filali-Ansary, Abdou. "Muslims and Democracy." In *Islam and Democracy in the Middle East*, edited by Larry Diamond, Marc F. Plattner, and Daniel Brumberg, 193–207. Baltimore, MD and London: The Johns Hopkins University Press, 2003.

Fukuyama, Francis. "The End of History?" *The National Interest* no. 16 (Summer 1989): 3–18.

Gellner, Ernest. "Forward." In *Islam, Globalization and Postmodernity*, edited by Akbar S. Ahmed and Hastings Donnan, x-xii. London: Routledge, 1994.

Postmodernism, Reason and Religion. London: Routledge, 1992.

Ghamari-Tabrizi, Behrooz. "Contentious Public Religion: Two Conceptions of Islam in Revolutionary Iran Ali Shariati and Abdolkarim Soroush." *International Sociology* 19, no. 4 (December 2004): 504–523.

Ghaneirad, Mohammad Amin. "A Critical Review of the Iranian Attempts at the Development of Alternative Sociologies." In *Facing Unequal World: Challenges For a Global Sociology*, Volume Two: Asia, edited by Michael Burawoy, Mau-kuei Chang, and Michelle Fei-yu Hsieh, 36–70. Taiwan: Institute of Sociology at Academia Sinica, Council of National Association of the International Sociological Association, and Academia Sinica, 2010.

Göle, Nilüfer. "Snapshots of Islamic Modernities." *Daedalus* 129, no. 1, Multiple Modernities (Winter 2000): 91–117.

Grand, Stephen R. "Starting in Egypt: The Fourth Wave of Democratization?" Washington, DC: Brookings Institution, February 10, 2011, www.brookings.edu/research/opinions/2011/02/10-egypt-democracy-grand (accessed January 7, 2013).

Griffith, William E. "The Revival of Islamic Fundamentalism: The Case of Iran." *International Security* 4, no. 1 (Summer 1979): 132–138.

Gülen, Fethullah. "An Interview with Fethullah Gülen," interview and translation by Zeki Saritoprak and Ali Unal. *The Muslim World* 95, no. 3 (2005): 447–467, quoted in John Esposito and Ihsan Yilmaz, *Islam and Peacebuilding: Gülen Movement Initiatives*. New York: Blue Dome, 2010.

Habermas, Jürgen. "Modernity: An Unfinished Project." In *Habermas and the Unfinished Project of Modernity*, edited by Maurizio Passerin d'Entreves and Seyla Benhabib, 38–55. Cambridge: The MIT Press, 1997.

"Religion in the Public Sphere." *European Journal of Philosophy* 14, no. 1 (2006): 1–25.

The Philosophical Discourse of Modernity: Twelve Lectures, translated by Frederick G. Lawrence. Cambridge, MA: MIT Press, 1990.

"'The Political': The Rational Meaning of a Questionable Inheritance of Political Theology." In *The Power of Religion in the Public Sphere*, edited by Eduardo Mendieta and Jonathan VanAntwerpen, 15–33. New York: Columbia University Press, 2011.

The Theory of Communicative Action, vol. 1, *Reason and Rationalization of Society*, translated by Thomas McCarthy. Boston, MA: Beacon Press, 1984.

Halliday, Fred. "The Iranian Revolution." *Political Studies*, xxx, no. 3 (September 1982): 437–444.

Hardt, Michael, and Antonio Negri. "Arabs are Democracy's New Pioneers," The Guardian – Comment is Free (February 24, 2011), www.guardian.co.uk/commentisfree/2011/feb/24/arabs-democracy-latin-america (accessed April 11, 2013).

Hashemi, Nader. *Islam, Secularism, and Liberal Democracy: Toward a Democratic Theory for Muslim Societies*. New York: Oxford University Press, 2009.

"The Multiple Histories of Secularism: Muslim Societies in Comparison," *Philosophy and Social Criticism* 36, no. 3–4 (March 2010): 325–338.

Hassan, Riffat. "Islamic Modernist and Reformist Discourse in South Asia." In *Reformist Voices of Islam: Mediating Islam and Modernity*, edited by Shireen T. Hunter. 159–186. Armonk, NY: M. E. Sharpe, 2008.

Hossein-zadeh, Ismael "Neoliberal Economics Comes to Iran," *CounterPunch* (October 17, 2014), www.counterpunch.org/2014/10/17/neoliberal-economics-comes-to-iran (accessed February 17, 2016).

Howard, Philip N., and Muzammil M. Hussain. *Democracy's Fourth Wave? Digital Media and the Arab Spring.* New York: Oxford University Press, 2013.
Hunter, Shireen T. "Introduction." In *Reformist Voices of Islam: Mediating Islam and Modernity,* edited by Shireen T. Hunter, 3–32. Armonk, NY: M. E. Sharpe, 2008.
"Islamic Reformist Discourses in Iran: Proponents and Prospects." In *Reformist Voices of Islam: Mediating Islam and Modernity,* edited by Shireen T. Hunter, 33–95, Armonk, NY: M. E. Sharpe, 2008.
"Preface." In *Reformist Voices of Islam: Mediating Islam and Modernity,* edited by Shireen T. Hunter, xix-xxii. Armonk, NY: M. E. Sharpe, 2008.
Huntington, Samuel P. "The Clash of Civilizations?" *Foreign Affairs* 72, no. 3 (1993): 22–50.
The Clash of Civilizations and the Remaking of World Order. New York: Simon & Schuster, 1996.
Iqbal, Muhammad. *The Reconstruction of Religious Thought in Islam.* Lahore: Ashraf, 1962.
Iran Daily Brief. "Mohammad Zamiran and Dr. Ehsan Shariati are Suspended," March 8, 2013, www.irandailybrief.com/2013/03/08/mohammad-zamiran-and-dr-ehsan-shariati-are-suspended/ (accessed July 10, 2013).
Jahanbakhsh, Forough. *Islam, Democracy and Religious Modernism in Iran (1953–2000): From Bazargan to Soroush.* Leiden, Boston, Koln: Brill, 2001.
Kamali, Masoud. *Multiple Modernities, Civil Society and Islam: The Case of Iran and Turkey.* Liverpool: Liverpool University Press, 2006.
Kaufmann, David. "Adorno and the Name of God." *Flashpoint* 1, no. 1 (1996): 65–70, http://webdelsol.com/FLASHPOINT/adorno.htm (accessed May 2, 2011).
Keddie, Nikki R. *An Islamic Response to Imperialism: Political and Religious Writings of Sayyid Jamal ad-Din "al-Afghani".* Berkeley: University of California Press, 1983.
"Sayyid Jamal al-Din 'al-Afghani'." In *Pioneers of Islamic Revival* – Second Edition, edited by Ali Rahnema, 11–29. New York: Zed Books, 2005.
Kepel, Gilles. *Muslim Extremism in Egypt,* translated by Jon Rothschild. Berkeley: University of California Press, 1986.
Khatab, Sayed. *The Political Thought of Sayyid Qutb: The Theory of Jahiliyyah.* London and New York: Routledge, 2006.
Kuru, Ahmet T. "Fethullah Gülen's Search for a Middle Way between Modernity and Muslim Tradition," in *Turkish Islam and the Secular State: The Gülen Movement,* edited by M. Hakan Yavuz and John L. Esposito, 115–130. Syracuse, NY: Syracuse University Press, 2003.
Kurzman, Charles (ed.). *Liberal Islam: A Sourcebook.* New York: Oxford University Press, 1998.
Lakoff, Sanford. "The Reality of Muslim Exceptionalism." *Journal of Democracy* 15, no. 4 (October 2004): 133–139.
Lazega, Emmanuel. "Network Analysis and Qualitative Research: A Method of Contextualization." In *Context and Method in Qualitative Research,* edited by Gale Miller and Robert Dingwall, 119–138. London: SAGE, 1997.
Leezenberg, Michiel. "Power and Political Spirituality: Michel Foucault on the Islamic Revolution in Iran." In *Cultural History after Foucault,* edited by John Neubauer, 64–73. New York: Aldine De Gruyter, 1999.

Lerner, Daniel. *The Passing of Traditional Society: Modernizing the Middle East.* New York: Free Press, 1958.

Lewis, Bernard. *The Crisis of Islam: Holy War and Unholy Terror.* New York: Random House, 2004.

——. "The Roots of Muslim Rage: Why So Many Muslims Deeply Resent the West, and Why Their Bitterness Will Not Be Easily Mollified." *The Atlantic Monthly* 26, no. 3 (September 1990): 47–58.

——. "What Went Wrong?" *The Atlantic Monthly* (January 2002): 43–45.

——. *What Went Wrong: The Clash between Islam and Modernity in the Middle East.* New York: Oxford University Press, 2002.

Mahdavi, Mojtaba. "Beyond Culturalism and Monism: The Iranian Path to Democracy." *Iran Analysis Quarterly* 2, no. 3 (Winter 2005): 2–10.

——. "Islam/Muslims and Political Leadership." In *The Ashgate Research Companion to Political Leadership,* edited by Joseph Masciulli, Mikhail A. Molchanov, and W. Andy Knight, 287–306. Burlington, VT: Ashgate, 2009.

——. "Max Weber in Iran: Does Islamic Protestantism Matter?" Paper presented at the 77th annual meeting for the Canadian Political Science Association, London, Ontario, June 2–4, 2005, www.cpsa-acsp.ca/papers-2005/Mahdavi.pdf (accessed on March 2, 2012).

——. "Middle East Has Truly Reached Turning Point," *Edmonton Journal,* 12 March 12, 2011, www2.canada.com/edmontonjournal/news/ideas/story.html?id=824ac4a2-5a7e-4974-a8d4-a5bc049e145f (accessed March 28, 2013).

——. "One Bed and Two Dreams? Contentious Public Religion in the Discourses of Ayatollah Khomeini and Ali Shariati." *Studies in Religion / Sciences Religieuses* 43, no. 1 (2014): 25–52.

——. "Post-Islamist Trends in Post-Revolutionary Iran." *Comparative Studies of South Asia, Africa, and the Middle East* 31, no. 1 (2011): 94–109.

——. "Universalism from Below: Muslims and Democracy in Context." *International Journal of Criminology and Sociological Theory* 2, no. 2 (December 2009): 276–291.

Mahdavi, Mojtaba, and Andy Knight. "Introduction." In *Towards the Dignity of Difference?: Neither End of History Nor Clash of Civilizations,* edited Mojtaba Mahdavi and W. Andy Knight, 1–23. London, UK: Ashgate, 2012.

——. "On the 'Dignity of Difference': Neither the 'End of History' nor the 'Clash of Civilizations.'" *Journal for the Study of Peace and Conflict,* (Winter 2008): 27–41.

——. "Preface." In *Towards the Dignity of Difference?: Neither End of History Nor Clash of Civilizations,* edited Mojtaba Mahdavi and W. Andy Knight, xxi–xxv. London, UK: Ashgate, 2012.

Mahmood, Saba. "Secularism, Hermeneutics, Empire: The Politics of Islamic Reformation." *Public Culture* 18, no. 2 (2006): 323–347.

Mamdani, Mahmood. *Good Muslim, Bad Muslim: America, The Cold War, and the Roots of Terror.* New York: Three Leaves Press, 2005.

Manoochehri, Abbas. "Critical Religious Reason: Ali Shari'ati on Religion, Philosophy and Emancipation." *Polylog: Forum for Intercultural Philosophy* 4 (2003), http://them.polylog.org/4/fma-en.htm (accessed January 28, 2012).

Masud, Mohammad Khalid, and Armando Salvatore. "Western Scholars of Islam on the Issue of Modernity." In *Islam and Modernity: Key Issues and Debates*, edited by Mohammad Khalid Masud, Armando Salvatore, and Martin van Burinessen, 36–53. Edinburgh: Edinburgh University Press, 2009.

Mather, Yassamine. "Iran's Political and Economic Crises." *Critique: Journal of Socialist Theory* 38, no. 3 (2010): 503–518.

Matin, Kamran. "Decoding Political Islam: Uneven and Combined Development and Ali Shariati's Political Thought." In *International Relations and non-Western Thought: Imperialism, Colonialism, and Investigations of Global Modernity*, edited by Robbie Shilliam. 108–124. London: Routledge, 2010.

Mendieta, Eduardo, and Jonathan VanAntwerpen. "Introduction: The Power of Religion in the Public Sphere." In *The Power of Religion in the Public Sphere*, edited by Eduardo Mendieta and Jonathan VanAntwerpen, 1–14. New York: Columbia University Press, 2011.

Mignolo, Walter D. "Delinking: The Rhetoric of Modernity, the Logic of Coloniality and the Grammar of De-Coloniality." *Cultural Studies* 21, no. 2 (2007): 449–514.

Local Histories/Global Designs: Coloniality, Subaltern Knowledges, and Border Thinking. Princeton, NJ: Princeton University Press, 2012.

"Prophets Facing Sidewise: The Geopolitics of Knowledge and the Colonial Difference." *Social Epistemology: A Journal of Knowledge, Culture and Policy* 19, no. 1 (2005): 111–127.

The Darker Side of Western Modernity: Global Futures, Decolonial Options. Durham and London: Duke University Press, 2011.

"Yes, We Can: Non-European Thinkers and Philosophers." Al-Jazeera, February 19, 2013, www.aljazeera.com/indepth/opinion/2013/02/20132672747320891.html (accessed March 13, 2013).

Milani, Abbas. *Lost Wisdom: Rethinking Modernity in Iran*. Washington, DC: Mage, 2004.

Mirsepassi, Ali. "Intellectual Life after the 1979 Revolution: Radical Hope and Nihilistic Dreams." *Radical History Review* 2009, no. 105 (October 2009): 168–176.

Political Islam, Iran, and the Enlightenment: Philosophies of Hope and Despair. New York: Cambridge University Press, 2011.

"Religious Intellectuals and Western Critiques of Secular Modernity." *Comparative Studies of South Asia, Africa and the Middle East* 26, no. 3 (2006): 416–433.

Moghadam, Val. "Socialism or Anti-Imperialism? The Left and Revolution in Iran." *New Left Review* I, no. 166 (November-December 1987): 5–28.

Moghadam, Valentine M. "What Is Democracy? Promises and Perils of the Arab Spring." *Current Sociology* published online (April 17, 2013): 1–16, http://csi.sagepub.com/content/early/2013/04/16/0011392113479739 (accessed April 21, 2013).

Moin, Baqer. "Khomeini's Search for Perfection: Theory and Reality." In *Pioneers of Islamic Revival* – Second Edition, edited by Ali Rahnema, 64–97. New York: Zed Books, 2005.

Moslemi, Mehdi. *Factional Politics in Post-Khomeini Iran*. Syracuse, NY: Syracuse University Press, 2002.

Nandy, Ashis. "Cultural Frames for Social Transformation: A Credo." In *Between Tradition and Modernity: India's Search for Identity: A Twentieth Century Anthology*, edited by Fred Dallmayr, G. N. Devy, 248–262. Delhi: Altamira Press, 1998.

Norris, Pippa, and Ronald Inglehart. *Sacred and Secular: Religion and Politics Worldwide*. New York: Cambridge University Press, 2004.

Pantham, Thomas. "Some Dimensions of the Universality of Philosophical Hermeneutics: A Conversation with Hans-Gerog Gadamer." *Journal of Indian Council of Philosophical Research* 9 (1992): 130–142.

Parsons, Talcott. *The Evolution of Societies*. Englewood Cliffs, NJ: Prentice-Hall, 1977.

Rahnema, Ali. "Ali Shariati: Teacher, Preacher, Rebel." In *Pioneers of Islamic Revival* – Second Edition, edited by Ali Rahnema, 208–250. New York: Zed Books, 2005.

An Islamic Utopian: A Political Biography of Ali Shari'ati. London and New York: I.B. Tauris, 2000.

"Introduction." In *Pioneers of Islamic Revival*– Second Edition, edited by Ali Rahnema, 1–10. New York: Zed Books, 2005.

"Introduction to 2nd Edition: Contextualizing the Pioneers of Islamic Revival." In *Pioneers of Islamic Revival*– Second Edition, edited by Ali Rahnema, ix-ixxiv. New York: Zed Books, 2005.

Rahnema, Saeed. "Retreat and Return of the Secular in Iran." *Comparative Studies of South Asia, Africa and the Middle East* 31, no. 1 (2011): 34–45.

Rawls, John. "The Idea of Public Reason Revisited." *University of Chicago Law Review* 64 (Summer 1997): 765–807.

Sachedina, Abdulaziz. "Ali Shariati: Ideologue of the Iranian Revolution." In *Voices of Resurgent Islam*, edited by John L. Esposito, 191–214. New York: Oxford University Press, 1983.

Sacks, Jonathan. *The Dignity of Difference: How to Avoid the Clash of Civilizations*. London and New York: Continuum, 2002.

Sadri, Mahmoud, and Ahmad Sadri. "Introduction." In *Reason, Freedom, and Democracy in Islam: Essential Writings of Abdolkarim Soroush*, edited by Mahmoud Sadri and Ahmad Sadri, ix-xix. New York: Oxford University Press, 2000.

Sadria, Modjtaba (ed.). *Multiple Modernities in Muslim Societies*. London: I.B. Tauris, 2009.

Said, Edward W. "Orientalism Reconsidered," *Cultural Critique*, no. 1. (Autumn 1985): 89–107.

Culture and Imperialism. New York: Alfred A. Knopf, 1993.

"Orientalism," *The Georgia Review* 31, no. 1 (Spring 1977): 162–206.

Orientalism: 25th Anniversary Edition. New York: Vintage Books, 1994.

"The Clash of Definitions." In *The New Crusades: Constructing the Muslim Enemy*, edited by Emran Qureshi and Michael A. Sells, 68–88. New York: Columbia University Press, 2003.

"The Clash of Ignorance," *The Nation* 273, no. 12 (October 22, 2001): 11–14.

Sajoo, Amyn B. "Introduction: Civic Quests and Bequests." In *Civil Society in the Muslim World: Contemporary Perspectives*, edited by Amyn B. Sajoo, 1–34. London: I.B. Tauris, 2002.

"Muslim Modernities and Civic Pluralism." *ISIM Review*, no. 21 (Spring 2008): 28–29.

(ed.). *Muslim Modernities: Expressions of the Civil Imagination*. London: I.B. Tauris, 2008.

Salehi-Isfahani, Djavad. "Iranian Youth in Times of Economic Crisis." *Iranian Studies* 44, no. 6 (2011): 789–806.

Salvatore, Armando. "From Civilizations to Multiple Modernities: The Issue of the Public Sphere." In *Multiple Modernities in Muslim Societies: Tangible Elements and Abstract Perspectives*, edited by Modjtaba Sadria, 19–26. London: I.B. Tauris, 2009.

"Tradition and Modernity within Islamic Civilization and the West." In *Islam and Modernity: Key Issues and Debates*, edited by Muhammad Khalid Masud, Armando Salvatore, and Martin van Bruinessen, 3–35. Edinburgh: Edinburgh University Press, 2009.

Sayyid, S. *A Fundamental Fear: Eurocentrism, and the Emergence of Islamism*. London and New York: Zed Books, 1997.

Schluchter, Wolfgang. *Rationalism, Religion, and Domination: A Weberian Perspective*, translated by Neil Solomon. Berkeley: University of California Press, 1989.

Sevindi, Nevval. *Contemporary Islamic Conversations: M. Fethullah Gülen on Turkey, Islam, and the West*, edited by Ibrahim M. Abu-Rabi, translated by Abdulah T. Antepli. New York: State University of New York, 2008.

Shilliam, Robbie. "Non-Western Thought and International Relations." In *International Relations and Non-Western Thought: Imperialism, Colonialism and Investigations of Global Modernity*, edited by Robbie Shilliam, 1–11. New York: Routledge, 2011.

"The Perilous but Unavoidable Terrain of the Non-West." In *International Relations and Non-Western Thought: Imperialism, Colonialism and Investigations of Global Modernity*, edited by Robbie Shilliam, 12–26. New York: Routledge, 2011.

Soroush, Abdolkarim. "The Idea of Democratic Religious Government." In *Reason, Freedom, and Democracy in Islam: Essential Writings of Abdolkarim Soroush*, edited by Mahmoud Sadri and Ahmad Sadri, 122–130. New York: Oxford University Press, 2000.

"The Sense and Essence of Secularism." In *Reason, Freedom, and Democracy in Islam: Essential Writings of Abdolkarim Soroush*, edited by Mahmoud Sadri and Ahmad Sadri, 54–68. New York: Oxford University Press, 2000.

Subrahmanyam, Sanjay. "Connected Histories: Notes towards a Reconfiguration of Early Modern Eurasia." *Modern Asian Studies* 31, no. 3 (July 1997): 735–762.

Swatos, Jr., William H., and Kevin J. Christiano. "Secularization Theory: The Course of a Concept," *Sociology of Religion* 60, no. 3 (Autumn, 1999): 209–228

Tavakoli-Targhi, Mohamad. "The Homeless Texts of Persianate Modernity." *Cultural Dynamics* 13, no. 3 (November 2001): 263–291.
Taylor, Charles. "A Catholic Modernity?" In *A Catholic Modernity?: Charles Taylor's Marianist Award Lecture with Responses by William M. Shea, Rosemary Luling Haughton, George Marsden, Jean Bethke Elshtain*, edited by James L. Heft. New York: Oxford University Press, 1999.
Modern Social Imaginaries. Durham and London: Duke University Press, 2004.
Sources of the Self: The Making of the Modern Identity. Cambridge, MA: Harvard University Press, 1989.
"Two Theories of Modernity." *Public Culture* 11, no. 1 (1999): 161.
"Why We Need a Radical Redefinition of Secularism." In *The Power of Religion in the Public Sphere*, edited by Eduardo Mendieta and Jonathan VanAntwerpen, 34–59. New York: Columbia University Press, 2011.
Tibi, Bassam. *The Crisis of Modern Islam: A Preindustrial Culture in the Scientific Technological Age*, translated by Judith von Sivers. Salt Lake City: University of Utah Press, 1988.
Tripp, Charles. "Sayyid Qutb: The Political Vision." In *Pioneers of Islamic Revival – Second Edition*, edited by Ali Rahnema, 154–183. New York: Zed Books, 2005.
Tohidi, Nayereh. "Modernity, Islamizaiton, and Women in Iran." In *Gender and National Identity: Women and Politics in Muslim Societies*, edited by Valentine M Moghadam, 110–147. London: Zed Books, 1994.
Vahdat, Farzin. "Critical Theory and the Islamic Encounter with Modernity." In *Islam and the West: Critical Perspectives on Modernity*, edited by Michael Thompson, 123–139. Oxford: Rowman & Littlefield, 2003.
God and Juggernaut: Iran's Intellectual Encounter with Modernity. Syracuse, NY: Syracuse University Press, 2002.
"Metaphysical Foundations of Islamic Revolutionary Discourse in Iran: Vacillations on Human Subjectivity." *Critique: Critical Middle Eastern Studies* 8, no. 14 (1999): 50–73.
"Religious Modernity in Iran: Dilemmas of Islamic Democracy in the Discourse of Mohammad Khatami." *Comparative Studies of South Asia, Africa and the Middle East* 25, no. 3 (2005): 650–664.
Wallerstein, Immanuel. "Eurocentrism and its Avatars: The Dilemmas of Social Science." *New Left Review* 226 (1997): 93–107.
Weber, Max. *The Protestant Ethics and the Spirit of Capitalism: The Relationship between Religion and the Economic and Social life in Modern Culture*, translated by Talcott Parsons. New York: Charles Scribner's Sons, 1958.
West, Cornel. *Democracy Matters: Winning the Fight against Imperialism.* New York: The Penguin Press, 2004.
"Dialogue: Judith Butler and Cornel West." In *The Power of Religion in the Public Sphere*, edited by Eduardo Mendieta and Jonathan VanAntwerpen, 101–108. New York: Columbia University Press, 2011.
"Prophetic Religion and the Future of Capitalist Civilization." In *The Power of Religion in the Public Sphere*, edited by Eduardo Mendieta and Jonathan VanAntwerpen, 92–100. New York: Columbia University Press, 2011.

The American Evasion of Philosophy: A Genealogy of Pragmatism. Madison: University of Wisconsin Press, 1989.
Yazbeck Haddad, Yvonne. "The Revivalist Literature and the Literature on Revival: An Introduction." In *The Contemporary Islamic Revival: A Critical Survey and Bibliography* edited by Yvonne Haddad Yazbeck et al., 3–22. Westport, CT: Greenwood Press, 1991.
Yousefi Eshkevari, Hassan. "Autobiography." In Ziba Mir-Hosseini and Richard Tapper, *Islam and Democracy in Iran: Eshkevari and the Quest for Reform*, 41–45. London: I.B. Tauris, 2006.
"Reformist Islam and Modern Society." In Ziba Mir-Hosseini and Richard Tapper, *Islam and Democracy in Iran: Eshkevari and the Quest for Reform*, 155–163. London: I.B. Tauris, 2006.
"Rethinking Men's Authority over Women: 'Qiwāma', 'Wilāya' and Their Underlying Assumptions," translated by Ziba Mir-Hosseini. In *Gender and Equality in Muslim Family Law: Justice and Ethics in the Islamic Legal Tradition*, edited by Ziba Mir-Hosseini, Kari Vogt, Lena Larsen, and Christian Moe, 191–213. London and New York: I.B. Tauris, 2013.
"Women's Rights and the Women's Movement." In Ziba Mir-Hosseini and Richard Tapper, *Islam and Democracy in Iran: Eshkevari and the Quest for Reform*, 163–173. London: I.B. Tauris, 2006.

Persian Sources

Abdolkarimi, Bijan. "Davate bozorg-e Shariati, tajdid-e ahd ba sonat-e tarikhi-e mast" ("Shariati's Major Invitation Was to Renew Our Historical Traditions"), Academy of Iranian Studies in London, January 17, 2012, http://iranianstudies.org/fa/ (accessed August 23, 2012).
"Ma va moderniteh beh revaiat-e Shariati" ("Modernity and Us as Narrated by Shariati"), Bijan Abdolkarimi Information Center, June 22, 2013, http://abdolkarimi.blogfa.com/post/83 (accessed November 29, 2014).
Ajoudani, Mashallah. *Mashrooteh Irani (Iranian Constitutionalism)*. Tehran: Akhtaran, 1387/2008.
Alatas, Syed Farid. "Goftegoo" ("Interview"). In *Shariati dar daneshgah (Shariati in the Academy)*, edited by Bonyad Shariati, 109–130. Tehran: Bonyad Farhangi-e Doctor Ali Shariati, 1390/2011.
Ali Shariati Information Center. "Erfan, barabari, azadi beh masabeh yek projeh" ("Spirituality, Equality, Freedom as a Project"), (no date), http://drshariati.org/show/?id=626 (accessed December 22, 2012).
"Mizgerd-e nasim-e bidari dar Barresi amoozeh-hay-e Shariati" ("Nasim-e Bidari's Panel on Shariati's Teachings"), (no date), http://drshariati.org/show/?id=212 (accessed July 27, 2012).
"Mizgerd-e dovom nashrieh nasim-e bidari dar bar-rasi shenakht shakhsiat Shariati," ("Nasim-e Bidariy's Second Panel on Examining Shariati's Character"), (no date), http://drshariati.org/show/?id=213 (accessed December 11, 2012).
"Shariati va gofteman-e edalat" ("Shariati and the Discourse of Justice"), (23 Azar 1390/December 14, 2011), http://drshariati.org/show/?id=539 (accessed March 5, 2012).

Aliakbari, Masoomeh. "Derangi dar zehniat-e ba vaseteh: naghdi bar nazar farzin Vahdat" ("A Reflection on Mediated Subjectivity: A Critique of Farzin Vahdat's Theory." In *Din va ideolojy (Religion and Ideology)*, edited by Bonyad Shariati, 367–389 (no publisher/no date).

Ghera-ati falsafi az yek zed-e filsoof: derang-hayi degar-andishaneh dar matni bi-payan beh nam-e doctor Ali Shariati (A Philosophical Reading of an Anti-Philosopher: Alternative Reflections on an Endless Text Called Dr. Ali Shariati). Tehran: Ghalam, 1386/2007.

Alijani, Reza. "Chera zan dar matoon moghadas?" ("Why the Question of Woman in Sacred Texts?"), Shariati Discourse Forum (no date), http://talar.shandel.info/showthread.php?tid=683&pid=3036#post_3035 (accessed July 2, 2011).

"Din, zan, va donyay-e jadid: goftegoo ba Reza Alijani" ("Religion, Women, and the Modern World: A Conversation with Reza Alijani"), *Cheshmandaz-e Iran* no. 44 (Tir-Mordad 1386/July-August 2007): 99–108.

Interview by author (Internet/Skype). November 20, 2012.

"Jonbesh zanan: jonbeshi mostaghel ama mortabet" ("Women's Movement: Independence and Interdependence"), *Baztab-e Andisheh* no. 70 (Bahman 1384/February 2006): 57–59.

"Motoon-e moghadas va doniaye jaded" ("Sacred Scriptures and the Modern World"), Shariati Discourse Forum (no date), http://talar.shandel.info/showthread.php?tid=683&pid=3036#post_3036 (accessed July 2, 2011).

Rend-e kham: shariati-shenasi jeld-e yekom: zamaneh, zendegi, va arman-ha (The Pure Noncomformist: Shariatiology Volume One: Era, Life, and Ideals) – Second Edition. Tehran: Ghalam, 1387/2008.

Seh Shariati dar ayineh zehn-e ma : eslam-garay-e enghelabi, motefaker-e mosleh, rend-e aref (Three Shariatis in Our Perceptions : Revolutionary Islamist, Refomist Intellectual, Artful Mystic). Tehran : Ghalam, 1389/2010

"Shariati dar bastar sonati gozashteh va jameh-e motakaser konooni" ("Shariati in his Traditional Social Context and our Pluralistic Contemporary Society"), Ali Shariati Information Center (no date) www.alishariati.ir/show/?id=205 (accessed May 14, 2012).

Shariat va gharb (Shariati and the West). Tehran: Ghalam, 1388/2009.

"Shariati va naghadi-e sonnat" ("Shariati and the Critique of Tradition"), *Iran-e Farda* no. 4, (Tir 1377/July 1998): 20–23.

"Tashaio sorkh, ya tashaio seh-rang-e irani" ("Red Shi'ism or Tricolored Iranian Shi'ism"), *Iran-e Farda* no. 34 (Tir 1376/July 1997): 30–34.

Arkoun, Mohammed. "Naghd-e aghl-e eslami va mafhoom-e khoda" ("The Critique of Islamic Reason and the Concept of God"), interview with Hashim Salih, translated by Mehdi Khalaji, *Kian* 27 (Khordad-Tir 1378/June-July 1999): 17–27.

Bonyad Shariati (ed.). *Shariati dar daneshgah (Shariati in the Academy)*. Tehran: Bonyad Farhangi-e Doctor Ali Shariati, 1390/2011.

Dabbagh, Soroush. "Tarikh-e ghara-at-e ideologik az din tamam shodeh ast" ("The History of Ideological Readings of Religion Has Reached its End"), *Nasim-e Bidary*, no. 7 (Khordad 1389/June 2010) http://soroushdabagh.com/home/pdf/58.pdf (accessed March 4, 2012).

Farasatkhah, Maghsoud. "*Roshanfekri dini: istadeh bar sar*" ("Religious Intellectuals: Standing on Its Head,"). Paper presented at Religion and Modernity seminar, Tehran, September 2007, http://e-b-a.blogfa.com/post-11.aspx (accessed February 20, 2012).

"*Shesh tip roshanfekri dini*" ("Six Types of Religious Intellectualism"). Islah Web, November 15, 2009, www.islahweb.org/node/2879 (accessed November 17, 2012).

Ghaneirad, Mohammad Amin. "Panel." In *Shariati dar daneshgah (Shariati in the Academy)*, edited by Bonyad Shariati, 64–68. Tehran: Bonyad Farhangi-e Doctor Ali Shariati, 1390/2011.

Tabar-shenasi-e aghlaniat-e modern: ghara'ati post-modern az andisheh doktor Ali Shariati (The Genealogy of Modern Rationality: A Post-Modern Reading of the Thought of Dr. Ali Shariati). Tehran: Naghd-e Farhang, 1381/2002.

Ghouchani, Mohammad. "Shesh nasl farzandan-e Shariati" ("Six Generations of Shariati's Children"), *Khordad* 28 (Khordad 1383/June 17, 2004).

Hajarian, Saeed. "Shariati mojadad bood va na motajaded" ("Shariati was a Revivalist not a Modernizer"), *Nasim-e Bidary*, no. 7 (Khordad 1389/June 2010), http://drshariati.org/show.asp?id=210 (accessed March 4, 2012).

Iqbal, Jawid. "Moghaddameh" ("Introduction"). In *Koliat-e iqbal lahori (The Poetry Collection of Iqbal Lahori)*, 19–34. Tehran: Elham, 1384/2005.

Jahanbegloo, Ramin. *Zir asmanhay-e jahan: goftegooye Dariush Shayegan ba Ramin Jahanbegloo (Under the World's Skies: Dariush Shayegan in Conversation with Ramin Jahanbegloo)*. Tehran: Farzan Rooz, 1387/2008.

Khatami, Farid. "Panel." In *Shariati dar daneshgah Shariati in the Academy)*. 22–28. Tehran. Bonyad Farhangi-e Doctor Ali Shariati, 1390/2011.

Mahdavi, Mojtaba. "Radikalism az do didgah: gofteman-e kelasik va noradikalism-e Shariati" ("Radicalism from Two Perspectives: The Classical Discourse and Shariati's Neo-Radicalism"). In *Ghoghnoos-e osian: revaiati digar az andisheh doktor Shariati (The Rebellious Phoenix: Another Account of the Thought of Dr. Shariati)*, edited by Amir Rezaei, 237–264. Tehran: Ghasidehsara, 2002.

(Mesbahian) Rahyab, Hossein. "Defa-e johari az mantegh darooni-e ideolojy: rooyarooyee ba bardasht-haye nadorost," ("A Foundational Defense of the Internal Logic of Ideology: Challenging Misconceptions"). In *Dar hashiyeh matn (On the Margins of the Text)*, edited by Bonyad Shariati, 37–130. Tehran: Shahr-e Aftab, 1379/2000.

Interview by author (Internet/ooVoo). April 23, 2013.

"Jameheh bi arman morde ast" ("A Society without Ideals is a Society without Life"), *Shargh* 1497 (19 Farvardin 1391/April 7, 2012): 26–29, http://old.sharghdaily.ir/pdf/91-01-19/vijeh/29.pdf (accessed August 8, 2012).

"Mahiat, mavane' va emkanat-e no-sazi-e hoviat-e irani" (Nature, Possibilities and Challenges of the Restructuring of Iranian Identity). In *Khodkavi-e melli dar asr-e jahani shoda (National Self-Examination in the Age of Globalization)*, edited by Bonyad Shariati, 54–96. Tehran: Ghasidehsara, 1381/2002.

(Mesbahian) Rahyab, Hossein. "Shariati va nam-e khoda" ("Shariati and the Name of God"). In *Din va ideolojy (Religion and Ideology)*, edited by Bonyad Shariati, 185–255 (no publisher/no date).

Motamed-Dezfooli, Faramarz. *Kavir: tajrobeh moderniteh irani: tafsir va bazkhani kavir doktor Ali Shariati (The Desert: The Experience of Iranian Modernity: Revisiting and Reinterpreting Dr. Ali Shariati's The Desert)*. Tehran: Ghalam, 1387.

Naraghi, Ehsan. "Tafakor gheir-demokratik-e Shariati amel-e nakami eslahat" ("Shariati's anti-Democratic Thought Responsible for the Failure of Reformism"), *Etemad Melli*, 29 Khordad 1385/June 19, 2006, http://talar.shandel.info/showthread.php?tid=237#post_486 (accessed May 14, 2013).

Nasr, Seyyed Hossein. "Goftam ba taraghi mokhalefam, cheh resad beh kanoon taraghi," ("Firmly Opposed to Taraghi Center") interview with Hamed Zare, *Mehrnameh* 2, no. 23 (30 Tir 1391/July 20, 2012): 111–115.

Rahmani, Taghi. "Azadi dar marhaleh eradeh, shenakht, va ghanoon" ("Freedom in Three Phases: Will, Recognition, and Law"), *Payam-e Hajar* no. 269 special issue, Shariati and Freedom (25 Khordad 1378/June 15, 1999): 26–34.

———. "Dar rastay-e moderniteh sharghi" ("Toward an Eastern Modernity"), *Iran-e Farda* 6, no. 34 (Tir 1376/July 1997): 25–27.

———. "Protestantism va fahm-e Shariati az an: goftegooy-e Susan Shariati va Taghi Rahmani" ("Protestantism and Shariati's Understanding of It: A Conversation between Susan Shariati and Taghi Rahmani"), interview with Lotfollah Meisami, *Cheshmandaz Iran* 65 (Day-Bahman 1389/January-February 2011), http://drshariati.org/show/?id=472 (accessed September 17, 2012).

———. "Zaban Soroush, zaban-e tanafor" ("The Language of Hate in Soroush's Discourse"), interview with Hossein Sokhanvar, *Etemad* no.1927 (27 Farvardin 1388/April 17, 2009), www.etemaad.ir/Released/88-01-27/256.htm (accessed June 7, 2012).

Sadr, Musa. "*Sokhanrani emam Musa Sadr dar arbaeen-e Shariati*" ("Lecture by Imam Musa Sadr at the Fortieth day of Shariati's Death"). Ali Shariati Information Center, http://drshariati.org/show/?id=182 (accessed on May 27, 2013).

Shariat-Razavi, Pouran. *Tarhi az yek zendegi (Portrait of a Life)*. Tehran: Chapakhsh, 1376/1997.

Shariati, Ali. "Arezooha" ("Aspirations") 1355/1976, C.W. 25, *Ali Shariati: The Complete Collection of Works* [CD ROM]. Tehran: Shariati Cultural Foundation, 2010.

———. "Azadi, khojasteh azadi," ("Freedom, Joyous Freedom"), (no date), C.W. 2, *Ali Shariati: The Complete Collection of Works* [CD ROM]. Tehran: Shariati Cultural Foundation, 2010.

———. "Ba to ei mehrban javdan-e asib napazir" ("With You, O Eternal and Imperishable Kindness"), 1356/1977 C.W. 1, *Ali Shariati: The Complete Collection of Works* [CD ROM], Tehran: Shariati Cultural Foundation, 2010.

———. "Bahs-e kolli raje beh tamadon va farhang" ("General Discussion about Civilization and Culture"), 1348/1969, C.W. 11, *Ali Shariati: The Complete

Collection of Works [CD ROM]. Tehran: Shariati Cultural Foundation, 2010.

Bazgasht: majmooeh asar 4 (Return: Collected Works 4). Tehran: Entesharat-e Elham, 1373/1994.

"Bazgasht beh khish" ("Return to the Self"), 1350/1971, C.W. 4, *Ali Shariati: The Complete Collection of Works* [CD ROM]. Tehran: Shariati Cultural Foundation, 2010.

"Bazgasht beh kodam khish?" ("Return to Which Self?"), 1350/1971, C.W. 4, *Ali Shariati: The Complete Collection of Works* [CD ROM]. Tehran: Shariati Cultural Foundation, 2010.

"Chegooneh Mandan" ("How to Stay"), 1355/1976, C.W. 2, *Ali Shariati: The Complete Collection of Works* [CD ROM]. Tehran: Shariati Cultural Foundation, 2010.

"Cheh bayad kard?" ("What Is To Be Done?"), 1350/1971, C.W. 20, *Ali Shariati: The Complete Collection of Works* [CD ROM]. Tehran: Shariati Cultural Foundation, 2010.

"Chera asatir rooh-e hameye tamadon-hay-e doniast?" ("Why Mythology is the Spirit of All World Civilizations"), 1348/1969, C.W. 11, *Ali Shariati: The Complete Collection of Works* [CD ROM]. Tehran: Shariati Cultural Foundation, 2010.

"Ensan, eslam va maktab-hay-e maghreb zamin," ("Human, Islam, and Western Schools"), (no date), C.W. 24, *Ali Shariati: The Complete Collection of Works* [CD ROM], Tehran: Shariati Cultural Foundation, 2010

"Ensan va Islam" ("Humanity and Islam"), (1347/1968), C.W. 24, *Ali Shariati: The Complete Collection of Works* [CD ROM], Tehran: Shariati Cultural Foundation, 2010.

"Erfan, barabari, azadi" ("Spirituality, Equality, Freedom"), 1355/1976, C.W. 2, *Ali Shariati: The Complete Collection of Works* [CD ROM]. Tehran: Shariati Cultural Foundation, 2010.

"Eslam Chist?" ("What is Islam?"), (1345/1966), C.W. 30, *Ali Shariati: The Complete Collection of Works* [CD ROM], Tehran: Shariati Cultural Foundation, 2010.

"Eslam shenasi: dars-e aval va dovom," ("Islamology: Lessons One and Two"), (1350/1971), C.W. 16, *Ali Shariati: The Complete Collection of Works* [CD ROM], Tehran: Shariati Cultural Foundation, 2010.

"Eslam shenasi: dars-e chahardah" ("Islamology: Lesson Fourteen"), 1351/1972, C.W. 17, *Ali Shariati: The Complete Collection of Works* [CD ROM], Tehran: Shariati Cultural Foundation, 2010.

"Eslam shenasi: dars-e haftom" ("Islamology: Lesson Seven"), (1351/1972), C.W. 16, *Ali Shariati: The Complete Collection of Works* [CD ROM], Tehran: Shariati Cultural Foundation, 2010.

"Eslam shenasi: dars-e hashtom," ("Islamology: Lesson Eight"), (1351/1972), C.W. 16, *Ali Shariati: The Complete Collection of Works* [CD ROM], Tehran: Shariati Cultural Foundation, 2010

"Estekhraj va tasfieh manabe farhangi" ("Extraction and Refinement of Cultural Resources"), 1348/1969, C.W. 20, *Ali Shariati: The Complete Collection of Works* [CD ROM]. Tehran: Shariati Cultural Foundation, 2010.

Select Bibliography

"Farhang va ideolojy" ("Culture and Ideology"), 1350/1971, C.W. 23, *Ali Shariati: The Complete Collection of Works* [CD ROM]. Tehran: Shariati Cultural Foundation, 2010.

"Fatemeh Fatemeh ast" ("Fatemeh Is Fatemeh"), (1350/1971), C.W. 21, *Ali Shariati: The Complete Collection of Works* [CD ROM], Tehran: Shariati Cultural Foundation, 2010.

"Haj-e bozorgtar," ("The Greater Haj"), (1350/1971), C.W. 6, *Ali Shariati: The Complete Collection of Works* [CD ROM], Tehran: Shariati Cultural Foundation, 2010.

Hoboot (The Descent). Tehran: Soroush, 1359/1981.

"Horr," 1355/1976, C.W. 2, *Ali Shariati: The Complete Collection of Works* [CD ROM], Tehran: Shariati Cultural Foundation, 2010.

"Jahatgiri-e tabaghati dar Islam; daftar-e avval" ("Class Orientation in Islam; Book One"), 1356/1977, C.W. 10, *Ali Shariati: The Complete Collection of Works* [CD ROM]. Tehran: Shariati Cultural Foundation, 2010.

"Khodsazi-e enghelabi" ("Revolutionary Self-Preparedness"), 1355/1976, C.W. 2, *Ali Shariati: The Complete Collection of Works* [CD ROM]. Tehran: Shariati Cultural Foundation, 2010.

"Khosoosiat-e ghoroon-e moasser" ("The Characteristics of the Modern Centuries"), 1347/1968, C.W. 12, *Ali Shariati: The Complete Collection of Works* [CD ROM]. Tehran: Shariati Cultural Foundation, 2010.

Ma va Iqbal: majmooeh asar 5 (Iqbal and Us: Collected Works 5). Aachen, Germany: Hosseinieh Ershad, 1978.

"Mazhab alaih-e mazhab" ("Religion versus Religion"), 1349/1970, C.W. 22, *Ali Shariati: The Complete Collection of Works* [CD ROM]. Tehran: Shariati Cultural Foundation, 2010.

"Meraj va Esra" ("Ascension and Isra"), 1355/1977, C.W. 2, *Ali Shariati: The Complete Collection of Works* [CD ROM]. Tehran: Shariati Cultural Foundation, 2010.

"Moghadameh" ("Introduction"), *Kolliat-e Iqbal Lahori (The Poetry Collection of Iqbal Lahori)*, 1–18. Tehran: Elham, 1384/2005.

"Nameh beh aghayan Homayoun va Minachi," ("Letter to Mr. Homayoun and Mr. Minachi") 1351/1972, C.W. 1, *Ali Shariati: The Complete Collection of Works* [CD ROM], Tehran: Shariati Cultural Foundation, 2010.

"Nameh beh Ehsan" ("Letter to Ehsan"), Azar 1355/December 1967, C.W. 1, *Ali Shariati: The Complete Collection of Works* [CD ROM]. Tehran: Shariati Cultural Foundation, 2010.

"Nameh beh Ehsan" ("Letter to Ehsan"), Farvardin-Ordibehesht 1356/April-May 1977, C.W. 1, *Ali Shariati: The Complete Collection of Works* [CD ROM]. Tehran: Shariati Cultural Foundation, 2010.

"Nameh beh pedar" ("Letter to Father"), 1351/1972, C.W. 1, *Ali Shariati: The Complete Collection of Works* [CD ROM], Tehran: Shariati Cultural Foundation, 2010.

"Nameh beh yek baradar," ("Letter to a Brother"), 1355/1976, C.W. 1, *Ali Shariati: The Complete Collection of Works* [CD ROM], Tehran: Shariati Cultural Foundation, 2010.

Select Bibliography

"Ommat va imamat" ("Community and Leadership"), 1348/1969, C.W. 26, *Ali Shariati: The Complete Collection of Works* [CD ROM], Tehran: Shariati Cultural Foundation, 2010.

"Tamadon chist?" ("What is Civilization?"), 1349/1970, C.W. 11, *Ali Shariati: TheComplete Collection of Works* [CD ROM]. Tehran: Shariati Cultural Foundation, 2010.

"Tamadon va tajadod" ("Civilization and Modernization"), 1348/1969, C.W. 31, *Ali Shariati: The Complete Collection of Works* [CD ROM]. Tehran: Shariati Cultural Foundation, 2010.

"Vijegihaye tamadon-e emrooz" ("The Characteristics of Today's Civilization"), 1348/1969, C.W. 12, *Ali Shariati: The Complete Collection of Works* [CD ROM]. Tehran: Shariati Cultural Foundation, 2010.

"Yek bar-e digar Abuzar," ("Once Again Abuzar"), (1351/1972), C.W. 3, *Ali Shariati: The Complete Collection of Works* [CD ROM], Tehran: Shariati Cultural Foundation, 2010.

Shariati, Ehsan. "Bar-e digar enghelab, yad-avar enghelab" ("Once More Revolution, A Reminder of Revolution"), *Shargh* (18 Bahman 1389/ February 7, 2011), http://talar.shandel.info/showthread.php?tid=318#post_3691 (accessed May 19, 2011).

"Cheh cheshm-andazi bara bahar-e Arab?" ("What Prospects for the Arab Spring?"), Rahnameh (no date), http://ehsanshariati.org/show/?id=60 (accessed January 4, 2013).

"Edalat zeil-e azadi ast: andisheh-hay-e eghtesadi-e Ali Shariati dar goftegoo ba Ehsan Shariati" ("Equality is a Part of Freedom: Discussing Ali Shariati's Economic Ideas with Ehsan Shariati"), *Ta'adol* (Khordad 1393/June 2014), http://taadolnewspaper.ir/ (accessed June 19, 2014).

"Ehsan az Shariati migooyad: dar goftegoo ba Ham-Mihan" ("Ehsan Talks about Shariati: In Conversation with Ham-Mihan") interview with Mohammad Ghouchani and Mehdi Ghani, *Ham-Mihan* (29 Khordad 1386/ June 19, 2007), 17–18.

"Goftegoo, hoghoogh-e bashar: rahyabi va rahkar" ("Dialogue, Human Rights: Approaches and Methods"), Shariati Discourse Forum (no date), http://talar.shandel.info/pdf/ehsan1003.pdf (accessed August 3, 2012).

"Goftegooye rooznameh etemad ba Ehsan Shariati" ("Etemad Newspaper's Interview with Ehsan Shariati"), Ali Shariati Information Center (no date) http://drshariati.org/show/?id=96 (accessed September 9, 2013).

"Hamchenan armangara, enghelabi, va ideolojik hastam" ("I Remain Utopian, Revolutionary, and Ideological"), interview with Susan Shariati, *Shahrvand-e Emrooz*, 10 Tir 1387/June 30, 2008, http://shahrvandemroz.blogfa.com/post-557.aspx (accessed November 3, 2011).

"Manaviat dar sepehr-e omoomi: dar astaneh sio panjomin salyad amoozgare 'erfan, azadi, Barabari'" ("Spirituality in the Public Sphere: On the Thirty Fifth Anniversary of the Teacher of 'Spirituality, Freedom, and Equality'") *Etemad* no. 2421 (28 Khordad 1391/June 17, 2012), www.etemadnewspaper.ir/Released/91-03-28/226.htm#204247 (accessed December 4, 2012).

"Mavane estemrar rah-e Shariati" (The Challenges of Continuing Shariati's Path"), Rahnameh, (no date) http://ehsanshariati.org/show/?id=6 (accessed January 4, 2013).

"Na-e bozorg" ("The Big No"), *Vijenameh Yekomin Salgard*, no. 1 (Khordad 1357/June1979): 51–56.

"Nayandishideh mandeh haye falsafi andisheh ye mo'alem Shariati" ("The Philosophical Unthoughts of the Thought of Teacher Shariati"). In *Dar hashiyeh matn (On the Margins of the Text)*, edited by Bonyad Shariati, 9–35. Tehran: Shahr-e Aftab, 1379/2000.

"Pas az seh daheh" ("After Three Decades"), interview with Shariati Cultural Foundation, Ali Shariati Information Center (no date), http://drshariati.org/show/?id=483 (accessed August 20, 2011).

"Pedaran va pesaran: ehsan shariati va soroush dabagh az andisheh khod va pedaraneshan migooyand" ("Fathers and Sons: Ehsan Shariati and Soroush Dabagh on their Own Ideas and their Fathers' Legacies") interview with Reza Khojasteh Rahimi, *Mehrnameh* 1 (Esfand 1388/March 2010), www.mehrnameh.ir/article/133/ (accessed January 7, 2013).

"Rah-e Shariati" ("Shariati's Way"), *Jaras*, 10 Tir 1390/July 1, 2011, www.rahesabz.net/story/38930 (accessed November 14, 2011).

"Safar-e bozorg" ("The Big Journey"), *Mehrab* no. 1 special issue Rendezvous with Shariati (1359/1980): 15–17.

"Shahrvand kist? shaharvandi chegooneh raftarist?" ("Who is the Citizen? What Kind of Behavior is Citizenship?"), Rahnameh (no date), http://ehsanshariati.org/show/?id=4 (accessed August 14, 2012).

"Shariati andishmand-e azadi: matn-e kamel sokhanrani-e Ehsan Shariati dar marasem siomin salgard shahadat-e doktor Ali Shariati dar hosseinieh ershad – khordad 1386" ("Shariati the Thinker of Freedom: The Full Text of Ehsan Shariati's Talk at the Thirtieth Anniversary of Shariati's Martyrdom at the Hosseinieh Ershad – June 2007"), Ali Shariati Information Center (no date), http://drshariati.org/show.asp?id=30 (accessed November 2, 2012).

"Shariati si-o seh sal bad" ("Shariati after Thirty Three Years"), Ali Shariati Information Center (no date) www.drshariati.org/show.asp?ID=171&q= (accessed September 9, 2012).

"Shekast-e tajadod talabi mashrooteh va nakaramadi-e fekri-e roshanfekran mosalman" ("The Failure of Constitutionalist Modernism and the Ineffectiveness of Muslim Intellectuals") interview with Ruhollah Mohajeri, ILNA: Iranian Labor News Agency (August 5, 2010), http://old.ilna.ir/newsContext.aspx?ID=138817 (accessed October 7, 2011).

"Talfigh dar projeh: goftegoo ba Ehsan Shariati dar bareh haghighat va nakami 'demokrasy motahed,'" ("Synthesis in Project: Interview with Ehsan Shariati about the Promise and the Failure of 'Guided Democracy'"), interview with Parvin Bakhtiar-Nejad, *Shargh* (24 Tir 1386/July 15, 2007), http://talar.shandel.info/showthread.php?tid=443#post_1997 (accessed May 20, 2012).

"Zamaneh Shariati-e pesar sakht-tar ast" ("The Times are Harder for Shariati the Son"), interview with Samina Rastegari, *Etemad* no. 1992 (13 Tir 1388/July 4, 2009), www.etemaad.ir/Released/88-04-13/150.htm (accessed June 7, 2012).

Shariati, Sara. "Chehreh jahani-gar, chehreh jahani-zadeh: siasat jahani kardan va ravand tarikhi jahani shodan" ("The Globalizer Face and the Globalized Face: An Evaluation of Globalizing Policies and the Process of Globalization"). In *Khodkavi-e melli dar asr-e jahani shodan (National Self-Examination in the Age of Globalization)*, edited by Bonyad Shariati, 121–174. Tehran: Ghasidehsara, 1381/2002.

"Dar bareh sharaiet-e emkan-e moderniteh dini" (On the Conditions for the Possibility of Religious Modernity"). In *Dar hashiyeh matn (On the Margins of the Text)*, edited by Bonyad Shariati, 131–166. Tehran: Shahr-e Aftab, 1379/2000.

"Din-e ma va dine anha" ("Our Religion and Their Religion"), Kanoon-e Arman-e Shariati (no date), www.slideshare.net/sco1385/ss-17593 30 (accessed July 13, 2013).

"Eslah dini beh masabeh eslah ejtemaei?" ("Religious Reform as Social Reform?"), Sara Shariati Internet Archives, April 17, 2011, http://sarahshariati.blogspot.ca/2011/04/blog-post_3728.html (accessed February 6, 2013).

"Faghr, chaleshi barai-e din" ("Poverty, a Challenge for Faith"), Sara Shariati Internet Archives. January 30, 2014, http://sarahshariati.blogspot.com/2014/01/blog-post.html (accessed November 21, 2014).

Interview by author (telephone). November 28, 2012.

"Karbord-e farhang" ("The Function of Culture"), Sara Shariati Internet Archives, April 17, 2011, http://sarahshariati.blogspot.ca/2011/04/blog-post_5280.html (accessed February 25, 2013).

"*Zaman-e omid*" ("The Era of Hope"), Sara Shariati Internet Archives, April 17, 2011, http://sarahshariati.blogspot.ca/2011/04/blog-post_1023.html (accessed December 23, 2012).

Shariati, Susan. "Chand kalameh harf-e zananeh: beh bahaneye rooz-e jahani-e zan" ("A Few Feminine Words: On the Occasion of the International Women's Day"). In Susan Shariati, *Don kishot dar shahr (Don Quixote in the City)*, 235–238. Tehran: Rasesh, 1388/2010.

"Dar mian-e do-ganeh-hay-e terajik: Shariati olgoo ya ravesh" ("Between Tragic Binaries: Shariati, Model or Method"), *Shargh* (29 Khordad 1386/June 19, 2007), http://drshariati.org/show/?id=36 (accessed April 13, 2011).

Don kishot dar shahr (Don Quixote in the City). Tehran: Rasesh, 1388/2010.

"Moghadameh: tafakor dar taghato" ("Introduction: Thinking at Crossroads"). In Faramarz Motamed-Dezfooli, *kavir: tajrobeh moderniteh irani: tafsir va bazkhani kavir doktor Ali Shariati (The Desert: The Experience of Iranian Modernity: Revisiting and Reinterpreting Dr. Ali Shariati's* The Desert*)*, 9–20. Tehran: Ghalam, 1387/2008.

"Paradox-hay-e vojdan-e asheghaneh dar negah-e Shariati" ("The Paradoxes of the Loving Consciousness in Shariati's Thought"), *Madreseh* no. 3 (Ordibehesht 1385/May 2006), http://drshariati.org/show/?id=123 (accessed March 2, 2011).

"Popolism: khizeshi baray-e tashakhos" ("Populism: A Movement for Recognition"). In Susan Shariati, *Don kishot dar shahr (Don Quixote in the City)*, 103–108. Tehran: Rasesh, 1388/2010.

"Protestantism va fahm-e Shariati az an: goftegooy-e Susan Shariati va Taghi Rahmani" ("Protestantism and Shariati's Understanding of It: A

Conversation between Susan Shraiati and Taghi Rahmani"), interview with Lotfollah Meisami, *Cheshmandaz Iran* 65, (Day-Bahman 1389/January-February 2011), http://drshariati.org/show/?id=472 (accessed September 17, 2012).

"Shaieh-ei beh nam-e Shariati" ("A Rumor Called Shariati"), *Etemad*, 2 Esfand 1386/February 2008, www.slideshare.net/sco1385/ss-1762423 (accessed July 11, 2011).

"Shariati, moalem kodam enghelab?" ("Shariati, the Teacher of Which Revolution?"), *Shahrvand Emrooz*, Bahman 1386/February 2008, www.slideshare.net/sco1385/ss-1762422 (accessed July 11, 2011).

"Simay-e yek zendani: negahi beh ketab-e Shariati beh revaiat-e asnad-e savak," ("The Portrait of a Prisoner: A Look at a Book Titled Shariati as Narrated by SAVAK Documents"). In *Ghoghnoos-e osian: revaiati digar az andisheh doktor Shariati (The Rebellious Phoenix: Another Account of the Thought of Dr. Shariati)*, edited by Amir Rezaei, 133–178. Tehran: Ghasidehsara, 2002.

"Zanan dar projeh Shariati" ("Women in Shariati's Project"), interview with Parvin Bakhtiarnejad, *Etemad* (15 Aban 1386/November 6, 2007), http://drshariati.org/show.asp?id=106 (accessed April 17, 2011).

Shayegan, Dariush. "Ayin hendoo va erfan eslami" ("Hindu Tradition and Islamic Mysticism"), interview with Aliasghar Seyed Abadi, *Baztab-e Andisheh*, no. 77 (Shahrivar 1385/September 2006), www.noormags.com/view/fa/articlepage/110528 (accessed February 8, 2012).

Soroush, Abdolkarim. *Az Shariati (On Shariati)*. Tehran: Serat, 1384/2006.

Bast-e tajrobe-ye nabavi (The Expansion of Prophetic Experience). Tehran: Serat, 1378/1999.

"Din-e aghalli va aksari" ("Minimal and Maximal Religion"). *Kyan* no. 41 (1377/1998): 2–9.

Tabatabei, Seyyed Javad. "Maktab-e Tabriz va mabani-e tajadod-khahi" ("The Tabriz School of Thought and the Foundations of Modernism"), www.javadtabatabai.org/search/label/978-600-5003-06-2 (accessed June 20, 2011).

Vahdat, Farzin. "Shariati: bohran-e hoviat-e irani va zehn-bonyadi" ("Shariati: The Crisis of the Iranian Identity and Subjectivity"), translated by Simin Fasihi, in *Khodkavi-e melli dar asr-e jahani shodan (National Self-Examination in the Age of Globalization)* edited by Bonyad Shariati, 222–237. Tehran: Ghasidehsara, 1381/2002.

Yousefi Eshkevari, Hassan. "Edameh projeh na-tamam" ("Continuing an Unfinished Project"), interview with Reza Khojasteh Rahimi, *Toos* no. 764 (Khordad 1377/June 1998): 30–31.

"Ma va miras-e Shariati" ("Us and Shariati's Legacy"), (1385/2006), http://talar.shandel.info/showthread.php?tid=439#post_2222 (accessed October 11, 2011).

"Pasokhi beh pendar-hay-e Akbar Ganji dar mored-e Ali Shariati" ("A Response to Akbar Ganji's Assumptions about Ali Shariati"), Ali Shariati Information Center (no date), http://drshariati.org/show.asp?id=97 (accessed March 3, 2012).

Index

Abdolkarimi, Bijan, 38–39
Abduh, Muhammad, 23, 53–54, 56, 62, 169
Abrahamian, Ervand, 10, 13, 27–29, 37, 54, 82
Abrahamic religions, 91
Abu-Rabi, Ibrahim M., 52–53, 56–58, 60–62, 64
Abu Zar, 30
Abu Zayd, Nasr Hamid, 4, 18, 58, 62–66, 73, 120, 169, 172
Adorno, Theodor, 18, 47, 111, 119, 129
Afghani, Sayyid Jamal al-Din, 23, 25, 53–56, 62, 66–69, 72, 169
Afghanistan, 2, 12, 49, 57
Africa, 23, 88, 137–139, 143, 145–146, 148, 155, 160
aggiornamento, 79, 82. *See also* Second Vatican Council
Aghajari, Hashem, 14
Ahmed, Leila, 4, 62, 176
Akhavi, Shahrough, 13, 102–103
Akhundzadeh, Mirza Fatali, 51
Alatas, Syed Farid, 12–13, 180
Alatas, Syed Hussein, 24
al-Banna, Hassan, 58
Al-Farabi, 63, 155
al-Ghannouchi, Rachid, 171
Al-Ghazali, 155
Al-Jahiz, 63, 155
Al-Kindi, 63, 155
al-Qaradawi, Yusuf, 58
Al-Razi, 63, 155
al-Sadr, Musa, 10
Al-Tawhidi, 63
al-Turabi, Hassan, 58
Ale Ahmad, Jalal, 22
Algar, Hamid, 13, 29
alienation, 7, 22, 72, 126, 158
Alijani, Reza, 10, 14, 71, 84–86, 92–101, 122–123, 159–160, 175, 177
Algeria, 7, 12, 31, 62, 149
Aliakbari, Masoumeh, 123, 131–132
An-Na'im, Abdullahi Ahmed, 4, 62, 81
anticolonial
  cosmopolitanism, 135
  discourses, 23, 25, 67, 101, 150, 161, 163
  intellectuals, 13, 68, 72
  modernity, 165, 178
  struggles, 7, 37, 91, 139, 145, 147, 149
antimodernism, 34, 76, 144
Arafat, Yasser, 9
Arab Spring, 4, 169–171, 174
Arkoun, Mohammed, 4, 18, 62–66, 73, 169, 172
armed struggle, 7, 31–32, 42. *See also* guerrilla warfare
Arnason, Johann P., 80
Asia, 16, 57, 88, 138, 143–144, 146, 155, 160
authenticism, 33, 35–40, 43, 58, 60–61, 103–104, 134–135, 149–150, 178
authoritarianism, 25, 36, 38, 63, 67, 88, 101, 105, 118, 130, 172

autonomous will, 69, 86, 102, 124, 133.
    See also free will
Averroes, See Ibn Rushd
Avicenna, See Ibn Sina

Bacon, Francis, 122
Bayat, Asef, 171–172, 174
Bazargan, Mehdi, 62–63
Beirut, 9
Benjamin, Walter, 119
Benvenist, Émile, 136
Berque, Jacques, 7, 157
Best, Lloyd, 24
Bible, 75, 124, 126
binary analysis
    East/West, 15, 39, 135, 141–143,
        149–150, 157, 160–162, 165
    Enlightenment/counter-Enlightenment,
        35, 105
    Islam/modernity, 3–4, 13–14, 18, 39, 81,
        135, 161, 165
    public/private, 78
    reason/non-reason, 120
    religious/secular, 74, 78, 81
    religious reason/secular reason, 74, 105,
        108, 111, 114, 117, 124
    sacred/secular, 112–113, 115,
        117–121, 124
    self/other, 128–129, 155
    tradition/modernity, 40, 44, 82, 135,
        161, 165
    West/rest, 49, 155, 179
Bloch, Ernst, 119
Borda, Orlando Fals, 24
Boroujerdi, Mehrzad, 34–37, 82, 134–135
Borzoui, Mohammad Bagher, 10
bottom-up change, 19–20, 27, 39, 41,
    71–72, 81, 85, 88, 93, 100, 135, 175
Britain, 6, 48, 53, 67
Butler, Judith, 116, 119–120

Caliph Uthman ibn Affan, 30
caliphate
    Ottoman, 48
    post-Muhammad, 28, 30, 58
    Umayyad, 26, 58
capitalism
    decentralization of, 151
    global expansion of, 5, 25, 82, 95,
        138–139, 147–148, 168, 175
    and human freedom, 96, 111
    industrial, 84, 95
    and Islamic thought, 56, 72, 175
    and rise of European modernity, 15, 78,
        112. See also modernity
Cartesian doubt, 122
Cartesian subjectivity, 130
Casanova, José, 15, 47–48, 78–79
Catholicism, 78, 79, 82
Césaire, Aimé, 3, 68, 145
Christian Reformation, 44, 67, 69, 83, 168.
    See also Protestant Reformation
Christianity
    and civilizational analysis, 136
    and Islam, 35, 75, 135
    and modernity, 46, 83
    prophetic, 18
    and secularism, 79
    and the West, 49
civil society, 19, 45, 49, 80, 88–89,
    107, 167
civilization
    African, 137–138
    Assyrian, 142
    Babylonian, 142
    Chinese, 136–138, 147
    and colonialism, 138
    Confucian, 75–76
    Eastern, 136, 142–143
    and Eurocentrism, 3, 61, 67, 116, 138,
        140–141, 147, 152–154
    global, 137, 139
    Indian, 136–138, 147
    Iranian, 137
    Islamic, see Islamic civilization
    and modernity, 67, 84, 117, 138, 142
    multiple civilizations, 147
    new, 139–140
    particular vs. general meaning, 136
    rise and fall, 137
    robotic, 139
    Sumerian, 142
    Western, 84, 136–139, 142–143, 147,
        151, 153
civilizational cosmopolitanism, See
    cosmopolitanism
civilizational dialogue, 153–154, 156, 162
civilizational diversity, 20, 80, 136, 140,
    143, 150, 155, 160–161
civilizational framework, 20, 134–164, 180
civilizational stagnation, 123
clash of civilizations, 49, 75–76, 154

Index

clerical class, 29, 34, 94. *See also* ecclesiastical class
clerical institution, 22, 82
Cold War, 2, 37, 76
collectivism, 104–105, 109–110, 125, 128, 130, 133
colonial periphery, 3, 22, 146
colonialism, 1–5, 7, 13, 15, 17–20, 22–26, 47–48, 53–54, 57, 67–68, 82, 84, 101, 108, 115, 137–138, 140–141, 143–145, 148, 150–151, 159–163, 165–168, 172, 178–179
committed democracy, 70, 87. *See also* guided democracy
communitarianism, 15
community, 64, 104, 121, 146, 152
Connell, Raewyn, 13, 179
consciousness
   civilized, 142
   collective, 7, 21, 24, 70–71, 125, 155
   critical, 5, 89
   individual, 125
   national, 146
   political, 30, 70
   public, 29
   revolutionary, 12, 28, 72, 87
   self-, 24, 55, 86, 107, 109, 122–126, 136, 139, 166. *See also* self-awareness
   social, 146
   transformative, 37, 45–46
comparative political theory, 16–17
Constitutional Movement, 23
Continental philosophy, 151
Corbin, Henry, 104, 157
cosmopolitanism
   from below, 179
   civilizational, 140
   genuine, 5, 152
   postcolonial, 17, 20, 135, 162, 165, 168
critical theory, 39, 112, 119
cultural diversity, 13, 84, 152, 154
cultural essentialism. *See* essentialism
cultural hybridity, 49, 158
cultural reform, 44, 85, 143, 162
culturalism, 13, 67, 85, 169

Dabashi, Hamid, 13, 16, 20, 29–30, 37, 147–150, 156, 161, 163, 167–168, 180
Dallmayr, Fred, 13, 15–16, 18, 46–48, 81, 119–120, 144, 150–156, 162, 164
Damascus, 9
declericalized Islam, 82
decolonization, 13, 20, 24, 179
deity, 108, 128, 132–133. *See also* God
democracy
   electoral, 88
   and government, 43
   guided, *see* committed democracy
   indigenous, 41, 65–66, 70, 120, 156, 169–173
   liberal, 5, 49, 76, 82, 90–91, 110, 114, 118, 166, 173
   and neoliberalism, 152
   and religion, 34, 42, 51, 58, 63, 65, 114, 116–119, 128, 130, 133
   and rights and freedom, 40, 107–108, 110–112, 123
   secular, 40, 113, 116–119
   social, 41, 72, 95–98, 100, 101, 175
democratization, 12, 14, 40, 48, 118, 169, 173–174
Descartes, René, 36
development
   and modernity, 44, 79, 168
   socioeconomic, 3, 48, 51, 78, 173, 175–176
   sociopolitical, 3, 19–20, 24, 38, 65, 68, 74, 78, 89, 98, 100, 120, 162, 172
   and underdevelopment, 155, 160
   uneven, 57
   Westerncentric, 57, 140
dialectical movement of history, 26–28
dialogical comparison, 16–18
dictatorship, 70, 96, 152, 155
dignity of difference, 154–155. *See also* recognition of difference
Duara, Prasenjit, 16, 146–147, 161
Durkheim, Émile, 118
Dussel, Enrique, 20, 47, 166–167

Eastern bloc, 2, 111
Eastern Europe, 79
ecclesiastical class, 73, 83. *See also* clerical class
egalitarianism, 12, 19, 26–27, 30, 41, 73, 92, 96–98, 100–101, 103, 106, 175–176
Egypt, 12, 53, 57–59, 62, 166, 171–172
Eisenstadt, Shmuel N., 15, 80
el-Sisi, Abdel Fattah, 174
end of history, 49, 154, 158

Index

Enlightenment
  counter-Enlightenment thought, 35–36, 66, 103–106, 110, 134
  critique of, 17–18, 20, 26–27, 101, 111–112, 117, 121, 128, 133, 163
  and Eurocentrism, 3, 45, 111, 120, 146, 165
  and modernity, 15, 26, 35–36, 44, 46, 63, 64, 67, 73, 80, 83–84, 96–97, 105, 107, 121, 158, 163, 168, 177
  post-Enlightenment thought, 2, 74, 146
epistemology, 35, 39, 45, 102, 107, 116–117, 120–121, 159, 169, 171, 178–180
essentialism
  civilizational, 157
  critique of, 152, 154–155, 157, 159, 161–162, 165
  cultural, 1, 5, 73, 76, 81, 93–95, 98, 101, 153
  particularist, 5, 20, 50. *See also* particularism
  racialized, 141
ethnocentrism, 179
Euben, Roxanne, 17, 54–55
Eurasia, 47, 167
Europe, 1–3, 5, 8–9, 15–19, 21–22, 24, 26–27, 36, 39, 42, 44–50, 53, 57–58, 63, 67–69, 73–74, 78–80, 82–84, 89, 91, 95–97, 100, 105, 111–113, 115–116, 121, 129, 134, 137–148, 159–160, 165–169
Eurocentrism, 2–5, 12–13, 18, 21–24, 43, 46–47, 50, 62, 73, 79–80, 84, 101, 115, 120, 124, 137–138, 140–141, 143, 145–146, 150, 153, 156, 165–167, 169, 179–180
existentialism, 7, 69, 125, 127, 131, 149

fascism, 111, 119, 141, 155
Fanon, Frantz, 3, 7, 22, 28, 33, 35, 68, 72, 84, 139, 145–146, 149, 159, 161
Farasatkhah, Maghsoud, 38, 41
fiqh, 92. *See also* Islamic jurisprudence
France, 7, 48, 82, 104
Frankfurt School, 39, 112
free will, 85, 102, 124. *See also* autonomous will
freedom
  bourgeois, 90
  of expression, 90
  human, 40, 64, 105–108, 120, 123–126, 130, 170
  from imperialism, 13
  individual, 52, 79, 81, 84, 91, 95, 100, 102, 110–112, 123, 127, 129
  religious, 114, 123
  universal value of, 26, 56, 83, 96–97, 156, 162
French Revolution, 30, 127
Fukuyama, Francis, 49, 152, 154, 158, 166
fundamentalism, 75–76, 89, 142, 157, 172–173

Gadamer, Hans-Georg, 15–16, 153, 156
Gandhi, Mahatma, 3, 97, 147, 161
gender equality, 12, 91–93, 176–178. *See also* rights, women's
Genesis, the book of, 126
Gellner, Ernest, 75
geographical
  boundaries, 91
  differences, 136
  entities, 158
  zones, 47, 136–137
geography of discourse, 21, 24
German Romanticism, 134
Ghaneirad, Mohammad Amin, 38, 132
Ghouchani, Mohammad, 41
global North, 47, 179
global South, 13, 47, 77–78, 161, 165, 168, 174–175, 179
globalization, 17, 26, 47–48, 91, 101, 148, 151, 158–159, 175–177
God, 28, 30, 36, 40, 49, 59, 60, 62, 64–65, 90, 94, 96, 102, 104–105, 107–109, 118–119, 123–126, 128–133. *See also* deity
Gramsci, Antonio, 88
Green Movement, 4, 169–171
Guevara, Ernesto Che, 7, 149–150
guerrilla warfare, 7, 32. *See also* armed struggle
guided democracy, 87–88, 105, 110–111. *See also* committed democracy
Gülen, Fethullah, 4, 18, 62, 64–66, 73, 120, 169, 172
Gurvitch, Georges, 7, 69

Habermas, Jürgen, 46–47, 105, 108, 111–117, 119–120, 166
Hardt, Michael, 169

Index

Hegel, G. W. F., 3, 26, 36, 105, 107–109, 111, 120–122, 124–125, 166
Heidegger, Martin, 36, 66, 103–105, 134
heresy, 9, 63
hijab, 92
historical determinism, 44
Hongming, Gu, 147
Horkheimer, Max, 18, 111, 119
Hosseinieh Ershad, 8–9, 31–32, 34, 70
human dignity, 81, 83, 91, 96, 121, 123, 132, 153
human nature, 124, 126
human reason, 45, 68, 73, 121, 124, 130, 166
human rights, *see* rights
humanism
    literary, 168
    modern, 35, 69, 84, 127, 139, 168
    religious, 127, 132–133. *See also* Islamic humanism
    secular, 116
    spiritual, 97, 101, 128. *See also* Islamic humanism
Hunter, Shireen T., 13, 32–33, 41, 53–54, 65–66
Huntington, Samuel, 2, 49, 75–77, 154, 158
Husserl, Edmund, 131

Ibn Miskawayh, 63
Ibn Rushd, 63, 155
Ibn Sina, 63, 155
identity
    civilizational, 23, 27, 145
    collective, 12, 25, 93, 104, 121, 172
    colonially constructed, 145
    crisis of, 52
    cultural, 48, 56, 141
    hybridity of, 71, 93, 101, 158
    indigenous sources of, 13, 22, 26, 161
    individual, 12, 121, 172
    Iranian, 25, 141, 163
    religious, 61, 71
identitarianism, 18, 72, 93–94, 116, 145, 147, 149, 156, 158, 161, 180
ideological awareness, 25, 31
ideological religion, 25, 34, 43, 98
ideology
    anti-imperialist, 109
    class-based, 25
    definition of, 24, 33, 38, 42–43

indigenous, 24, 25, 68
Islam as, 43. *See also* Islamic ideology
revolutionary, 21, 24, 28–29, 33–34, 37, 44, 70
of sameness, 152, 156, 164
and state, 43
ijma, 94
ijtihad, 55
Imam Hussain, 26
Imam Mahdi, 26, 59
imperialism, 5, 7, 12, 25, 45, 54, 61, 67, 108, 111, 138–139, 145–147, 151–152, 160, 173
indigenization, 20, 179–180
indigenous social theory, 38, 179
individual autonomy (agency), 45, 69, 83, 86, 95, 110, 112, 124, 128, 130, 132
individualism, 69, 90, 110, 127, 133
industrialization, 51, 95, 175–176
Inglehart, Ronald, 77
intellectual responsibility, 19, 23–27, 31, 39–40, 69–71, 87–89, 91, 111
intellectuals
    authentic, 23–25, 27, 29, 44, 69–70, 72, 86–87
    committed, 71, 87, 105
    Eurocentric, 21–23
    religious, 12, 34, 42, 99, 103
    revolutionary, 7, 88, 96
    self-alienated, 7, 22–23, 139
    Third World, 33, 139
    vanguard, 7
Iqbal, Muhammad, 22–23, 53, 55–56, 62, 66–70, 72, 85, 95, 101, 106, 120–121, 169
Iranian Revolution, 2, 5, 10, 11, 14, 18, 27–29, 33, 61, 66, 103, 108
Islam
    and democracy, 34, 42, 51, 75–76
    history of, 26, 28–30, 45, 90
    in Iran, 25, 141, 143, 163, 178
    and modernity, 1–5, 16, 48, 49, 50, 55, 60, 62–64, 73, 76, 163, 165, 169–171, 176, 178
    ontological-inspirational capacities of, 15, 19, 26, 40, 52, 85, 92, 98, 121, 132
    and revolution, 34, 42
    and secularism, 49, 52, 65, 73, 75–76, 94, 171–173

Islam (cont.)
  social-mobilizational capacities of, 15, 19, 25–26, 52, 85, 98
  and socialism, 12
  and the West, 66, 163
Islamic
  authenticity, 37, 103–104
  civilization, 8, 53–54, 84, 143, 148, 155, 159, 163
  democracy, 51, 65. See also Islam and democracy
  discourse, 10–12, 14, 17, 21, 27–28, 32–33, 35–38, 40–41, 43, 92, 102–106, 108–109, 111, 115, 131–135, 174, 178, 180
  exceptionalism, 15, 76–77, 170
  humanism, 40, 63, 73, 94, 103, 120
  ideology, 8, 25–31, 33–35, 34, 41, 43, 51, 66, 134
  jurisprudence, 43, 55–56, 64, 173. See also fiqh
  law, 55, 59–60, 176
  liberalism, 73, 98–101
  modernism, 52–54, 56–58, 66
  political thought, 48
  Protestantism, 81–82, 85, 89
  reformism, 18, 52, 62–65, 73, 81, 98, 101, 172, 175
  revival, 29, 67, 75, 79
  state, 15, 27, 38, 44, 58–59, 62, 64, 70, 76, 94, 171. See also religious state
  thought, 5, 8, 13, 15, 17–20, 38, 45, 50–53, 55–56, 62, 66, 68, 73, 85, 90–91, 94, 97, 106, 132, 134, 157, 163, 176, 178, 180
  tradition, 1, 4, 15, 33, 50, 51, 58, 68, 130–131, 133
  traditionalism, 62, 95
  Weltanschauung, 60
Islamic Nahda Party (Tunisia), 171, 174
Islamic Republic, 2, 11, 27, 34, 60, 61, 63, 103, 178
Islamism, 2, 4, 11, 14, 15, 19, 27, 40–41, 51–52, 56–63, 66, 71–72, 86, 93–95, 98–99, 101, 103, 110, 130, 159, 161, 170–172, 178–180
Islamization, 27, 178, 180

Jahiliyya, 59
Jewish
  intellectuals, 129
  -ness and Zionism, 116
  ontology, 18, 119, 129
jihad, 53
justice, 7–8, 26, 28, 31, 72, 79, 81, 88, 94, 96, 100, 117–118, 156, 174–175

Kahak, 6
Kakuzo, Okakura, 147
Kant, Immanuel, 3, 36, 115
Kaufmann, David, 129
Kenyatta, Jomo, 68
Khamenei, Ali, 58
Khan, Syed Ahmad, 53, 67
Khomeini, Ruhollah, 29, 39, 51, 58–63, 66, 71, 102–103, 108, 110, 179
khums, 59
King, Jr., Martin Luther, 117
knowledge production, 5, 12–13, 17, 20–24, 101, 143, 166, 168, 178–180

laicism, 114
Laoust, Henri, 157
Latin America, 149, 169
Lebanon, 9, 12
Left, the, 12, 23, 32–33, 37, 41, 95, 99–100
Lerner, Daniel, 1, 75–76
Lévinas, Emmanuel, 129
Lewis, Bernard, 2, 76
liberal democracy, see democracy
liberalism, 90, 96, 114, 118, 155, 174
liberation theology, 15, 17, 35, 82, 148–150
liberty
  individual, 110–111, 118, 123
  political, 64
  positive and negative, 90–91
Libya, 171
Lukács, György, 42
Luxemburg, Rosa, 88

Machinism, 84
Mahdavi, Mojtaba, 39–40, 154–156, 163
Malcolm X, 149–150
Malekian, Mostafa, 99
Malkom Khan, Mirza, 23
Mamdani, Mahmood, 2
Marx, Karl, 3, 95

Marxism, 25–26, 30, 32, 88, 95–96, 110–111
Marxism-Leninism, 88
Mashhad, 6, 8–9
Massignon, Louis, 7, 82, 157
materialism, 27, 126
Maududi, Abul Ala, 51, 58, 61–62, 66, 71
Medieval thought, 83, 113
Mediterranean region, 157
Memmi, Albert, 68
Mernissi, Fatima, 4, 62, 176
Mesbahian, Hossein, 42, 72, 128–130, 159
metanarrative, 15, 18, 23, 44, 77–78, 80, 120, 137, 142, 158, 179
metaphysics, 36, 65, 67, 103, 105, 108–109, 113, 127, 129, 141
Middle East (and North Africa), 1, 12, 20, 48, 57, 75, 148, 150, 169, 174
Mignolo, Walter, 2, 13, 20, 179
minimal religion, 98–99
Mir-Hosseini, Ziba, 13, 176
Mirsepassi, Ali, 19, 35–37, 65–66, 103–106, 110, 125, 134–135
modernism, 2, 4, 6, 19, 22, 38, 40, 44, 51, 53, 62, 98, 169
modernity
   alternative, 26, 35, 85, 96–97, 158, 163, 165–168
   anticolonial, 178
   capitalist, 25, 118–119, 138–139, 147–148
   colonial, 13, 17, 19–20, 24, 26, 45–46, 48, 52, 66, 68, 141, 148, 161, 163, 165, 167, 172, 179
   dark side of, 39, 166
   emancipatory consequences of, 39, 73, 80, 83, 95–96, 168
   Enlightenment, 3, 15, 18, 20, 26, 35–36, 45–46, 66, 80, 96–97, 101, 105–106, 110, 112, 120–121, 128, 146, 158, 163, 177
   European, 3, 5, 21–22, 48, 50, 53, 67, 69, 73, 78, 82–83, 85, 121, 137, 139–140, 146, 165, 168
   indigenous, 5, 15, 19–20, 27, 38, 44, 62, 66, 82, 87, 89, 96, 99, 100, 135, 141, 158–159, 161, 168–169, 171–175
   Iranian 76, 130–131
   Islam and, *see* Islam

multiple modernities, 3–4, 15, 49, 78–81, 167
Persianate, 47
project of, 46, 55, 112, 168
rejection of, 27, 50–51, 76, 134, 156
tradition and, 40, 44, 67
Western, 11, 15, 20, 35, 39, 47, 51, 53, 58, 61–62, 82–85, 93–95, 97, 106, 109, 117, 119, 127, 134–135, 138, 156, 160–161, 168
modernization, 1, 4, 12, 15, 18, 20, 25, 35, 38, 40, 43, 45, 50, 52–53, 55–57, 74–76, 78, 82, 101, 104, 120, 135, 139, 158
Moghadam, Valentine M., 174
Mojtahed Shabestari, Mohammad, 99
Monoculture, 84
Monotheism, 27, 31, 56, 83, 85, 96, 107–109, 123
Morsi, Muhammad, 172, 174
Mosaddegh, Mohammad, 6, 11
Motamed-Dezfooli, Faramarz, 131
Mounier, Emmanuel, 82
Movement of God-Worshipping Socialists, 31
Muslim Brotherhood, 58, 172
Muslim societies, 1–5, 10, 12–13, 19–20, 48–50, 52–56, 58, 65–66, 69, 75–77, 79–80, 85–86, 92, 98, 107, 119–120, 143, 145, 163, 165, 170–173, 176, 180
Mutazila, 63

Nadwi, Abul Hassan Ali, 58
Nandy, Ashis, 160
Naraghi, Ehsan, 11, 33
Nasr, Seyed Hossein, 51
Nasser, Gamal Abdel, 59
nation-state, 15, 48, 51, 57, 147, 150, 175
National Front (Iran), 6–7
National Liberation Front (Algeria), 31
Nationalism, 57, 145, 147
Nationalist-Religious Coalition, 11
National Resistance Movement, 6
nativism, 34–35, 38, 93, 133–134, 145, 149–150, 156, 159, 161, 169, 178–180
natural sciences, 24
naturalism, 142
Negri, Antonio, 169

Neo-Shariatis, 4–5, 14–15, 17, 19–20, 40–45, 71–73, 86–88, 91, 93–101, 120–121, 156, 158–159, 161–163, 165, 171–173, 175, 177–178, 180
neocolonialism, 5, 82, 101, 151
neoliberalism, 101, 152, 174–175
nihilism, 109
Nimeiry, Gaafar, 63
Nkrumah, Kwame, 68
Norris, Pippa, 77
North America, 78, 91, 174
Nyerere, Julius, 68, 161

occidental rationalism, 3, 47, 112, 115, 166, 168
occidentalism, 5, 20, 134–135, 156–157, 161–162. *See also* orientalism in reverse
ontology, 15, 18–19, 26, 28, 30, 35–36, 39, 45, 52, 73, 85, 91, 96, 101–110, 112, 116, 119–133, 144, 159, 163, 169, 171, 178–180
Organization of People's Mojahedin of Iran, 32
Organization of Revolutionary Monotheists, 10–11
Organization of the Vanguard Fighters of the Oppressed, 10
orientalism, 1–2, 5, 7, 16, 20, 48–49, 63, 76, 134–135, 142–145, 147–150, 156–157, 162, 178–179
orientalism in reverse, 20, 134, 178–179. *See also* occidentalism

Pahlavi dynasty, 6, 8–9, 11, 25, 29, 38, 43, 45, 75, 106
Palestine, 9, 91
Paris, 6–7, 21, 31, 35, 139
parochialism, 16, 179
particularism, 5, 20, 36, 133–134, 154, 159, 162
Pax-Americana, 152
People's Fadaee Guerrillas, 32
permanent revolution, 28
phenomenology, 15, 39
pluralism, 36, 52, 83, 89, 100, 104, 113, 123, 133, 145, 155, 164–165
political legitimation, 94, 176
positivism, 63–64, 75, 96–97
post-Islamism, 4, 40, 169–172

postcolonialism, 3, 16–17, 19–20, 57, 59, 72, 74, 87–88, 133, 142–143, 145, 147, 151, 159–163, 165, 168, 170, 179
premodern, 65, 104, 107, 113
progress, 3, 25–26, 44–45, 50, 54, 67, 75, 80, 83–84, 138, 142–143, 154, 157, 167
Prophet Muhammad, 9, 29, 55, 58, 90
Protestant Reformation, 44, 78, 82–83, 89–90. *See also* Christian Reformation
public reason, 114–115
public religion, 15, 19, 39, 74, 78–79, 81–82, 86, 91, 96, 98–100, 112, 114, 131
public sphere, 37, 40, 75, 77–78, 112–118, 120, 170–173

Qichao, Liang, 147
Quran, 55–56, 58–60, 62, 67–68, 90, 92–94, 110, 124
Qutb, Sayyid, 51, 58–62, 66, 71, 179–180

Radhakrishnan, Sarvepalli, 68
Rahmani, Taghi, 14, 89, 100
Rahnema, Ali, 7, 9, 13, 30, 32, 127
Ramadan, Tariq, 4, 62
rationalism, 3, 18, 39, 43–44, 47, 53–54, 60, 63–64, 73–75, 96, 112–113, 115, 121, 128–129, 141–142, 144, 166, 168
Rawls, John, 114–115, 118
Raziq, Ali Abdel, 58
recognition of difference, 97, 154, 156, 159. *See also* dignity of difference
relativism, 4, 52, 81
religion
  emancipatory vs. oppressive, 12–13, 18, 25, 28, 35, 82, 99–100, 117–119, 125, 128–129, 133, 173
  public vs. private, 30, 75, 89, 98–99, 114, 116, 173. *See also* public religion
  return of, 78, 121
religious intellectualism, 33
religious reform, 40–41, 45, 53, 72, 78, 82, 91–93, 98
religious state, 40, 73, 94–95. *See also* Islamic state
Renaissance, 67, 83–84, 89, 168
Renan, Ernest, 49, 54
republicanism, 41, 51

revolutionary reform, 42
revolutionary consciousness, 7, 12, 72, 87
revolutionary vanguard, 33. *See also* vanguardism
Rida, Muhammad Rashid, 53
rights
  civil, 111, 118, 149
  citizenship, 12, 45, 107, 109, 171
  democratic, 90, 108, 123
  equal, 102
  human, 64–65, 91, 105, 112, 120, 154, 170
  individual, 52, 79, 81, 100, 105–106, 110–112, 129–130
  negative, 90–91
  political, 56, 100
  women's, 91–93, 176–177
rights-bearing individual (subject), 19, 105–106, 126, 130, 131, 133
Rodinson, Maxime, 157
Rorty, Richard, 118
Russia, 48, 69

Sachedina, Abdulaziz, 13, 29
Sacks, Jonathan, 154
Said, Edward, 3, 16, 143–147, 150, 156, 161–163
Salvatore, Armando, 80
Sartre, Jean-Paul, 7, 125, 127, 131, 149
SAVAK, 8–9
Sayyid, S, 57
science, 53, 61, 63–65, 67, 102, 121, 136, 140–141, 166
Seal of the Prophets, 55
Second Vatican Council, 79, 82. *See also* aggiornamento
secularism, 12, 41, 49, 59, 65, 73, 75–79, 94, 98–99, 104–106, 110, 114, 116, 118, 170–173
secularization, 15, 18, 43, 50, 74–75, 77–78, 82, 112–113, 118, 120, 158, 173
Senghor, Léopold Sédar, 68
self-awareness, 123–125, 139. *See also* consciousness
separation of church and state, 75
September 11, 2001, 2, 49, 76
Shariat-Razavi, Pouran, 11
Shariati, Ali
  "Ascension and Isra," 132
  "Aspirations," 83

"Civilization and Modernization," 135–136
"Class Orientation in Islam: Book One," 69
"Community and Leadership," 70, 83, 87
"Culture and Ideology," 136
Dialogues of Solitude, 124
"Extraction and Refinement of Cultural Resources," 140–142
"Fatemeh Is Fatemeh," 177
"Freedom, Joyous Freedom," 90
"General Discussion about Civilization and Culture," 136, 142
"Horr," 26
"How to Stay," 26–27, 139
"Human, Islam, and Western Schools," 90
Iqbal and Us, 21–22, 24, 67–70, 111
"Islamology: Lesson Eight," 90
"Islamology: Lesson Seven," 176
kaviriat, 123
"Letter to a Brother," 26
"Letter to Ehsan," 22, 25, 83, 96
"Letter to Father," 82
"Letter to Mr. Homayoun and Mr. Minachi," 25
life and legacy, 5–16
"Once Again Abuzar," 90
philosophical thought, 120–126
Prisons of humanity, 110, 125
Religion versus Religion, 28, 94
Return, 14, 24–25, 70–71
"Return to Which Self?," 22, 122, 143
return to the self, 5, 35–36, 45, 71–72, 84, 134, 138, 140, 161–163
"Return to the Self," 84, 138–142
"Revolutionary Self-Preparedness," 32, 86, 90, 96, 123
"Spirituality, Equality, Freedom," 87, 96–97, 142
"The Characteristics of the Modern Age," 137–139
"The Characteristics of Today's Civilization," 139–140
The Descent in the Desert, 123–126
"The Greater Haj," 90
"What is Civilization?," 136, 138, 141–142
"What is Islam?," 94, 176
"What Is To Be Done?," 138

Shariati, Ali (*cont.*)
  "With You, O Eternal and Imperishable Kindness," 121
  Worldview and Ideology, 122
Shariati, Ehsan, 14, 42–45, 72, 85, 87–91, 94–97, 100–101, 127–128, 157–158
Shariati, Mohammad-Taghi, 6
Shariati, Sara, 44, 71–72, 87, 93–94, 98–99, 101, 121, 156–160, 163, 175
Shariati, Susan, 41–42, 71, 91, 97, 128, 157–158, 176–177
Shayegan, Dariush, 33–34, 42
Shi'ism, 6, 8, 9, 12, 25–26, 28–30, 34, 37, 59–60, 63, 92, 141, 149
Shilliam, Robbie, 115
shura, 94
Siahkal uprising, 31
social libertarianism, 97
social sciences, 6, 24, 166, 178–180
social welfare, 100, 127, 173–174
socialism, 12, 25–26, 28, 30–31, 51, 69, 72, 83, 106, 111, 127, 149, 175
solidarity, 17, 56, 79, 96–97, 127, 129, 140, 149, 153, 176
Sorbonne, 6, 69, 104
Soroush, Abdolkarim, 4, 18, 33–34, 42, 62, 64–66, 73, 81, 98–100, 120, 169, 172
Southampton, 9
sovereignty
  divine, 8, 36, 59–60, 62, 64, 109, 123, 132–133
  human, 59, 64, 126
  popular, 45, 51, 64, 73, 87, 89, 102, 106–108, 171–172
Soviet Union, 2, 49, 84
spirituality, 19, 30, 32, 40, 43, 64, 66, 69, 70, 72, 84–85, 96–98, 100–101, 104, 106, 109, 112, 115, 121–124, 126–128, 131, 136, 138–139, 141–142, 154, 162, 173, 175
state neutrality, 116
subjectivity
  collective, 108, 111
  individual, 19, 36, 91, 101, 105, 110, 122, 124–125, 130–131, 133
  mediated, 20, 37, 102, 106–109, 130–131, 168
Subrahmanyam, Sanjay, 3, 20, 47, 167
Sudan, 58, 62–63
Sunnism, 12
Syria, 9, 12, 53

Tabatabaei, Javad, 8, 33, 34, 42
Taghizadeh, Seyed Hassan, 23, 51
Tagore, Rabindranath, 147
Taha, Mahmoud Mohammad, 62–63
Taliqani, Azam, 176
Taliqani, Mahmoud, 62–63, 103
Tavakoli-Targhi, Mohamad, 47
tawhid
  ideology, 27
  ontology, 91
  worldview, 15, 28, 85, 102, 106, 132
Taylor, Charles, 15, 116–117, 119–120
Tehran, 8–10, 31, 139
theocracy, 60, 94. *See also* religious state.
Third World, 25, 28, 33, 35, 84, 87, 111, 138–139, 159, 161
top-down change, 50, 56, 70, 72, 75, 105, 135, 178
Touré, Ahmed Sékou, 68
Tracy, Destutt de, 42
traditionalism, 8, 19, 38, 41, 44, 51–54, 62–63, 85, 93, 95, 98, 130, 133, 142
translation proviso, 114–115
Tunisia, 171, 174
Turkey, 12, 57, 62, 75–76, 169

ulama, 8, 29, 51, 54, 56, 59–61, 85, 169
United States (America), 6, 9, 19, 23, 49, 62, 76, 84, 114, 118, 149, 151–152, 159
universalism
  from below, 177, 180
  blind, 80
  false, 80, 164
  hegemonic, 1, 3, 5, 16, 20, 36, 48, 50, 94, 133, 141, 151, 153–154, 162, 165, 180
  homogenizing, 152, 159, 168
  inclusive, 180
  rejection of, 134, 162, 179

Vahdat, Farzin, 19, 36–37, 105–112, 115–119, 122–123, 125, 130, 134–135
vanguardism, 7, 27, 59, 70, 88. *See also* revolutionary vanguard
velayat-e faqih, 11, 59–60, 63, 65

Wadud, Amina, 176
Wallerstein, Immanuel, 166, 168
War on Terrorism, 49, 76

Watt, William Montgomery, 157
Weber, Max, 74, 78, 112–113, 119–120, 166
welfare state, 100, 175
West, Cornel, 15, 18, 117–120, 133
West, the, 1, 2, 5, 11, 17, 34–35, 37–38, 47, 49, 50, 54, 56–57, 66, 68, 75–77, 84, 89, 116, 134–135, 137–139, 142–145, 147–148, 150–152, 154, 157, 160, 168–169, 176, 179
Westerncentrism, 13, 17, 57, 68, 84, 142, 152, 154, 157. *See also* Eurocentrism
Westernization, 12, 15, 20, 23, 25, 29, 50, 53, 56, 57, 134, 139, 178
Westoxication, 22–23
World War I, 48, 140
World War II, 151
worldview, 15, 27–28, 33, 43, 82, 85, 97, 101–102, 106, 112–114, 121, 122, 124, 126–127, 132, 140, 158, 163

Yacine, Kateb, 68
Yousefi Eshkevari, Hassan, 14, 88, 92, 93, 177

Printed in the United States
By Bookmasters